Just as I
promised
will write
love Lou

Our Days
Are Like Full Years

A Memoir with Letters from Louis Kahn

HARRIET PATTISON

Yale University Press
New Haven and London

Letters of Louis I. Kahn reproduced by permission of Sue Ann Kahn.

Illustration credits appear on page 437.

yalebooks.com/art

This project has been supported by a grant from the Graham Foundation for Advanced Studies in the Fine Arts, by an Arnold W. Brunner Grant administered by the AIA New York Chapter and the Center for Architecture Foundation, by a grant from Alphawood Foundation Chicago, and by Larry and Korin Korman and the Korman family. The author is grateful for this generous support and for the ongoing assistance provided by the Architectural Archives of the University of Pennsylvania.

Graham Foundation　　**ALPHAWOOD** FOUNDATION CHICAGO

Designed and set in Janson Text by Laura Lindgren

Printed in China by 1010 Printing International Limited

Library of Congress Control Number: 2020935117
ISBN 978-0-300-22312-5

A catalogue record for this book is available from the British Library.

The paper in this book meets the requirements of ANSI/NISO z39.48-1992 (Permanence of Paper).

10 9 8 7 6 5 4 3 2 1

Part One: Harriet Pattison, Belmont Harbor, Chicago, 1946.
Part Two: Harriet Pattison, Nathaniel Kahn, and Bonnie Pattison, Maine, 1963.
Part Three: Aristide Maillol, *L'Air.* Kimbell Art Museum, Fort Worth, Texas, c. 1972.
Part Four: Louis Kahn at the Bishop Field Estate, Lenox, Massachusetts, 1973.

No act no thought can
separate us as long as
love makes no other demand
of us than to be pure and true
—LK

A Note on Transcriptions

In transcribing the selection of letters contained in this book, I have tried to be as accurate as possible. It is important to note, however, that many of the letters were written quickly and while Lou was traveling from place to place, so inevitably there are words and passages that are fragmentary or difficult to decipher. To aid the reader, therefore, I have occasionally added a word or two enclosed in [brackets] to clarify meaning or to supply contextual information. Lou often used irregular spacing of words in his writing as a kind of punctuation, and in some cases I have added a comma or period where I felt he intended a pause or break. Spellings of places and names have been standardized and misspellings have been corrected, except where I thought they were intentional. A few letters have been edited for length or nonrelevant content, in which case an ellipsis (. . .) was used.

—HP

Contents

Harriet Pattison
1809 Delancey Place
Philadelphia Pa

PROLOGUE: A Box of Letters

There is a Chinese cinnabar box on a bookshelf by my bed. It is filled with letters from the architect Louis Kahn, who died in 1974. Lou—as he was called by nearly everyone—was my teacher, my inspiration, my companion, and the love of my life. Yet he was twenty-seven years older and had been married for nearly as many years when we met. It was my hope that someday we would live together, but that was not to be, and we were perhaps apart more than we were together in the fifteen years between our meeting and his death. This is a small portion of time in most lives, and yet measureless in intensity and effect in ours. Because of our separations, his travels, and our feelings, Lou wrote to me often, and I kept his letters in my treasure box. Once read, they rested there, undisturbed. Like much of my life, they were unexamined, put off for a later time. But it is a later time now, for I am past ninety. One day, suddenly curious as the cat that sat beside me, I lifted the lid of the box and the letters spilled out, as if they'd been waiting with their contents eager to be read.

And there was Lou! Thinking, dreaming, traveling, drinking in the world, with boundless enthusiasm and wonder. I found him in every phrase. He was by turns confiding, poetic, funny, and wise, and I remembered the anticipation of opening each of his letters. I found myself inside them, too—young again, in love, and challenged to raise our child on my own and venture on a career. They brought back events I had shared in—events of his most productive years, when opportunities came from across the world to create masterworks for a great variety of people and their institutions. In them Lou's voice, unmistakable and haunting, lives again, calling for my accompanying narrative and reflections on being liberated from the dark forgetting of the cinnabar box.

—HP

PART ONE

The Holly Branch

1959–1962

Louis Kahn, Yale University Art Gallery, 1953.

1959

I first saw Louis Kahn on a snowy day in New Haven. It was 1953, several years before our story together really began. I was twenty-five and in my second year at the Yale Drama School, where I had applied to study scene design, but had been accepted instead into the acting program. I was crossing Chapel Street to the Waldorf Cafeteria with several friends from the art school when we saw what appeared to be a large man in a sheepskin coat and leather shoes who was slipping and sliding between snowbanks. One of my companions darted ahead to offer him a hand and persuaded him to join us for coffee.

Once inside the cafeteria, the man wrestled off the coat and emerged, much smaller than expected—but broad-shouldered and agile in a suit and bow tie. His graying hair, I remember, seemed long, and when he swept it back, I saw that his face was badly scarred, giving him a fierce look. But his blue eyes sparkled like the snowflakes he brushed off, and he had a soft, hoarse chuckle that was disarming and that punctuated the stunning monologue he launched into about the arts at Yale. He never mentioned the Yale University Art Gallery going up across the street, or that he was its architect, but rather spoke broadly, framing his ideas in such poetic images and stories that we listened spellbound until it was almost dark. I tried to record a few of his phrases afterward, and then gave up, realizing I hadn't even caught his name, so I simply wrote, "I met an amazing man."

I left Yale that summer to go abroad and lost these notes in the ensuing restless years. Though my love for theater remained, I had decided not to continue at drama school. Since my father's death a few years earlier, my elderly mother had indulged my every venture; I was the last, and most spoiled, of their six children to be launched with his funds. The others had moved on in their lives, validated by wartime service, except for one sister who had also sought a life in the theater.

After a year and a half in Europe I returned to my hometown, Chicago, where I had deep roots and fond memories of my education at the University of Chicago. But I found that my network of friends and family had become thin, and I had trouble finding a job, any job, which I now needed to do. My dreams of a career in the arts, or of falling in love with expectations of "settling down," as my friends had done, seemed destined to be lost along with the sense of my own promise, and I was haunted by foreign cities and people I'd known. I moved to New York City, where I worked for a filmmaker down on his luck and then in an editing job at *Publishers Weekly*. I tried to imagine how I might assemble my intellectual and artistic interests and abilities into a way of life and some kind of a career, but without backing by a university or mentor, I didn't know how to begin. It was a lonely time that resists being remembered, except for one constant—music—which, on an August day in 1958, brought an odd proposal that changed my life.

I was in Maine, where my widowed mother kept the family house by the sea that drew its three generations together over the course of forty summers. I had resumed playing the piano and was taking lessons with Edith Braun, a fine musician who taught at the Curtis Institute of Music in Philadelphia. Mrs. Braun, who summered in Maine along with many Curtis musicians, recognized my lostness and knew better than my mother how to give wise counsel and affection. "Child," she said to me after a lesson, "come to Philadelphia. I'll teach you there," though I was almost thirty, and a performing career was not in the cards. I believed her when she then said, "Philadelphia is a wonderful city, and something good for you will come of it."

I moved in the fall to the top of a row house on Delancey, a tree-lined street of mid-nineteenth-century brick mansions. Although I spent long hours at the piano, I managed to make new friends. Several were architects, young men aspiring to build ideas of their own and challenge the city's established firms. Two were especially fascinating, if a study in contrasts: one, Wilhelm von Moltke, was a city planner and Prussian émigré, and the other, Robert "Bob" Venturi, an irreverent Princeton-trained architect. Bob knew my Yale friend Mariette Russell, who brought us together for what was to become a sweet, courtly romance.

At Christmastime Bob invited me to a holiday party at the rustic workshop of sculptor Wharton Esherick, nestled in the woods outside the city near Valley Forge. Once again it was snowing, and the forested scene was just right for a reappearance of the amazing man—though I did not at first recall where I had seen him. Lou, who had designed the workshop, was Esherick's pal and the party's host. Bob had worked for Lou for a few years, and Lou had championed him throughout the 1950s. The party was a little wild, with lots of drinks, a blazing fire, and a version of pin-the-tail-on-the-donkey that involved a poster of Santa Claus. Bob was reserved in this reveler's environment but eager for me to meet his mentor and friend. He introduced us in the middle of the raucous scene, and suddenly I remembered where I had seen Lou before. I dared to ask if he had a sheepskin coat "for a snowy day like this." "No," he replied. But after a pause, he recalled with a little laugh that a Yale student had loaned him one, once, because of a snowstorm on a day when he didn't have a coat. How like Lou—he never caught up with the weather, trusting it would work out like everything else!

At midnight, with a kiss from Bob, I boarded the Chicago-bound train at Paoli Station to join my family for Christmas. I stayed awake on that long trip, dreaming—as gray morning light overspread trackless snowfields of Ohio and Indiana—about Lou Kahn and the touch of his beautiful hand.

In Tuscany after leaving Yale, 1953.

Sometime that spring I invited friends to a party, which included an architectural scavenger hunt. Several architects came, and to my delight, they brought Lou with them. He handed me a holly branch loaded with red berries as an offering, and I carefully put it in a tall vase. Lou would later remind me of that holly branch, and it was to become our symbol, marking the signal moment of fifteen years to follow. But not until the end of May did I recognize, with a kind of astonishment, that I was falling passionately in love for the first time, with a man twenty-seven years older than me and unlike anyone I had ever known. That spring evening, I had gone with Bob to a reception for Fellows of the American Academy in Rome. On a penthouse terrace above the treetops of Philadelphia's Rittenhouse Square, Lou gave a brief talk about his time at the Academy and the gift of seeing the ruins of Rome, Greece, and Egypt, which had deeply inspired him and given him a new sense of direction in his work.

Lou (at right) in front of the Temple of Apollo at Corinth, Greece, 1951.

It was late when the gathering broke up and Lou rushed to join Bob and me, disengaging himself from other colleagues and friends. The three of us walked through the square and stopped at the Barclay Hotel bar. We ordered drinks, and Bob and Lou compared notes about Rome, sparring with each other—two friends putting on a show of quick comments and jokes, partly for my benefit. But I knew Rome too, and soon all of us were talking about Italy and art and music. Lou mentioned his daughter, a musician, of whom he was quite proud. Several times Lou caught my eye, and I felt a rush of excitement. What was this? I knew he was married, although Bob had told me that Lou and his wife lived rather separate lives.

At closing time, instead of leaving us, Lou chose to walk with Bob and me the few blocks to my door on Delancey Street, where they left me, the two of them standing under the streetlight. I raced upstairs and stood in the dark, knowing somehow that Lou and I would be together. Looking back, even now I wonder at myself. I was inexperienced with men and brought up to have a "normal" life, to marry someone appropriate, and yet suddenly none of that mattered.

I was about to leave Philadelphia to help my mother over the summer in Maine with a houseful of teenage grandchildren, and I had taken a job at an auction house in New York City, starting in September, but the prospect of never seeing Lou again left me hollow, and that night I sat with a pounding heart and wrote a bold note to him. I invited him to dinner (and to Maine, if he happened to be in the state!) and mailed it the next morning before I could stop myself. This was his reply.

Dear Harriet

I reread your note It is so deeply good
Always it will be a delight to meet you wherever
Likely not that I will get to Maine though I
picture myself there wanted as you beautifully
implied.

Lou

Dear Harriet,
I reread your note. It is so deeply good.

 Always it will be a delight to meet you wherever. Likely not that I will get to Maine though I picture myself there wanted as you beautifully implied.

Lou

 When I realized that Lou was actually coming for dinner, I was panic-struck. What would we talk about? I called up a worldly friend, asking her to join us. "Just for cocktails," she said. Cocktails? I rarely drank them, so I was guessing at what to serve and rushed out and bought little bottles of liquor and a Burgundy with a handsome label. Elaborate dinner preparations of favorite French recipes kept my mind off possible scenarios until the day and very moment when the two arrived. I pressed the buzzer to open the street door and heard them chatting as they mounted the stairs. It's all a blur except that I served martinis, following a brother's formula. The iced stems rattled on the tray I held. I remember that, and the pause that followed. Then each reached for a glass, later a refill, and Lou never after wanted any but "my" martinis. When I accompanied my friend down to the street, she turned at the door and, instead of "Goodbye," said to me, "Be careful!"

 Suddenly not careful, I ran up the three flights. Lou was struggling to open the wine with the cheap corkscrew. He must have been nervous too, because he spilled the Burgundy all over his gray suit, the sofa, and the rug. "Don't worry," he said. "Get some salt." And we began to laugh and couldn't stop, taking turns flinging the Morton salt in swipes and arabesques across the stains and into the air, until the box was empty. And the fancy dinner was never touched.

"Faraway," Lincolnville, Maine.

In June I left Philadelphia and went to Faraway, our family's summer house in Maine. The name described how I felt leaving Lou behind.

The house stood on a rise between pine and spruce woods and a field of wildflowers, above a rock beach on Penobscot Bay. There I could only connect with Lou using a rural party-line telephone, which meant that neighbors might listen in on our evening calls. Lou was alone at the office then, but there was no real privacy for me with boisterous, curious nieces and nephews around, so I would pull the phone out onto the front porch to listen and talk, sometimes for hours, as moonlight spangled the bay or fog chalked out the islands in its chill drift. I would nestle into the enveloping warmth and fascination of Lou's words, and afterward, very late in a quiet house, I would stay up to write down what he'd said or compose a letter and address it, marked "Private," to Lou's office. In the morning I would take it up the long dirt drive to the mailbox, always with a hope that a letter from him might await me there. Between the morning mail and the night call, I would wonder if what was happening to my life was too fantastic to be real.

Wonderful Wonderful Harriet,
Your lovely face feels harbouring in mine. Even as a boy in Arthur's court there was a girl and now as then it is you. Snow in the morning sun white and gold. When a beginning is come nothing that stems from it is as full. Time changes Form. What gives it life is eternal. Three precious words you sent me. Those same words, only mine, I send you. I love you.

Lou

PHILADELPHIA TO FARAWAY, AUGUST 2, 1959

Wonderful Wonderful Harriet,
Many many times I read your letter—Yes how does one answer to these happenings—How full of wonder is the moment of inception. At that moment the new being is already inherently singular and instantly too it is open to the play of circumstance. Yet no form is possible except what is answerable to its unique tendencies.

But even more full of wonder is the first meeting of one with another when streams of harmony instantly exchange, when distance has no measure, when life is love all of feeling, the feeling of a heavenly entering. Inception of no earthy form, singular, yet in one and in the other, it lives separately.

My work is delightful. Everything I am now designing costs too much. Realities are good if they serve art.

Your loving clown,
Lou

PHILADELPHIA TO FARAWAY, AUGUST 16, 1959

Dearest Wonderful Harriet, I love you.
I love you is the only prayer in the Sanctuary. Am I worthy of you? should never be answered for it is the soul in conflict. It should always remain a question to the one in love.

Do you love me? "Yes" is no answer. "No" is no answer. The answer is I love you or silence.

I love you is more wonderful than the Sun. The Sun is a measure—a quantity. "I cannot do without you" is also just a measure. I love you and am I worthy of you? should be together the expression of love and the reflection from the well from which it came.

Gosh Harriet how I felt this all when I spoke with you on the phone. You tried and I tried to say something we couldn't. Can you imagine what will happen when we meet again? Do you think you'll give the sun and the stars a single thought.

Lou

10

Lou in his office at the corner of Twentieth and Walnut Streets, Philadelphia.

As much as our calls were about how we missed each other, they were also about Lou's work and his excitement over beginning to receive the kind of commissions he had always desired. Lou's rise in the architecture world had been slow, progressing from private homes and housing projects in the 1940s to a commission for a psychiatric hospital, which had allowed him to establish a private practice in 1947. When the breakthrough commission for the Yale University Art Gallery came in 1951, after his return from Rome and the ancient world, Lou was already fifty years old. Several modest projects had followed Yale, but now, a decade later, with a major medical research building under construction at the University of Pennsylvania, Lou felt he was finally on the verge of great success.

TOP AND BOTTOM: The Yale University Art Gallery, completed in 1953—a fusion of modern and ancient, with its glass curtain walls and heavy, brooding concrete stair and ceiling.

TOP: The Trenton Bath House, in Ewing Township, New Jersey, completed in 1955. Lou felt that it was in this building, with its clarity of plan and structure, that he "discovered himself."

BOTTOM: The workshop Lou designed for the artist Wharton Esherick, in Malvern, Pennsylvania, where I attended the Christmas party in 1958.

I marveled at Lou's Civic Center Studies for Philadelphia, 1956–57, which included the geometric City Tower and castle-like parking garages—reserving the city core as a car-free zone.

Lou's Richards Medical Research Laboratories at the University of Pennsylvania, under construction in 1959. After Philip Johnson, the influential architect, examined the plans in Lou's office, he reportedly exclaimed, "When this building is finished, you will be world famous."

One of Lou's pastels of the Pyramids at Giza, Egypt, 1951. The glass and steel of sleek modernism never suited Lou. He wanted, instead, to capture the silence and power of ancient ruins in his work.

Lou was also a sought-after teacher, giving master classes first at Yale and then at the University of Pennsylvania, and now there was a demand for him overseas as well. In September he traveled to Holland to give the keynote address at a conference in Otterlo organized by Team 10, a group of young architects searching for new directions in the profession that included the English husband and wife Peter and Alison Smithson and the Dutch architect Aldo van Eyck.

Lou's letters from this trip came to me in a bundle, which is often how he sent them when he traveled. He would jot notes and letters, sometimes with sketches, over several days, then post them together when he had the chance. This first bundle of letters details events of the conference and records his visits to several places in southern France: the medieval city of Carcassonne and the Gothic cathedral of Sainte-Cécile at Albi, as well as recently completed buildings of the Swiss French architect Charles-Édouard Jeanneret, known as Le Corbusier. I felt as if Lou were taking me along with him, introducing me to places and landscapes I didn't know—including me as he was in the midst of discovering Le Corbusier, whose work would come to mean more to Lou than that of any other living architect.

Le Corbusier's Couvent Sainte-Marie de La Tourette, near Lyon, France.

Geneva, 15th

Darling Harriet,

Today I saw a wonderful building—Couvent de La Tourette-Eveux-sur-Arbresle—near Lyon, a monastery. I had a letter from Andre Wogenscky (Corbusier's assistant) to allow me in. Wogenscky was one of the French representatives at the conference in Otterlo. The building is a coming together of spaces boldly and even violently meeting each with its own light quality. I felt all humility before this masterpiece of Corbusier's. I kept telling the monk who guided me thru of my reactions—the meaning profound in the nakedness of every form, the joyous courage that comes from realization in art, and that only a religious man could act with such fearless invention for the sheer need [or] rather desire for the creation. All the time I talked to him I was thinking of course of my own realizations and testing against what I saw. I felt nothing but humility and strength and a powerful will to continue more than ever.

This monk, a South African, spoke English very intelligently. He readily saw my point that an artist never sets out to solve a problem for which there is a known solution and a known appearance (or feeling). He draws from the circumstances and need the essence of new clusters of affinities which he models into a new image.

The monks with the problem may well have envisioned a Gothic monastery. Now in the hands of the Master it becomes a tough environment of spaces religious all Corbusier's and all Everyone's.

I didn't know of this work until the meeting at Otterlo. To go back to southern France from where I had just come seemed crowding it (and damned exhausting) for so short a stay. But I couldn't resist it after it was described to me. So back to Paris—Paris to Lyon—Lyon to Eveux-sur-Arbresle by taxi. Then to Ronchamp from this unfriendly place, Geneva.

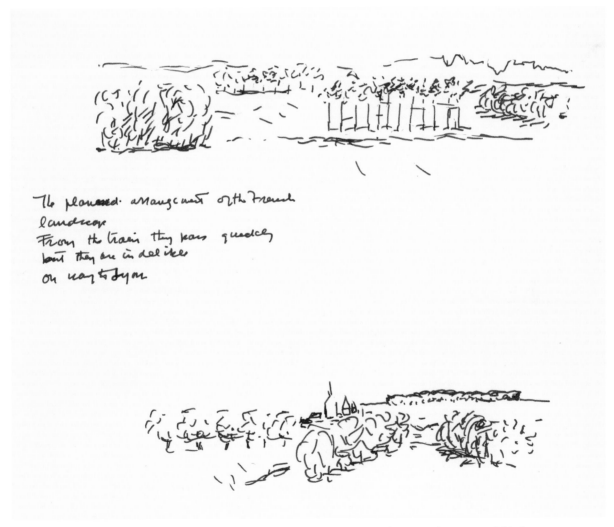

The planned arrangement of the French landscape. From the train they pass quickly but they are indelible. On way to Lyon.

Sweetheart my wonderful sweetheart how your image and all that I feel gives radiance to it is ever with me. Once it appeared unbelievably real. The wife of Aldo Van Eyck, a Holland architect of unusual ability, reminded me right away of you — without that her beautiful face and graceful body, but above all I felt you in me by the loving closeness of her husband and in her artful way of showing her faith in him.

After my talk at the conference it was expressed as the presence of a new beginning. Harriet it was a good moment. Already I told you of deciding to go once more again to Couvent de la Tourelle and then to Ronchamp which I found to be a great great work. I am now ready to learn. The thought of seeing you is everything.

Love Lou

Ronchamp —
The wound is the earth left after excavation (an idea of myself Lou). All the evidence of making is present.

The chapel
The inverted roof is the concrete form. In acoustical effect it matters demonstrated by standing below then not visiting the chapel

Pyramid erected to view the chapel at its own elevation —

Paris, 17th

Sweetheart my wonderful sweetheart how your image and all
that I feel gives radiance to it is ever with me. Once it appeared
unbelievably real. The wife of Aldo Van Eyck, a Holland architect
of unusual ability, reminded me right away of you—in the cut of
her beautiful face and graceful body. But above all I felt you in me
by the loving closeness to her husband and in her artful way of
showing her faith in him.

   After my talk at the conference it was expressed as the presence
of a new beginning. Harriet, it was a good moment.

   Already I told you of deciding to go south again to Couvent de
La Tourette and then to Ronchamp which I found to be a great,
great work. I am now ready to leave. The thought of seeing you is
everything.

Love,
Lou

Ronchamp—The mound is the earth left after excavation (an idea I myself had). All the evidence of making is present.

The Chapel. The inverted roof is the correct form for acoustic effects. The monks demonstrated it by chanting before then twisting the clapper.

Pyramid erected to view the chapel at various elevations.

The wing ga bird
wiee
wiee
a wiee a wiee
a wiee to fly
a wiee to fly
to fly
to fly
fly — fly — fly . . .
is the wing ga bird.

Existence wiel — Is it not an element of the Psyche.?
I must insist on other element of the Psyche the 'Ina' a name I chose arts to give to what I thought symbolizes primordial conscious ness ι.

INA
The beginning of all conscious existence

INA and WILL
The beginning of I am and of feeling, The entrance of will — conscious direction

Dearest. you will recognize that I was not satisfied with wing ga bird because the 'wiee' was suspended when I forgot consciousness THE most wonderful reason un measurable and un material. Also I did not like the word consciousness it sounds like a cheap perfume. So I invented INA. Another reason is that there can be no consciousness without wiee but there can be no wiee without consciousness So INA is pure consciousness with no wiee. [so far it makes no sense to me either].
I love you my dearest my dearest.
I dare to write you this undigested thought. I am really terribly interested to think into it
you are the only one I ever loved

In November an envelope arrived at my new address in New York City with a remarkable letter Lou wrote after one late-night phone call in which he speculated about nature, man, and creativity. I was learning that architecture for Lou wasn't only about making buildings. It was also a philosophical and spiritual investigation—a lens for looking at the world and understanding human beings—often expressing feelings that existed for him somewhere between words and drawings. This is not to say that Lou's speculations were meant to be academically rigorous, but they were gesturing at things that mattered greatly to him. In this letter he invented the word *Ina* as an attempt to express what he called "the unmeasurable." The unmeasurable was a place from which Lou felt artistic inspiration and realization arose.

This is the beginning of the odyssey of
conscious existence.

A rose wants to be a rose.
... is the same for all living things
The character of ... is different
This makes a rose different from a man.

There is no ... in rocks there is no consciousness
There is conscious existence and non conscious existence
Feeling is the book of the odyssey of the INA and will
This book is our ... — It is a book with only intuition no facts.

From all this I intend to develop the idea of
Realization.

So far I realize our own feeling and our
own Thought must reach out to the
Realm of Feeling and the Realm of Thought
which is so much as to say the recognition of
Thought and the recognition of Feeling,
Realization cannot come to us except
that the interaction in the Thoughts and Feelings
follows.
Realization is the sensing of a harmony
of systems. It is the sense of order, or one may
say that Order is the name given to a harmony
of systems.
The Scientist works from Realization
The Artist works from Realization (a discipline) to search for the elements ... in Nature ... is not
The scientist learns Realization turns to form. ... concerned with the making of
The artist thru his realization ... Form itself

... from which form may come

... none of these properly developed

The beginning of feeling — the experience of INA and conscious direction
The beginning of thought — the experience conscious direction.
This may be said another way — Feeling is the record of consciousness and will experienced
... the evolution.
(must work on this part ↑)

Dearest After I spoke to you on the phone I wrote this piece about ...

I love you

PHILADELPHIA TO 34 E. 62ND ST., NEW YORK, NOVEMBER 1, 1959

Dearest,
You will recognize that I was not satisfied with "wing of a bird"
because the "will" was suspended when I forgot consciousness—
THE most wonderful sense, un-measurable and un-material.
Also I did not like the word consciousness. It sounds like a cheap
perfume, so I invented INA. Now the reason is that there can
be consciousness without will but there can be no will without
consciousness. So INA is pure consciousness without will (so far it
makes no sense to me either).

I love you my dearest my dearest.

I dare to write you this undigested thought. I am really terribly
interested to think into it.

You are the only one I ever loved.

21

                    The wing of a bird
                         will
                         will
                      a will a will
                      a will to fly
                      a will to fly
                         to fly
                         to fly
                     fly—fly—fly . . .
                   is the wing of a bird

Existence will—is it not an element of the Psyche?
I must insert another element of the Psyche the "Ina" a name I should like to
give to what I thought symbolizes primordial consciousness.

                            INA
            The beginning of all conscious existence

                        INA and WILL
            The beginning of form and of feeling.
            The entrance of will—conscious direction

This is the beginning of the odyssey of conscious existence.

A rose wants to be a rose
Ina is the same for all living things
The character of will is different
This makes a rose different from a man.
There is no will in rock, there is no consciousness.
There is conscious existence and non-conscious existence
Feeling is the book of the odyssey of the Ina and will
This book is our richest inheritance. It is a book with only intuition. No facts.

The beginning of feeling—The experience of INA and conscious direction
The beginning of thought—The experience of conscious direction.
(This may be said another way—Feeling is the record of consciousness and will experienced in our evolution)
(must work on this part)

From all this I intend to develop the idea of <u>Realization</u>.
So far I sense our own feeling and our own thought must reach out to the Realm of Feeling and the Realm of Thought which is as much as to say the recognition of Thought with recognition of Feeling. Realization cannot come to us except thru its introspection in the Thoughts and Feelings of others.

Realization is the sensing of a harmony of systems. It is the sense of order, or one may say that order is the name given to a harmony of systems.
The Scientist works from Realization
The Artist works from Realization
The scientist leaves realizations to search for (or discover) the elements in Nature from which form may come. He is not concerned with the making of form itself.
The artist thru his realizations turns to form.

None of this is properly developed

Dearest, After I spoke to you on the phone I wrote this piece above. I said it to myself very much better before. I don't know what makes me want to explain these things. I don't need them for my work—maybe to be the teacher who does not rely on his own work as example I need this. In fact it is for my freedom in this sense.

After I spoke to you—How can I say I love you my dearest forever when I know you only a few months. Well I can say I love you forever because all of me holds nothing for anyone else because your love inspires me because I feel that my love inspires you. I am proud because my love is not divided and when you tell me of your undivided love my own feels indestructible.

Lou

ROCHESTER, NEW YORK, TO 34 E. 62ND ST., NEW YORK,
DECEMBER 18, 1959

Dearest,
It was lovely of you to see me off. Our days are like full years.
Every incident like this one is an event.
    I love you.

                                                                    Lou

Lou visited me in New York City whenever he could, often routing his travel through Idlewild Airport (now JFK) so that we might spend a day or an evening together. In Manhattan we could walk freely hand in hand, visiting museums and window-shopping, and I would cook us supper in my apartment, but I worried about where it would all lead.

Lou's napkin sketch of me, made in a café at Idlewild Airport as we waited for one of his flights.

With my brothers and sisters in Chicago on New Year's Day, 1940. Left to right are Priscilla (Posie), William (Willy), me, Abbott, Nancy, and Edwina (Eddie).

1960

When my brothers, sisters, and I were photographed in 1940, it was just two years before Pearl Harbor and probably the last time all of us were home together for our parents' New Year's Day open house. World War II would scatter us, sending my brothers into air and sea battles and two sisters into auxiliary services. The war brought brides to the boys and a West Point husband to Nancy, but Eddie, Posie, and I were still not married twenty years later—hardly our parents' expectation when they gave us girls good manners and college educations but no middle names, expecting us to acquire a husband's name for our final identities.

Despite a sixteen-year difference in their ages, my parents, William Lawrence Pattison and Bonnie Abbott, had a truly happy marriage. I was born in 1928, the last of their six surviving children (one daughter, Jean, had died in childhood of pneumonia). Like our parents, we were Chicago born, proud midwesterners of pioneer stock. I harbored the prairie in my bones, and its traditions were close to a living memory for my generation. I proudly repeated stories of how my great-grandparents built a log cabin on the Fox River, "fought off Indians" on land they seized for farming, and introduced the first piano to the Illinois territory.

We grew up on Chicago's North Side, considered a good neighborhood for raising a white, Protestant, middle-class family. It was separated by "the Loop," crowded with skyscrapers, from the African American neighborhoods on the South Side and the immigrant neighborhoods on the West Side, where some of our cousins lived in a gloomy mansion on Jackson Boulevard. Unifying this divided city was the primal void of Lake Michigan, which tempered the prairie heat waves in summer, blasted us with icy winds in winter, and provided the backdrop for what is still one of the most dramatic skylines in the world. In my time that skyline was bounded by two distinctive landmarks, Holabird & Root's Palmolive Building, with its revolving beacon, and Ernest Grunsfeld's domed Adler Planetarium, both Art Deco masterworks designed by the fathers of school friends of mine. (I adored the Grunsfeld house, with its stairway curved like a shell up to a spacious living room in flowing wood veneers with French modern furniture and tall windows surveying a walled garden.)

Our home was at the top of a three-story brick walk-up apartment building, built by my father near Belmont Harbor. It was crowded with shared bedrooms and closets, but had a study for my mother, a billiard room for the boys, and a tiny office where my father ran his modest real estate business. I recall winters with "Jack Frosted" windows and hissing radiators drying our snowsuits after sledding in Lincoln Park or a visit to the Christmas displays downtown at Marshall Field's, where our mother outfitted us when hand-me-downs wouldn't do. By April our windows would be unsealed and opened to the clop and rumble of horse-drawn delivery wagons and street vendors' calls through the alleys and concrete backyards where we played or zigzagged through to join friends for a twenty-five-cent double feature at the Lakeshore. My first movie was *Little Women* with Katharine Hepburn, over which I bawled when Beth's death shattered the March family. But Saturday matinees at the Goodman Theatre outweighed the best movie-screen memories. From the moment its chandeliers dimmed, I held my breath for the gold curtain to rise and the gossamer green curtains within to open onto a magical scene.

My mother wasn't particularly taken by the theater, but she cared about literature and art. She had a diverse group of friends and was active in women's clubs and on the education council of our school. She read to us with a wonderfully expressive voice and frequented auctions where she acquired all manner of objects, furniture, and prints, which were always "undervalued."

My father was a provider in every way. He was gallant and galvanizing, rarely in repose, always filling one of many roles, whether managing his apartment buildings, fixing furnaces and painting walls, or going to market and hauling quantities of food from wholesale stalls. He was up before anyone, making breakfast, and home for dinner, where he presided over the table. He was our transport and guide to a city whose evolution and layout were layered, like business files, in his head from when he was a boy, just old enough to recall the Great Chicago Fire of 1871 and, vividly, the decade of rebuilding afterward. I can still hear his impromptu talks before the Historical Society's dioramas, those magical lighted scenes of our mythical origins: the wagon trains, the Fort Dearborn settlement, the railroad stockyards, Abraham Lincoln heading off to his inauguration, the terrifying night of the Great Fire, the Haymarket Riot, and even bootlegging gangsters in a shoot-out the year I was born.

I especially loved the Chicago Historical Society's collection of Mrs. James Ward Thorne's miniature rooms, and a curator allowed me to carefully dust them when I was eleven. I admired the historic American mansions of Salem and the James River, but it was the final room, an exquisite miniature

Me in the garden at Faraway, Lincolnville, Maine, 1933.   My parents, Bonnie and William Pattison, 1930s.

My father making breakfast at Faraway for my sisters Nancy and Posie, my brother Abbott, and me, before the long drive back to Chicago at the end of the summer, c. 1937.

of a modern penthouse, that drew me most. And I soon began to beg to be taken on drives to look for Frank Lloyd Wright's unmistakable houses in the suburbs, from which scandal had long since banished him. After I saw pictures of Fallingwater, my mother gave me a book on Wright's houses, and I spent long hours testing myself to see if I could remember and reconstruct his plans and elevations in my mind's eye. It never occurred to me that I might find a role for myself in the world of architecture.

All six of us Pattison kids attended Francis W. Parker School on the edge of Lincoln Park. Parker promoted John Dewey's progressive education theories with memorable teachers in a family-like community and inspired ceremonies that made relevant, even joyous, experiences of "learning by doing." The arts were not a luxury but on a par with civics and science, and a number of my schoolmates, including Joan Mitchell and Edward Gorey, went on to successful careers as artists. In my senior year my love for the theater flowered into creating sets for a play production whose hero and heroine were in my class. My classmates were deeply in love but destined to be torn apart by religious prejudice: she was Jewish, and he Protestant. The social mores of that time were powerful, and despite its humanism, our small private school on Chicago's North Side could only tentatively explore issues of oppression and exclusion. The reality of my classmates' anguish hit home to me, but I was sheltered from such experiences personally, never dreaming that my own life would be thrown into the turmoil of an impossible love in the coming years.

Recalling the easy grace of a privileged and sheltered childhood also conjures up the pageant of our summers in Maine, where our father drove us from Chicago with gloved hands in a plush LaSalle with a steamer trunk strapped on the back. By the end of three days we would arrive at Faraway, the summer house, where our mother took charge and filmed our life there with a Bell & Howell movie camera for our father, who returned to Chicago's blistering heat to support the family playground. Maine was a magical land and seascape for us. We sailed among its islands and bays, explored its hills and forests, rode horses, swam off the rocks, played tennis, golf, and baseball, and painted with the eccentric Miss Hackett, who lived across the road. We hayed, harvested apples, danced in barns, and were fascinated by raconteurs, visitors from afar, on the pillared porch at dusk. For me, the romance of this landscape and my love for it recall a performance of *A Midsummer Night's Dream* staged one long-ago summer afternoon in a garden amphitheater, nested between the library and the harbor in Camden, Maine.

In my New York apartment, early 1960s.

The world of New York City in 1960 was utterly different from the one I had grown up in. At thirty-one, with a job as a lowly assistant to a testy arts appraiser at Parke-Bernet Galleries, I didn't have the slightest idea of how to contend with the difference between what was anticipated for me by my family and what was actually happening in my life.

On the surface, the auction house seemed like a good fit, satisfying my penchant for beautiful things and giving me something to talk about with the family. It was fun to assess Bruegels and Beckmanns, and I found the drama of the auction floor irresistible. I was privy to remarkable treasure hunts, typing up on a portable Olivetti the contents of valuable collections in opulent estates and death-darkened apartments. In one such place I was astonished as a dustcloth was lifted to reveal the great Rembrandt painting *Aristotle with a Bust of Homer*, soon to be bought for the Metropolitan Museum of Art, but what kind of future was there in this? I didn't want to end up like a character in an Edith Wharton story, stuck in a tiny apartment, the lover of a man who showed up at his convenience, living in the quiet desperation of an unkind city bustling with the noise of commerce and other people's dreams.

I longed for advice and to tell someone in my family about Lou but dared not share what was going on even with my sister Eddie, who lived in an apartment in Murray Hill. I was afraid of what she would say, as she herself had already suffered the loss of her dreams of a career as an actress and was now selling cosmetics and juggling several boyfriends, none of whom had any intention of marrying her.

In a bold move, I decided I would try to introduce Lou to family friends, who I thought would be more accepting and less likely to judge me. My mother was a close card-playing friend of the opera singer Bidu Sayão and her husband Giuseppe Danise, who also summered in Maine, and they had been especially kind to me. They invited me to a party at their apartment in the Ansonia Hotel on Manhattan's Upper West Side, and I took Lou along. It was immediately awkward. Lou's magic failed to charm the sophisticated guests who in a single sentence segued between Italian, French, and Portuguese, with the occasional English word thrown in. Lou was nervous, which made him garrulous, anticipating that these fellow artists would welcome us and gather us both into their glamorous milieu. But they didn't. Bidu's husband, aged, venerable as a master opera singer, was especially disdainful. His look to me required no words. He'd seen enough operas to know how our kind of story would likely end.

My confidence was shaken. Rebuffed in my bid for acceptance, I felt desolate, doomed to protect my secret in silence. Lou salved my wounds with his letters and sketches bearing news of his growing success and his intent to take me along with him, entrusting me with concepts and plans as I curled up listening to him on the phone or reading his letters. On the instant of meeting, he could sweep away my solitude and anxieties, replacing them with the expanding compass of his world. I longed for a different kind of life, but also for the comfort of my family. How could I make it work both ways, resolving the rift between my past and an uncertain future with Lou?

A telegram from Lou arrived at my door one chilly morning, announcing, almost comically, "Africa Exciting." Going to work that day, I imagined Lou in grasslands, among the animals he loved and could draw beautifully from memory. In fact he had landed at the coastal Southwest African town of Luanda, Angola—then still under Portuguese colonial rule—where the US State Department was planning to build a consulate and diplomat's residence. The letters that arrived after this telegram capture the way Lou observed everything going on around him with great attention to detail.

LISBON TO 34 E. 62ND ST., NEW YORK, JANUARY 3, 1960

My Dearest:

I will be met on my arrival in Africa. Until then, I will not know where to send mail—if at all possible. Was told that the captain of our ship puts the stamps on which means special attention and that you will get this little letter. Have not a thought in my head. The few hours I had in Lisbon left the impression that the folk from the country must be infinitely more worthwhile. The few I saw selling their wares or looking over the big city were handsomer, more graceful, better dressed, vivid. The red-brown complexion is surely attractive. Gold looks very well against it.

I shouldn't know with so little time to see, but I sensed a warm love for children. What attracted me most was the offering of sweets to two strange children. A couple of well dressed "ladies" from Lisbon made endearing greetings to two country children who were with their most beautiful, natively dressed, mother. The mother didn't act like "Oh no you mustn't." She approved with wonderful dignity. The children accepted with eyes lowered in slight embarrassment. Even the "ladies" were gracious.

In a restaurant—little, 4 tables—I had a boiled fish and potato lunch and very good beer. A boy and his father got their order brought in. A heaping dish of steaming boiled something engulfed also in potatoes and boiled broccoli. The boy's eyes and mouth both laughed in glee. At the other tables everyone sympathized with the

33

boy and wished him a good appetite. I don't know what they said but whatever it was lasted several minutes; the boy expressing his delight and the others never tiring in expressing theirs. Indeed all the people somehow appear like children to me. Young and old.

Turning the corner of an old street the sudden excitement was the chasing of a little mouse from the door of a shop by four giggling men, one with a broom (like the witch's broom at Halloween). The poor mouse made it across the traffic'd street, ran hugging the opposite curb and disappeared in the culvert . . . It was time to return to the airport . . . Dearest most beautiful sweetheart you'll just have to accept the droning of this silly little letter by my telling you I love you.

Lou

LUANDA, ANGOLA, TO 34 E. 62ND ST., NEW YORK, JANUARY 5, 1960

Harriet,
If I were but as handsome as this animal. Saw nothing of real Africa. The natives in Luanda the most interesting people.

Lou

After a week in Luanda, on the eve of his return to the United States, Lou traveled to Leopoldville, in neighboring Belgian Congo, now Kinshasa, Democratic Republic of the Congo.

Dearest,

Yesterday I was invited to a party at the home of the American Consul General of the Belgian Congo at Leopoldville. Word got around that over a hundred were there. Black tie and white jacket was proper dress. The women came in their best. Everyone came masked. Our little party first had priming cocktails at the apartment of one of the secretaries. I was excused from the white jacket formality but I did have a red mask given to me by a certain person. When we arrived the party seemed a bit starchy. Foreigners mixed with Americans produced bits of French with the ring of third year culture and English learned for a reason. Candlelit tables on the lawn overlooking the Congo River which appeared lavender. The lawn shaded by Acacias—even in the warm dark of the sky— was ink green, only yellowed by the faint glow of the candles and merry faces at the tables. On the terrace, the HaChaCha. The party broke up at 7 this morning. I, good me, was in bed by two.

This morning, later, I was shown thru the consular buildings in Leopoldville and from there I had lunch with the consul and his wife. I saw some of the wreck of the night and morning. We then drove around the countryside to see the living ways of the black people, palm and acacia forests and the dramatic sight of the rapids of the Congo River. This may seem I saw a bit of Africa. No—from the stories I heard, I saw nothing.

The first day of my arrival, Sunday a week ago, I went sailing in the Atlantic off Luanda. The days that followed were all working and entirely too much customary drinking. I stayed at the house of the consul of Luanda.

In a way the whole assignment is a tour de force. The tropics is just a different life. I am asked to build for Americans who hope to express their culture in a world of utter mystery.

With all my love,
Lou

Sunset soon after takeoff over French Africa to Kano. The glow of an ebbing fire. The sun a single red ember. All in its light is of that red. The wool blue of the clouds away from its light accepts the red. Beyond and away from this cloud and sun play is the transparent light of angelical blue.

Only the next moment.

A Kano the engine was found faulty The delay of four hours made it possible to see the Sahara at daylight, Atlas Mountains

At Kano the engine was found faulty. The delay of four hours made it possible to see the Sahara at daylight. Atlas Mountains.

Political upheavals would ultimately scuttle the Luanda project, but Lou's response to the tropical climate of Angola, the harsh glare of the sunlight, and the rugged topography of the Atlas Mountains, which he saw on the flight back to Lisbon, primed him for another exciting commission closer to home. Dr. Jonas Salk, developer of the polio vaccine, was looking for an architect to design his new research institute, funded by the March of Dimes, on land at La Jolla, California, north of San Diego. Salk was impressed by the Richards Medical Research Laboratories in Philadelphia, and even more by Lou himself. They bonded at once over the desire to build a laboratory where, as Salk put it, "Picasso would feel at home." In late January Lou visited the site.

Dr. Jonas Salk, Lou, and Basil O'Connor, president of the March of Dimes, with an early model of the Salk Institute for Biological Studies.

It was a high mesa overlooking the Pacific—dramatic, like the settings of the temples he loved in the ancient world.

The excitement of the Salk project was powerful, not only for Lou but for me as well, as it was my first real exposure to how an architect looks at a problem and begins the search for form. Lou spoke about "what a building wants to be," and the importance of how the parts of a building are brought together—but I was not yet prepared to follow the technical subtleties of structure, hierarchical spaces, and material capabilities that Lou so greatly valued. I could relate to his drawings and frames of mind, if not the constraints of construction and the battles of the profession. When he spoke about the inspirations of the Acropolis, the monastic community at Assisi, and the garden courts at the Alhambra, in Granada, it sparked ideas in my head that I eagerly shared with him, sometimes sending along tentative drawings for him to look at.

In July, while I was in Maine—where I have managed to return almost every summer of my life—I finally told my mother about the man whose phone calls interrupted the routine of our daily activities. We were expanding the garden at Faraway, and she was a little surprised at my ability to project an organizing vision for its design. It felt like a good moment to break through our mutual reticence, and so I told her about the artist-architect who had enabled me to see the world differently.

I told her that he was Jewish, an immigrant, revered by a new generation eager for his words and work, almost twice my age, unhappily married, and that I loved him. My mother listened, paused, as she was logical and guarded, and thanked me for my truthfulness, but expressed a deep concern that I reported to Lou on the phone and that echoes through his next letter.

My sketch of spruce trees at Faraway.

PASADENA, CALIFORNIA, TO FARAWAY, LINCOLNVILLE, MAINE,
JULY 24, 1960

Dearest,
To think that anyone should question the true ring of Mr. K. Your Mother feels the stony road for the inordinate. She does not deny our being together. This is wise. It is to wait patiently for the play of experience.

What does it mean to love more than once? The sphere within which we meet kindredness is small. This limited sphere is where most of us dwell.

Only love is a blinding oneness from a limitless sphere so vast as to be intraversable in a lifetime. Only love is revelation, brilliant with desire.

Lou

Dearest Sweetheart,

Now I have witnessed the dividing of cells. Movies were taken at
precise time intervals of a single cell under the microscope. The
cell divided and the two divided to four, etc. The workings of the
interior and the quivering of the walls was something unbelievable
and exciting. Theodore Puck, the inventor of the method and famous
for the isolation of a single cell which he was able to make reproduce
itself (by discovering the importance of controlled environment),
demonstrated the film for me. He is to work at the Salk Institute.
The 12:05 [train] shakes so. . . . I was warned before I saw him that
he is the most insensitive to fields other than science. This was by a
Dr. Melvin Cohn of Stanford U. also a famous scientist.

When I arrived in Denver to meet Puck, he was there waiting
for me. The first place he took me to was a 60 foot broad stone
terrace, about 200 feet long, overlooking and paralleling a range of
mountains. On the terrace of stone was inlaid in marble a tracing
(drawing) of the mountain peaks ahead with explanation carved in
the stone. The platform raised above the road by a few steps was
bare of everything except for a large sundial, scientifically placed,
with markings of explanation on the stone platform on how to read
the dial. Puck said he comes here often to get religion about his
work. He wondered and doubted if San Diego could offer as much.
We waited for the sun to set. I needn't tell how beautiful it all was
and then drove in the half-light thru tree lined roads to my hotel. I
liked him, and wondered now a little about Cohn in Stanford.

Cohn talked much art. He was not too sure of my role as
architect and I sensed a confidence in all matters including a
cautious concern about architecture ready to become more
assertive—"K" willing.

We came to the medical school labs at Stanford U. which Ed
Stone designed. The description of this building I must leave to
when I see you again my sweet darling. For the moment it may
be visualized as composed of a heavy pierced concrete element
2½ x 2½ feet square prevailing overall. Walls (openings closed
in), open screen walls, piers, etc., courts, gardens, fountains (that
damned train) hanging bronze disks with flowers. The whole
thing is a colossal tour de force, completely forbidding, vacuous
on the interior. A 20 million $ joke. The open concrete pattern is

Tracing of peaks in stone
sundial   road   steps

Cohn Talked much art. He was not so sure of my
role as architect and I sensed a confidence in all
matters including a cautious concern about architecture
ready to become more assertive & willing. We came
to the Medical School Labs at Stanford U which Ed Stone
designed. The description of this building I must leave
to when I see you again my sweet darling. For the moment
it may be visualised as composed of heavy placed
concrete elements $2\frac{1}{2} \times 2\frac{1}{2}$ feet square prevailing over
all, — walls (openings closed in) open screen walls piers etc
courts gardens fountains (that damned Tracy) hanging
bronze dishes with flowers. The whole thing is a colossal
tour de force completely forbidding vacuous on the
exterior. A 20 million $ AKE. The open concrete pattern
is so insistant that the Dr. (and 20 others too) is leaning to
escape it. Many y cause there it beautiful as explained
to trustees who paid for it.

Cohn is a dry man but a good man million are a
scientist. Later, before departing for Los Angeles, I dropped
at his home for a drink. I met his wife writer on
comparative literature. We almost came to blows, Boy!
what an opinionated

Dr. Dulbecco of Pasadena (California Institute of Tech.
was wonderful. Also Dr. Meselsohn brilliant
young understudies. Both terrific guys.
The P. railroad is caput

Tracing of peaks in stone / sundial / road / steps

41

so insistent that the Dr. (and so others too) is leaving to escape it. Many of course think it beautiful, especially the trustees who paid for it.

Cohn is a dry man but a good man, brilliant as a scientist. Later, before departing for Los Angeles, I dropped in at his house for a drink. I met his wife, writer on comparative literature. We almost came to blows. Boy! what an opinionated —!

Dr. [Renato] Dulbecco of Pasadena (California Institute of Tech.) was wonderful. Also Dr. [Matthew] Meselson brilliant young undernourished. Both terrific guys. The P. [Pennsylvania] railroad is caput.

Dearest, most wonderful sweetheart, I was so glad to have spoken to you on arrival in New York. How I love to hear your voice. Your voice and all ever said is like a single cry wildly everywhere in me. Memories are real. Our moments together are jewels. All is a single faith.

The one and only love—those who know it know its simplicity. Those who could not experience it recognize it as the symbol of all love. . . . Sweetheart darling I love you. I want to tell you this before you turn over for this is the close of my little letter. . . .

All my love,

Lou

PHILADELPHIA TO FARAWAY, JULY 1960

Dearest,

The ring of your voice when we talked the morning you left for Maine. It remains as only the broken edge of a beautiful joy that presses its way into every moment that opens from my work . . .

As always my dearest, dearest, I have been working. Salk, Luanda, Bryn Mawr [dormitories], Rochester [Unitarian Church] all together and then each one separately. Your beautiful thought on Luanda is going to work well. There are endless little problems (inside the general idea) that need sharpening. The space is too much for the maximum area allowed by the State Department. I know it may prove fatal to the idea if it gets into doctrinaire hands (the book). I am relying on their liking its original submission to inspire exception.

Biology [addition to Richards] is also in trouble with budget. They are giving me no money. Maybe that's good for me. I may be forced to thin my office. Hate the idea. I may have to wait until the president gets back in September for action of the Trustees. Nobody likes to appear before trustees. They can be so destructive, so arbitrary. Again, though, I am looking at it from my point of view of the moment. They were really hellishly nice to me before. (My mind can get damned ordinary.)

How is my sweetest most wonderful darling sweetheart darling? How is the island? How tonight I wish I could call on a genie to take me in the palm of his hand and just lean over and place me beside you. How we both would cry without sound for joy. How heavenly a single moment can be. How years can be dust. How a moment can be a radiant ever light. Let us never falter in our love for the want of just all, all that is nought but expanded nothing. My love for you and your love for me is everlasting. It is a soul in itself. It has its own indestructible existence. We are only its harbor.

Am not in the mood for pictures, though I have some beauts in mind. It is now 11:30. Think I should knock off. I love you, I love you, I love you.

Love,
Lou

One of Lou's presentation drawings of the First Unitarian Church, Rochester, New York, c. 1960.

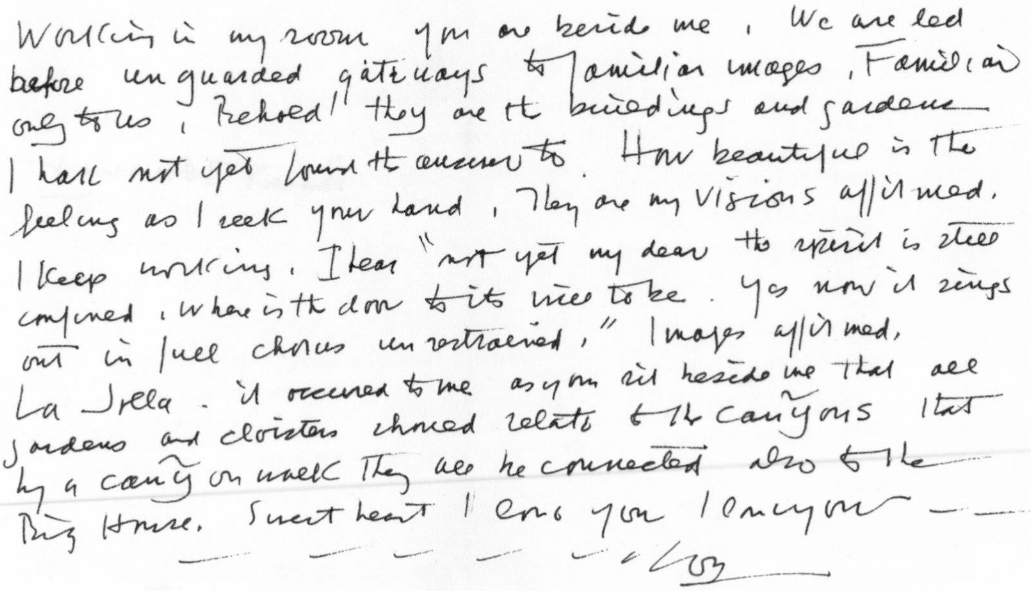

[handwritten letter reproduced above the typeset transcription]

[POSTMARKED] PHILADELPHIA TO FARAWAY, JULY 28, 1960

La Jolla
Dearest Harriet,
Working in my room, you are beside me. We are led before
unguarded gateways to familiar images. Familiar only to us. Behold!
They are the buildings and gardens I have not yet found the answer
to. How beautiful is the feeling as I seek your hand. They are my
visions affirmed.

I keep working. I hear "not yet my dear, the spirit is still
confined. Where is the door to its will to be? Yes, now it sings out
in full chorus unrestrained." Images affirmed.

La Jolla. It occurred to me as you sit beside me that all gardens
and cloisters should relate to the canyons, that by a canyon walk
they all be connected also to the Big House. Sweetheart I love you I
love you.

Lou

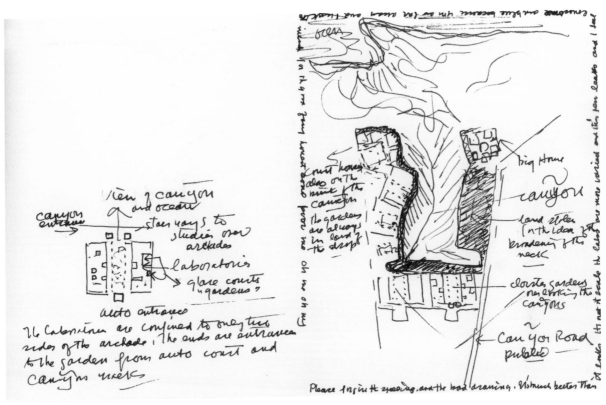

[LEFT: laboratory plan] *The laboratories are confined to only two sides of the arcades. The ends are entrances to the garden from auto court and canyon walks. Canyon entrance / view of canyon and ocean / stairways to studios over arcades / laboratories / glare courts "gardens" / auto entrance*

[RIGHT: site plan] *Ocean / court houses also on the brink of the canyon / The gardens are always in land of the drop / Big House / canyon / land stolen for the idea of the broadening of the neck / cloister gardens overlooking the canyons / canyon road, public*

Please forgive the spelling and the bad drawing. It's much better than it looks. It's not to scale. The labs are more varied and this pen leaks and I feel lonesome and blue because you are far away for the good of my honest soul poor me oh me oh my.

As shown in this sketch, the Salk Institute master plan included not only laboratories but also a meeting house, or "Big House," and residences for scientists. Lou found working simultaneously on the Salk and Luanda projects especially generative of new forms and ideas.

The house [consul's residence, Luanda] as it appears from the road. The living room on the 2nd floor is flanked by two porches from which the columns supporting the Sun Roof and its beams and girders may be seen. The living room (facing west) is screened. The lower floors are all screened. The middle room below is the dining on the level of the ground. The screens are of wood made to allow light to enter or be shut out. No glass.

(Don't forget West is East in Luanda or North is South. I don't know which now.)

Dearest Harriet,
Your sacred letter of love—love entered love—A shrine—A shrine
nature cannot make.

    Sweetheart, dear sweetheart, I love you.

                                    Lou

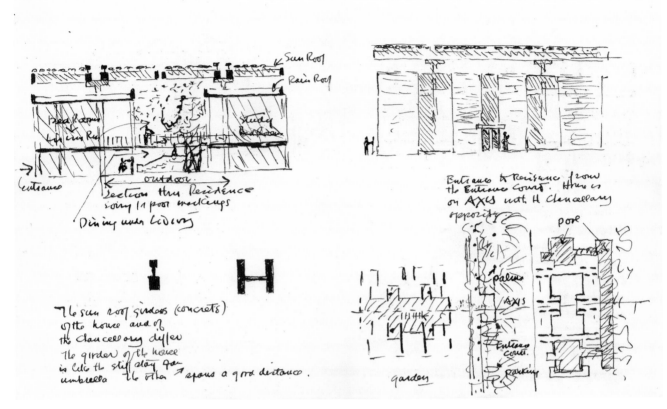

[TOP LEFT] *Section thru Residence (sorry for poor markings) entrance / bedrooms / living room / dining under living / outdoor / study / bedrooms / sun roof / rain roof*

[BOTTOM LEFT] *The sun roof girders (concrete) of the house and of the Chancellery differ. The girder of the house is like the stiff stay of an umbrella. The other spans a good distance.*

[TOP RIGHT] *Entrance to residence from the entrance court. House is on AXIS with the Chancellery opposite.*

[BOTTOM RIGHT] *garden / palms / AXIS / entrance court / parking / pool*

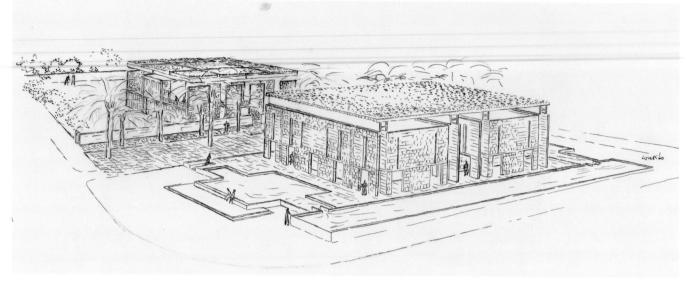

Lou's perspective of the Luanda consulate and residence, showing freestanding outer walls to control heat and glare that Lou called "ruins wrapped around buildings." He was soon to use this idea for the Salk "Big House" as well. The drawing incorporates the thought I'd suggested of a moat surrounding the consulate.

PHILADELPHIA TO FARAWAY, AUGUST 21, 1960

Dearest,

I made a few pictures illustrating the main parts of the Big House in San Diego which I am enclosing. I feel that now I have the beginning of a scheme of spirit.

Before I begin to describe let me tell you about my meeting with Salk on Wednesday. I had only the laboratories developed sufficiently to talk about. The Big House and Dwellings were most preliminary. We spent the whole day from 10 in the morning until about six in the evening. . . .

The meeting with Salk was really excellent and exciting. He helped strengthen the concept of the monastic courts and studies over the garden arcades. He extracted from my plans of the lab areas all studies and assigned them all to the court entrance. This really distinguished the "stainless steel" rooms (labs) from the "oak table–rug–pipe" rooms. Fundamental my dear Watson fundamental. Before dinner, just before, Jonas and I visited the Rosenthals who introduced him to me. They had been to the talk in Pittsburgh. The R's are art collectors, world travelers, good people, very friendly, short, quaint . . .

The Big House will present on its exterior the play of high walls with openings. Windows will not be seen, they will be in back of the shielding walls. The central area of the house (1) [see the following drawings] is a high walled room with only a sun roof over. The enclosing walls will have masonry openings (no glass), which look into walls behind, rising from small courts. This will give a glow of light in the entrance hall (1). The piers supporting the beams and sun tile [roof] form passages to the major space of the house. The walls are fitted with candelabra for night lighting. The room would be a wonderful place to hold a banquet or big gathering. Room #1 then leads to a fountain room (2), flanked by three walls with the axial wall overlooking the canyon scene and the ocean. This room leads down by steps to the ground level. These two rooms then form the axis of all other spaces.

All walls will reach up to the same height. The spaces enclosed that emanate from the central space will have several floors but will not in the aggregate exceed the height of the central area. They will all come to the same conclusion in height. It should give a firmness to the Big House as seen from the distance (my anxiety to explain has made me unselective and repetitive).

Building (3) is the dining place. Instead of a large dining room I show alcoved dining rooms served by a center station and bar (the center business I am not too sure about). The idea is that of creating comfortable places of chatting with visiting dignitaries and with natural friends. . . . The three tiered Building (3)—1st kitchen and cafeteria—main level alcove dining—level above seminar rooms and larger meeting rooms.

Building (4) is the library which on the main level is a lounge (magazines, technical and humanities—Esquire and the like) placed in a walled garden. The level below is for stack room, reading, and the level over the lounge is a reference library. Note connection of lounge to dining. Building (5) is the Auditorium, which with its sloping seat plan is a single story. Building (6) is the exercise room, lockers, Turkish Baths, and sunning roof. 4 levels in all. Area (7) is for the swimming pool and play (handball) courts.

The Details are lacking but I believe there is the beginning of a spirit. I know you will understand when I feel that my inspiration is the Alhambra. It resembles it in no way, still I am drawn to the analogy for reasons I believe we both, and only we, understand . . .

Lou

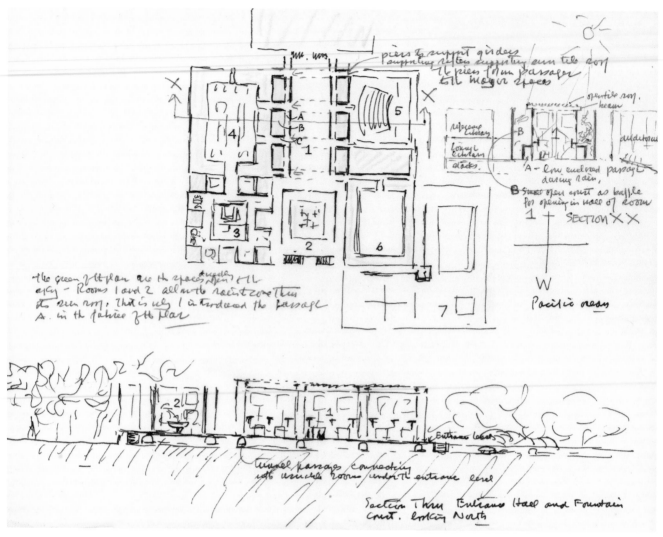

[TOP] *The green of the plan are the spaces directly open to the sky—Rooms 1 and 2 allow the rain to come thru the sun roof. That is why I introduced the passage A in the fabric of the plan*

piers to support girders, supporting rafters supporting sun tile roof / the piers form passages to the major spaces

[RIGHT] *SECTION XX reference library / lounge library / stacks / open tile roof / beam / A—low enclosed passage during rain / B—small open court as baffle for opening in wall of room / auditorium*

[BOTTOM] *Section thru Entrance Hall and Fountain Court, looking North / Tunnel passages connecting with useable rooms under the entrance level*

View from the West—The Fountain Court (1) overlooks the Pacific ocean. The Dining Room (2) The Exercise and Turkish Bath Building. The Pool Terrace

All windows (as in Luanda) will be shielded by walls with openings in the masonry. They will appear like windows but will have no glass. The size and shape of the openings will depend on the orientation and the outlook. The general appearance will be of a walled in building, no glistening of glass will be present.

Dearest Harriet,

Thought I'd write to you before they come for me. The Esherick party, always a good time, always a touch of Thoreau. Sure I'll meet some vixen, more beautiful than beautiful with virtues untold, talents sparkling but she will be but a foggy smudge in the light of you my sweetheart. . . .

This morning dearest I got your letter with "colored" drawings. It isn't the crayon sweetheart. Your drawings are wonderful. The house and surroundings are wonderful. Your whole letter is wonderful but I longed so much for more of your thoughts, your feelings. My mind keeps harking back to the first letter I wrote you, "When I was a boy" – – – "there is a girl." A year ago—but how timeless it feels to me, how utterly true its ring is! Here now almost the whole of me is out of me. The tiniest thread holds on to me . . . As though of tiny shrieks inaudible is this being from which I draw to write.

Tell me about your party last night. Esherick's daughter called for me last night. She is the one who works with Libby Holman (actress of the 20's. Torch singer, good gal). The party was real good. Cool fireplace steak, gin, good company. A feeling of living directly. Heard a story everyone thought terrific, well maybe. It's about the Lusitania (the boat). It was the fateful night. Entertainment (first class) supplied by a magician. A sizable table was loaded with bottles, glasses, silverware. The magician carefully rolled up one end of the table cloth and gave a sudden yank freeing the cloth from the mass on the table as the German torpedo struck!!! Moments later floating in the water was a lady naked except for a string of pearls around her neck. The magician was swimming around the same spot. Noticing him she sneered, "Hey! are you nuts or something!"

Please my darling hide those sketches I made too quickly at Carcassonne.

I love you Harriet. I will always love you.

Lou

Lou in his office at Twentieth and Walnut Streets, where I sent my letters and called him.

Sat. late.

Dearest,

Your long, long letter came this morning. I could have had it Friday only I disregarded a card slipped under my door last night thinking it was an advertisement. Actually it was from the post office announcing your letter undelivered because the door was closed. It was like watching a mystery. Each page I was eager for the next. I enjoyed so much your jokes, your most wonderful friends, and the private life and work of a loving witch.

I tried to think of a dream I had a few days ago. It was a sky of green light. Rays of gold in arpeggios, dutiful to laws yet unfound, inspiring to seek into their secret played with flowing effortlessness across its pale incandescence.

The ground rose below as a luminous purple, dense with mass alluvial, suddenly rent in long leveling gashes of red ever opening wider to a furnace. Overhead, the play continued, heedless of the other show of the same law below.

Vivid was the dream. The Northern lights you described. The darkness of all around. The distance we apart. The beautiful expansive virtuosity of nature—the relentlessness of its laws. Designs. Endless designs yet unborn, yet never to be born, yet inestimable, yet of the law. My sweet darling how uncaring is nature of us once we are. How concerned we are of ourselves once we are.

Sunday

I have been reading some Greek history. Homer. The play of the strong body, the honor to the mind. Both had equal station. Long life was worthy if the victorious warrior grew to legend and the man of mind became the teacher. The warrior is in some of us. He is asked to test his spirit and skill against resigned warriors and successful compromisers. The mind is honored yes but cunning is given the accolade (I say to hell with it. It probably isn't true anyway).

A year ago a note came to me. I felt like the sun turning to illuminate only the one who sent it. I felt duty bound only to life in its dearest joy, that of love. Now this love is a constant song in me. Someday, someday my darling our love will be in our little ones. They will be of love and give us back all that we gave them.

Lou

Lou's "someday, someday," and our talks over the summer gave me great hope for a future together. But I wanted it to become real, and the prospect of continuing my auction-house job in New York City now seemed an intolerable delay. There was also the promise of coming closer to a life in the arts, though at the moment there appeared to be no role beyond that of a good listener and sounding board for Lou's ideas. I recognized the world I wanted to belong to and the depth of an artist I might love forever. I couldn't return to a job where I was as expendable as its last consignment. How meaningless was that world of trading possessions compared to the unbounded world of *making* art that was Lou's! I felt that I would lose not just my soul but my life if I pretended at it much longer, and so, amid a flurry of excuses and explanations, I quit my job and gave up Manhattan for Philadelphia.

Rittenhouse Square, Philadelphia, early 1960s.

1961

Bob Venturi and Edith Braun welcomed me back to Philadelphia warmly, and I found a third-floor studio apartment on Spruce Street not far from Lou's office on Twentieth Street. Halfway between us was Rittenhouse Square, one of the original five squares brilliantly conceived by William Penn in his plan for Philadelphia, which with its giant sycamores, elms, and maples, its pathways, and its evergreen shrubs provided seven acres of repose to break up the noise and activity of the city. Lou and I would often meet in the square on a warm day and find a bench to ourselves near a favorite sculpture (his lion, my billy goat) or by the reflecting pool. He would bring along an apple or a bag of walnuts, both of which he could crack open with his strong bare hands to share with me along with our thoughts and laughter.

The pace of Lou's life was accelerating, but he rarely seemed too busy to step out of the office to meet for lunch at the Hoffmann House, which served the German food that he loved, or Bookbinder's, or L'Aiglon, a bistro run by a lively Greek family, or the Art Alliance on the corner of the square, where Lou was a member. After lunch we might stop at Joseph Fox, the bookseller in a basement shop on Sansom Street, or scout the shelves at Sessler's on Walnut Street, where, among the rare old books and prints, Lou found a Piranesi etching of the ruins of Rome that he bought for me. Occasionally we would even go for an afternoon movie.

Lou taught the Master's Studio at the University of Pennsylvania on Mondays and Wednesdays, and I would often sit in at the back, listening to the advanced architecture students presenting their projects. I recall one day in particular when a lovely redhead with a South African accent presented her work. It was Denise Scott Brown, already making her distinctive presence known and causing a stir.

Most of all, I looked forward to spending hours at Lou's office whenever he worked alone on evenings and weekends—I did not go during the day, as this would have aroused suspicion. As much as Lou needed to talk through ideas, he also needed solitude to think, and I would sit for long stretches beside him, with just the scratch of the charcoal, the rustle of yellow tracing paper, and the hourly tolling of the PNB bell, Philadelphia's Big Ben, to break the silence. Though unschooled, I had an intuitive sense of the way he thought, and it was thrilling when he would turn and ask what I thought. I realized then that there were openings, like unresolved in-between spaces, for a quality idea, or an insight, and I dared to think I might find a way to be useful somehow to his work. At midnight we would pause for cheese and deli leftovers, laid out like a tea ceremony to preface Lou's nip of aquavit. It was in easy times like these that Lou would speak also of his childhood, and I began to know more of the man I loved.

Lou was born in 1901 in Estonia. Although the actual city of his birth has been questioned in recent years, he always told me he was born on the island of Ösel (now Saaremaa) in the Baltic. His birth name was Leiser-Itze Schmulowsky. He never recited that full name; he said only that his name was Itzak. When he was three, he was captivated by coals glowing in a fire. He wanted to play with the light, so he gathered the coals into his apron, which flared up, burning his face and the backs of his hands—he had covered his eyes with them. His father, Leopold (born Lieb Schmulowsky), a stained-glass craftsman and officers' scribe in Czar Nicholas II's Russian army, felt his disfigured boy would be better off if he died, but his mother, Bertha (born Beila Mendelewitsch), was convinced that his scars would make him stronger and that he would grow up to be a great man. She was known as a healer and

Kuresaar — Loss.

The castle in Kuressaare, Lou's childhood town, on the Baltic island of Saaremaa.

Bertha Kahn, Lou's mother.

Leopold Kahn, Lou's father.

Sarah, Oscar, and Louis Kahn, c. 1908.

played the harp and sang lullabies to her firstborn. Those plaintive melodies, hummed by Lou, still linger in my ear, together with the stories of his early years. He spoke of a castle on the island and of seeing Cossacks in the streets "carving up Jews." He told of the boat trip to America when he was five, and that his drawings had so impressed the captain that he gave Lou's mother, little sister Sarah, and baby brother Oscar oranges and moved them up from steerage into a better cabin. Leopold—who had come to America first and adopted the name Kahn—met them at the port of Philadelphia in 1906, and young Itzak started a new life as Louis Isadore Kahn, an American boy.

Lou's myriad tales of scrambling together a destiny came alive in this place, his new city. I loved hearing how the boy found a wide world of possibilities in Philadelphia, though Leopold had to abandon his stained-glass craft for meager wages in this hive of mill workers, railroad builders, and bricklayers, and he needed income from Bertha's fine needlework to put bread on their table. They lived one step ahead of the landlord in too many Northern Liberties tenements for Lou to have a fixed sense of "home." Home was an idea; the word spelled a certain sacredness, culture, and delight. The street was where all the fun took place. You threw a football out the window and the game began. Lou was good at sports. He was shy because of his scars, but he was daring physically. In school he was on the wrestling team, and in that arena his scars were an advantage, unnerving the opponent.

The Philadelphia public schools provided the three Kahn children with an excellent education, and Lou won prizes for his drawings. Although he could not afford pennies for pencils or the horse-drawn tram, across-town weekend walks to the Fleisher Art Memorial rewarded him with free painting lessons and access to a piano, which he was teaching himself to play. Lou joked about the family's children being so underfed that when Oscar, yearning to be a parachutist, jumped off a roof one day, holding an umbrella, he didn't break any bones on the cobbles because he had sailed down so lightly. Lou was not as lucky; jumping from curb to curb in an alley, he tripped, hit his head, and was temporarily blinded. The blindness lasted long enough for him to accept that if he couldn't be a painter, he could always be a pianist. Art was his ticket in life, and he relied upon it far more than anything else.

One day a benefactor overheard Lou improvising on the Fleisher Steinway, and she was so impressed that she gave him a piano. But the tenement room he shared with his brother wasn't big enough for beds and the piano, so out went Lou's bed, and he slept on the piano. Lou's parents could not afford a music teacher for their son, but by listening in on a neighbor's lessons, Lou learned to play everything from Bach and Brahms to Gershwin and boogie-woogie by ear. It was a gift, and he got a job playing piano in the silent movie houses—his favorite stars were Charlie Chaplin and Tom Mix—saving the money earned for college. When the local movie house upgraded to an organ, there was a momentary panic, but overnight he became good at fiddling with stops and playing the double keyboard, while a friend operated the pedals on his hands and knees until Lou got the hang of that too. Lou told me this story while pounding out some hammy tremolo stuff on my piano until we both broke up laughing. He also told me of a night spent in a cold City Hall jail for protesting against police brutality in the arrest of an anarchist who had thrown a stink bomb in a theater, and of his childhood sweetheart, a girl from his neighborhood named Ada whom he adored.

Lou was blessed with luck. He intended to become a painter, but in his senior year at Central High School he took a class in Greek, Roman, and Gothic architecture taught by William Gray that so captivated him that he knew that "only architecture would be my life." He was admitted to Penn, scraping his way through by doing odd jobs, and graduating in 1924. He was hired as a draftsman in the office of his revered professor Paul Cret and befriended the debonair Philadelphia architect George Howe, who promoted his work and helped him ease his way into their "gentleman's profession." Ultimately, though, it was Lou's native talent and dogged labor that allowed him to advance into a career that was all but closed to one from his social position.

A fellowship abroad in 1928–29 allowed Lou to return to his native land, and he described to me spending two weeks sleeping on his grandmother's dirt floor in Saaremaa. He would never see any of that part of the family again—they were all lost in the cataclysm of the war or killed in the Holocaust. While in Europe he sought out modern work in Denmark and the Netherlands, especially, and then proceeded south to Italy, making sketches along the way, sensing that somewhere between the ancient and the modern he could find something new.

He hoped to marry Ada on his return to Philadelphia, but when he got back, he found she was engaged to someone else. It was a deep hurt that I could see still in his face when he spoke of it. Lou's parents and brother and sister all moved to California in 1930, and Lou married Esther Israeli the same year.

Lou in the late 1920s.

Lou did not speak much about the intervening years. He didn't mention other relationships he'd had, and I didn't ask. He said little about his marriage, other than that he had made a mistake. I knew this could hardly characterize thirty years of connection, but it was what I wanted to hear, and I accepted it. Over time I learned a few details: that Esther was from a successful family, a lawyer's daughter, a Penn honors graduate, and that her job as a medical research assistant had helped support Lou and his practice during the Great Depression and in later times too. Finally, I learned that Lou and Esther lived on the top floor of her parents' house on Chester Avenue in West Philadelphia, and had done so ever since their marriage.

When it came to Lou and Esther's daughter, Sue Ann, Lou was filled with enthusiasm. She was a talented flutist and graduate student at Penn, and Lou arranged for us to meet. Sue Ann was lovely and delicate, with long black hair, a sweet laugh, and a winning shyness. We had a lot in common, and despite a twelve-year difference in our ages, we became friends, as Lou hoped we would. I believed that Lou would level with his daughter about our relationship, as difficult as that might be, but it became distressingly clear that he was avoiding telling her. He seemed able to put different parts of his life in different places in his mind, and it occurs to me now that this was a kind of living equivalent of the way he sought a strong distinction between spaces in his architecture.

The Richards Medical Research Laboratories at the University of Pennsylvania (1957–61). The towers, which brought Lou international attention, owe something to the Italian hill towns he had seen in 1928–29 as well as Scottish castles, which he greatly admired.

Lou with his father, Leopold, at the Museum of Modern Art, 1961.

In June, Lou invited me to the opening of an exhibition at the Museum of Modern Art in New York City, devoted to his recently completed Richards Medical Research Laboratories, cocurated by architecture's kingmaker, Philip Johnson. Sue Ann was there, as was Lou's wife, Esther, whom I glimpsed amid a throng of well-wishers. She was tall and commanding, with a strong voice. A woman named Anne Tyng was also there, clearly at ease among the men from Lou's office. She and Lou had been lovers in the late 1940s and 1950s, and their daughter, Alexandra, had been born in 1954. Anne was small, very attractive and self-possessed, and I watched as she approached a frail but dignified elderly man. It was Lou's father, Leopold, who had flown in from California. I wondered what they had to say to each other, or if Leopold knew that he had a second granddaughter, and that Anne was her mother.

Through Bob, who was also a friend of Anne's, I knew of the profound influence she'd had on Lou's work, introducing him to the powers of pure geometry and giving him the courage to "go for it" with the design of the Yale University Art Gallery. Anne was an architect in her own right; she had gone to Harvard and had worked in Lou's office since 1945, where she designed the City Tower, the Yale building, and the Trenton Bath House with him. Although their romantic relationship had ended, they remained loyal friends. In the years that followed, I would come to admire Anne's conduct in maintaining her pride and professionalism in spite of the attacks on her private life—the balancing act of a charmer with a stunning intellect. Perhaps it was a combination of her Anne Hutchinson blood and missionary parents that reinforced Anne's righteous passion for her causes and her challenge to male dominion, Lou's included.

On that evening at MoMA, Lou was merry and nimble as he Fred Astaired among his well-wishers, pausing to greet, reminisce, and joke with them. At one moment he caught my eye, circled, and introduced me to Leopold Kahn. I wanted to tell him something meaningful—that I was in love with his son, that his son loved me—but a handshake and a smile were all that I could muster. While we never met again, I am glad I glimpsed that lively and endearing ninety-year-old, who could have played the good grandfather in a fairy tale. In spite of the warmth of this moment and the dazzle I felt at the celebration of Lou's accomplishment, the evening was bewildering: his wife, his daughter, his father, an ex-lover, his loyal staff, famous admirers, all in one space with his work—what a scene! I had always had Lou to myself, and now for the first time I was seeing him as a public person. I felt lost, melted into the crowd, and left for Maine soon afterward.

PHILADELPHIA TO FARAWAY, LINCOLNVILLE, MAINE, JUNE 1961

Dearest Sweetheart,
It was so hard to feel your disappointment in not being able to talk to me freely. The delight of the few nights we had alone before your leaving lingers like the feel of the breaker that has receded. Only prying words make our meeting less. Yet I can only remember their beauty as of their fullness in love.
Sweetheart, I love you my sweetheart.

Lou

I can't recall what I said to Lou following the MoMA opening, but I must have expressed my sense of insecurity and disappointment at being treated like just another person, one of many, in his life. His response felt like a subtle scolding. It was as if the doors and windows to the outer world might be shuttered, and that I would be kept to a secret place, trapped, silent, awaiting his release. It was paralyzing, like watching something falling and about to break.

I recall a prescient dream in which I protested because Lou was taking me through a doll-sized house that he had designed for me. It was charming but

Lilliputian. When I turned away, I saw in the far distance a vast, magnificent alabaster citadel. Its abstract beauty and purpose were somehow meant to assuage my disappointment. I was, it seemed, warned about entering into the space of this improbable love, where there was no room for me. However, it felt prophetic, as if I had caught a glimpse of the magnificent work Lou would build, which would outlast all of us. How could I ever retreat from the midst of such a breathtaking prospect in which, perhaps, even I was meant to share?

I tried to find distraction with friends visiting Maine, including Bob Venturi, who delighted everyone with his humor and whimsical ideas. He had no inkling of my involvement with Lou, and I didn't have the strength to tell him about it, not yet. I did not want to hurt him, or risk losing his respect.

With my mother (left), Bob Venturi (right), and other family and friends at Faraway, summer 1961.

Dearest Sweetheart Harriet,
Sunday more than any other day seems hollow without you.

Yesterday I got up feeling nauseous. Am sure it was a bug—for all day I had to from time to time rest on my bench. Last night my father came for dinner. I went thru the motions of entertaining him but gave in finally to what hit me—went upstairs to bed while everyone was talking away and slept on till this morning. Felt funny not having bid my father off.

Today, Sunday, I feel somewhat better—can judge because I am eager to work and what is more beautiful than ever is that I feel like working because of you. I am so anxious to show you my work after it is well developed I want you to hug me for joy of its worthiness. Have been taking snatches of the English History Volumes I bought. A popular History of England by Charles Knight. I might give them all to you if you love me and then of course I still have the cake and eat it too. Haven't eaten for nearly two days now and am proving to myself the comfort around the girth and that one can feed on oneself. Sweetheart sweetheart my little note is so self concerned. But no my darling, I feel so close to you as though I was just chatting alongside you in our bed. Your voice when I spoke to you feels now like an everlasting melody. I can remember not a single word only a quiet radiance of selflessness desiring to be mingled only with another song of a soundless harmony. It said I love you in the most beautiful way.

I love you.
Lou

Lou and I talked often about books and I gave him some of mine that I thought he would like to read—although he read slowly and rarely cover to cover. I had given him Goethe's *Wilhelm Meister's Apprenticeship*, which he did not love as I did, but *Faust* struck him deeply.

Dearest,

I have been taking snatches at a paperback Faust. So close is he to the edge where existence is and is not.

"For he whose strivings never cease Is ours for his redeeming."

Is the soul fed by deed? Do deeds remain but material? Is the edge the exchange? This reminds me of Wilhelm Meister. I am sure I will find it where I left it. Half our worries are over. I don't any longer have to look for it, I only have to remember where I put it.

I have had little time to read or draw which I want so much to do. I am in the midst of reading over contracts for Salk, Fort Wayne [performing arts center], Wayne U[niversity]. It's so contrary to shaking a hand in trust or giving your word and nowhere near as binding and inspiring. Still it is our way recognized by society and its rules. My tendency in reading over the conditions of a contract is to favor the owner and make it harder for myself. But then I find the client doubtful of my motives and cautiously asks for explanations. The best it seems is to take the standard form, an icicle framed document with a most sad countenance, and then everyone is full of trust and good intentions.

My sweet darling I miss you,

Lou

Dearest Harriet,

I read *Faust* thru for the first time and [was] struck dumb by the squareness of the tragedy. It all now lies in my mind solidly on the side of living. How masterful. How unbearably heart breaking. How invaluable is the soul. How the most fabulous treasures of the entire universe cannot tip the scale upon which this weightless endlessness is even not. How cheap is a whole life of delight to the faintest utterance out of love's openings. Mephistopheles is the soullessness of man. Faust, the singular, possesses the invalued. Faust feels not this treasure and longs for talents not his. Mephistopheles is all matter, solid and indestructible. Margareta is all soul, unfathomable and indestructible.

Let's read it together my dearest. You must add your love of "Faust" to mine.

With all my love,
Lou

Built of plain cinder block, Lou's Tribune Review building in Greensburg, Pennsylvania, resonates with a power beyond its size.

PHILADELPHIA TO FARAWAY, JULY 8, 1961

My dearest pussy cat,

Tomorrow midnight I am off to Greensburg (near Pittsburgh). Am going with Dave Wisdom, Marshall Meyers and Bill Huff. Monday morning till evening will be going over the check list of incomplete or badly done construction credits to owner, extras to builders. Our book keeping seems to be good. Monday evening we have fun at a country place of Bill's aunt, Pike Lodge (not a stream in site). There will be drinking. Bill's stories of his drinking relatives harken back to the bold stories of the Vikings and their inexhaustible propensities. Tuesday morning, if we get up, we drive back to Greensburg and continue with the builder and then fly back to Philadelphia at 6 p.m. Wednesday I am going to Washington, and when I get back I will continue the work I got into these few days of which I am very pleased.

Today I was visited by the minister of planning of Ahmedabad, India who explained to me some of the conditions in the design of the new capital city of this principality. He is a strict vegetarian and when lunch time came I took him over to the L'Aiglon and had Athena "Tina" prepare a salad and other dishes he likes. She is a vegetarian (she was taken to the slaughter house one day by her father and since then never touched meat). She is beautiful and friendly. He, bright looking short and vivid (though he teaches philosophy, is not very philosophic). After they exchanged lengthy explanations of their similar likes, yoga, Gandhi, and the healing powers of vegetables, we left for the office. He kept looking back and stopped to copy the name of the restaurant the address and her name on a piece of paper and kept telling me how beautiful she is. I noticed how little his expression changed from my talk with him and his remarks about his new acquaintance. He obviously had a good time. He left me soon after.

The sketch is of Albi. . . .

Love,
Lou

One of Lou's 1959 drawings of Albi Cathedral, which he sent to me. Albi's remarkable all-brick construction inspired Lou with the expressive and structural possibilities of this most basic building material.

Wed. night

My Dearest Sweetheart Darling,

My brilliant secretary booked me to Ottawa by way of Cleveland. I'm still mad! Connections are difficult to Ottawa. . . . I had no identification papers proving my citizenship. Not a blessed piece of paper except your letter and your photos. The American officer of immigration gave me a bad time holding me unnecessarily to call me down losing thereby precious time and finally he stamped my pass card and I had barely enough time to catch the plane to New York. . . . On the plane I read a piece in Esquire magazine. It documented the present trend of sex freedom; the trend of writers; of students; of even the "liberalism" of some ministers. I could only read up to [the] point when I could sense the utter futility of any relation with our love. The preoccupation, alone, with sex is enough to make it bloodless, wooden. Love is so much more . . . But I must admit that I need you to be near me . . .

All my love, my sweetheart,

Lou

Darling Harriet,

Away you come to me as the gentle rain or as the bird lighting on the bough. . . . Longing gives strength to the heart, emptiness is filled with sweetness . . .

I am going to California on Thursday and will be away about four to six days. Shall I call you from out there or shall we buy the pyramids instead?

With all my love,

Lou

Dearest,

Typical Mexican broadcast—Chile today. Hot Tomali.

The weather has been straight from Hades up in the 90's with humidity to match. And you sit there and say why suffer come to Maine where the fog comes up like thunder and puts you to sleep at night. Sunshine? That is for Italy.

I believe I told you about the playground I was asked to design with Isamu Noguchi. Went to see the park commissioner in New York; not enough money. Interesting site on Riverside Drive from 100th to 105th Street overlooking the Hudson River. Was nice to meet Noguchi again. The people in New York I have met seem so abrupt and arrogant, competition for commissions must be keen to prompt such conduct. I have been working steadily on my buildings and like it so much to feel development. . . .

A group of French Architects from the [Ecole des] Beaux Arts, 80 in all, came to the office and the site of the U of P building. A few of them came in privately and I had a delightful time talking to them (I told you all this last night—now I remember). But today a group of architects from Greece came. Really they were full of life (especially the true caryatids who accompanied them, also architects). When I saw those people I saw in their faces <u>Living</u> and can realize how few experience living at all. Even the rich with all at their disposal just go from one place to another to just sit. . . .

With all my love,
Lou

Lou and sculptor Isamu Noguchi at the proposed site for the Adele Levy Memorial Playground, Riverside Park, New York City.

Lou's bird's-eye perspective of the Salk Institute for Biological Studies, showing the three-part scheme: the laboratories face the sea at the head of the canyon, the Big House (later called the Meeting House) is in the foreground, and the residences for scientists are on the far side of the canyon. With construction on the laboratories about to begin, Lou went to California to set up the field office in July.

Dearest of all there is and will ever be,

Must tell you all that happened—Flight over in record time 4:05 hours really felt like no time with my father telling about his old friends and some of his exploits. It took longer from Los Angeles to San Diego (125 miles) than from Phila. [to] Los Ang. The delay taught me something about air. Thin air on mountain and thick air at sea level is air thick or thin except that the oxygen molecules are farther apart in thin air. So hard to breathe because the lungs need more than you get at one breath. Pressurizing is the compression of the thin air high up which also must be heated to a normal temperature. The delay was caused by the air system going berserk. Knowing all the time that it would take a long time to repair and in order to make us (the riders) captive, the company maneuvered us from the lobby to plane back to the lobby to another plane which needed servicing with gas etc. etc. back to the new plane on which we waited until after 4 hours we departed on our scheduled time of flight of 30 minutes to S.D.

I found Galen Schlosser frantic but full of enthusiasm for the project, the people helping us, the site, and the beautiful weather. He rented a car for the project which we could use only a little on the first day of my arrival. The day, you see, was already over (the business part) so we set out to have a good time. We ate at a German restaurant in La Jolla, so very German with potato Pfan Kuchen, Klop mit Sauerkraut, und Münchener bread and served by really beautiful girls I swear recently from Germany. After dinner saw "Sound of Murder," a comedy that starts like a Ngaio Marsh tragedy—played in the high school auditorium of La Jolla.

Next morning visited site and the ranch next to the site to look over a house we were told could be rented. I believe they (the ranch owner, a Mr. Black, very rich raiser of horses) is going to rent it to us for 250.00/mo. It's very close to the site, about 500 [feet].

I hope we get it. We should know tomorrow. We were discouraged from using it as an office and when we agreed with the city planning commission they suggested that we avail ourselves of a prefab classroom unit, which he offered to taxi over to our site for free. It's just perfect with its blackboards, appropriate lighting, good space measuring 24 by 48 feet. This

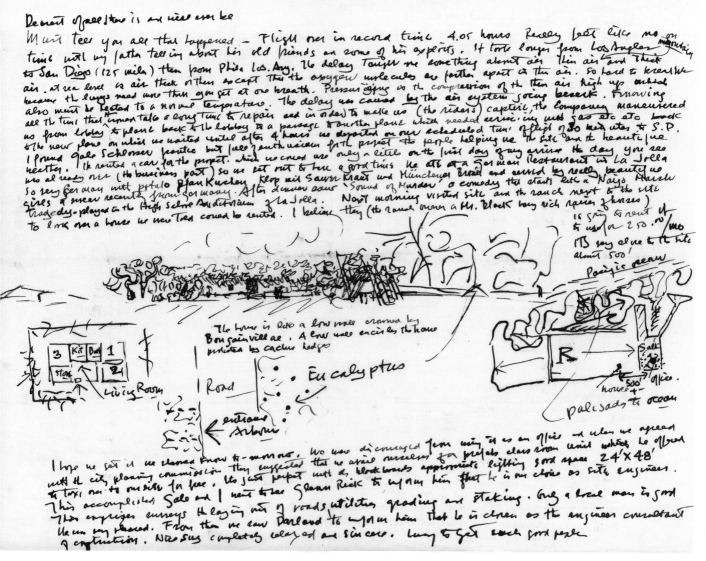

Lou's July 31 letter centers on a sketch not of his Salk design but of the proposed field office, a little house on a coastal ranch adjacent to the construction site. At left is a plan of the house and its approach, above is a perspective, and at far right is a site plan, with the coastal ranch denoted by a capital *R*.

[LEFT] *Living Room, study, kitchen, bath, 1, 2, 3 [bedrooms] / entrance arbor / road / Eucalyptus*

[ABOVE] *The house is like a low wall crowned by Bougainvillea. A low wall encircles the house protected by cactus hedges.*

[RIGHT] *Pacific Ocean / palisades to ocean / Salk [site] / R [ranch] / house 500' +- from office*

accomplished, Gale and I went to see Glenn Rick to inform him that he is our choice as site engineer. This comprises surveys, the laying out of roads, utilities, grading, and staking. Only a local man is good. He was very pleased. From there, we saw Dorland to inform him that he is chosen as the engineer consultant of construction. Nice guy, completely relaxed and sincere. Lucky to get such good people.

. . . Went to a play in the replica Globe Theatre in Balboa Park on the site of the San Diego Exposition of 1915. I remember having admired [Bertram] Goodhue's buildings when I was in school. They are really well studied Spanish Architecture. We were told that they are rotted on the interior (made to look like adobe or stone stuccoed over but made in reality in wood frame with hollow areas in the seemingly heavy walls). The effect is wonderful. . . . I suggested how they may preserve them—very costly of course— what was so nice—before the show the players put on a side play of dances of Shakespeare's time. The Queen, her retainers, were seated in one area on the lawn and the performer before her danced most gracefully and sang naughty and also love sick songs. This was all out in the open framed by the Spanish and Tudor buildings. Charming is the word. After that they entered the theater and beckoned the audience follow. The Merchant of Venice, very good indeed in the tiny intimacy of the interior.

The next day we visited Doyle, the man we chose to advise us on the landscaping and the sense of the atmosphere. A pixy sent from New England by Olmsted (famous Landscape Architect of great estates at the turn of the century) to San Diego to take charge of 1915 fair. He had it out with Goodhue and has been on his own ever since. He immediately liked my idea of the gardening—The gathering of rainwater in cisterns below the gardens leading to linear pools feeding the soil of the garden. The trees so fed will shield the water from evaporation. No green thumb garden. . . .

(Saturday) . . . From this to see a few stone yards on the way to Tijuana (Mexico) just across the border from San Diego. A real hell hole full of cafes and dancing girls. After walking the streets for a while we dared going into one for a beer. The floor show was the parade of practically nude girls bumping at the men seated with their drinks. Soon two came over to sit next to us not the dancers but those of the familiar game of ordering drinks which you pay for.

If you're a sucker you're congenial about it, for them the drinks pile up. It happened—you remember the story of Korsmo (Norwegian friend in Japan). . . . Later we went to the Jai Alai games the fast murderous catching and projecting of a lively ball. The game starts at 7:30 and lasts until midnight. Betting is part of the game. I am sure that dirty tactics are afoot though we couldn't catch on. We both lost 2 bucks. Then back to San Diego and the next morning Sunday drove around the gardens to catch the fantastic growth. Had lunch at Balboa gardens and took plane back to L.A. and then spent the rest of the day with Pop and Sarah. My sweetest love, all the time away I included you in all my fun and my thoughts. The house was yours, the site had to become the place where my work was partly yours with my people. I kept imagining how you would see them. Sweetheart, my letter is a wordy one. I love you, my darling. I love you.

Lou

Lou with Norwegian architect Arne Korsmo in Kyoto, Japan, 1960.

How my heart leapt at Lou's description of the bougainvillea-covered ranch house. The words "the house was yours" and his sketches of that enchanted place helped furnish some of the vacant space I was hosting in my imagination. It was a new way of nourishing our joint romantic fantasy of creating an alternative design for living to replace the present realities of our separate lives. I imagined the bougainvillea house with a view to the sea and Lou's new building beyond the eucalyptus grove, and thought about a place for my piano and the fun and music we would have if our lives were truly united. However, this reverie was somehow diminished by the description of the dancing girls in Tijuana, and Lou's reference to "the story of Korsmo." Arne Korsmo was an old friend. The year before, the two of them had attended the World Design Conference in Tokyo. One evening during their time in Japan, they met several geishas. Apparently one of the geishas had imagined that Korsmo was interested in a relationship and showed up later at his house in Oslo. A scene had ensued when Korsmo's wife came to the door. In Lou's telling of the story it was amusing, like a French farce, but to me it seemed more like Ibsen or Strindberg, and I couldn't help but identify with the woman and what she must have felt at having her hopes dashed on a doorstep so far from home.

LOS ANGELES AIRPORT TO FARAWAY, AUGUST 9, 1961

My Darling Harriet:
Yesterday I attended the funeral of a saintly woman of infinite sweetness and love. The cantor and rabbi sensed from all they had heard that this was no ordinary being. The beauty of the scripture and the words of praise fell like cotton pellets on basalt (no one could describe the beauty and piety that was felt in her presence). After the sad ceremony, I drove to the cemetery with Bernice. When I was going to college she and her brother were little people who would visit the Jacobsons over the weekend in the tiny house over their butcher shop. It was expected of me without fail to sit on edge of their bed on Saturday morning and invent stories about kings and fairies. She is now grown and slightly gray and full of delightful memories of her wonderful relations and also of me.

She was buried in a simple coffin dressed in a shroud as requested by orthodox rule. No one cried out. It was all so quiet so deeply good in its way that the feeling of beginning and end could just as easily be of the end to beginning. How great she was to have been of such spirit that the day of her interment gave a sense of eternity to all who saw her covered.

Then we drove to Ada's house where was held services by a Minyon (a synagogue may be formed by any 10 men gathered together. The most learned of the group takes over as the Rabbi). I returned to the office about eight in the night and was waiting impatiently for everyone to leave so I may call you. At 10, I went out for a walk when I got back the doors were closed. I had left my keys, all my money except a pitiful token, in the sweaty jacket hung up to dry. Lucky, I had the token. This morning, I had too little time to call before boarding the plane to San Diego. I will have called you, my wonderful darling, before you receive this letter. My thoughts are full of you. Often they are full of joy and often they are full of the purest love and also sometimes, I am troubled even by the slightest touch of misunderstanding and even, by what you hinted, by the intrusion of the clan. Away from you, my love says we are inseparable. This is the only religion I have.

With all my love,
Lou

The "saintly woman" was Mrs. Jacobson, the mother of Lou's lost childhood love Ada. How long had it been since Lou had last seen Ada? Reading this letter after so many years, I remember wanting to comfort him, to take away that history and to make our own story. But Lou cherished his past, even the hurts he had suffered as a youth. They were a part of him and he kept it all very close, like the token in his pocket.

My Sweetest Darling:

. . . All this time I did not write though I felt an urge to. Architects from many places kept barging in. I felt frustrated not knowing when to call you and when I did my darling was not in.

A few days ago, Sue mentioned she'd like to go to Maine for a few days "then," she said, I could visit Harriet. Now it seems Maine is too far away and time is too short. I got such a funny twitch when she mentioned you and wanted to tell her about you and me. Had we have been completely alone I could have. . . . A few nights ago I had a vivid dream in which I felt freed of a great burden. No one was around but I felt that all my friends were smiling at me. They were glad for me but I felt alone and unconquering. I entered a very beautiful old structure. There were good looking people there, they were interacting. I wanted to have reason to talk to them. I wanted to tell them that I am an architect. I knew no one. Then from around the corner I saw you. You came to me. You were so beautiful, a faint cry and you embraced me at once. We left together as though carried. "My love! My love!" I whispered. We found ourselves in cool low corridors which lead to the outside. I love you, I love you, came from me so freely. How beautiful was the ending. When I arose, I felt tears and alone but my belief in you and our love was as real as the dream felt in dreaming . . .

All my love,
Lou

The Friday after Labor Day, Lou did come to Maine. He met my mother at Faraway, before he and I went off to spend the afternoon on Indian Island. Indian Island Light had guarded Rockport Harbor in Maine's Penobscot Bay since 1854, until the last keeper retired and the light was decommissioned. In 1934 my mother had purchased the island at a government auction, with a bargain bid, and at my urging she had recently begun to restore it from damage by vandals during years of neglect.

The island was not much more than a windswept rock ledge with sparse vegetation and hovering seabirds, but it had a struggling, wild beauty. With no phone, no electricity, and a gasoline-powered pump for the well water, it was primitive and rugged. A lobsterman left the two of us off. We laughed as Lou, typically in city shoes, slipped on the seaweed in scrambling up the rocky beach. The island was uninhabited then, but at its tip was a cluster of whitewashed brick and wood structures: a lighthouse tower with the keeper's house and outbuildings.

Lou and I climbed the iron steps to the lantern room of the Egyptian Revival tower, flooded with light and with views of the Camden Hills, coastal islands, and the open sea on the horizon. We explored the house perched above the sea, its empty rooms awaiting a family but alive with light dancing off the water and the sound of breakers on the beach below. I rejoiced that Lou was there to see this, and to imagine its empty rooms becoming a lighthearted retreat for our own family in future times. In the evening we returned to the mainland, and Lou stopped again at Faraway. He later told me that in parting, my mother had firmly said, "Be good to my daughter."

Indian Island, Rockport, Maine, 1961.

The Margaret Esherick House in Chestnut Hill, Philadelphia, 1962.

1962

The fall and winter of 1961–62 was a golden time for Lou and me. It was a season of fantasy that we both indulged in, imagining often how wonderful it would be to live together and have a family—although when I tried to talk about specifics, Lou would fall silent or say something poetic that effectively put the discussion off. He was always eager for me to see his work, and one autumn day he took me to see a house near completion that he had designed for Margaret Esherick, the niece of his artist friend Wharton at whose studio we had met three years earlier. Margaret was a single woman who ran the Fireside Book Shop in suburban Chestnut Hill, and we took the local train there on a Saturday and walked the few leafy blocks to the house. I remember discovering how lovely autumn could be in that commuter community. Its traditional stone and clapboard family houses with landscaped front yards had the charm of an English village. They hardly prepared me for Lou's rectangular stucco building, which resembled no other on Sunset Lane. The house's T-shaped windows monogrammed a blank street facade, making it guarded and enigmatic, a little like Lou himself. The delayed surprise of a glass wall at the back, open to Pastorius Park, seemed somehow at odds with the stark entrance.

Once inside the vestibule, I turned to view a two-story living room, with a tall window slit that framed the fireplace, letting in sky views and slants of sunlight across the bare floor. I was struck by the room's stillness. I appreciated the many built-in bookshelves, but couldn't imagine how else to furnish it. The rest of the house struck me the same way: it was full of turns and niches, but it felt hermetic, with a tiny bathroom off the bedroom upstairs and a fussy kitchen below, fitted out with ship's-galley precision by Wharton himself.

I was surprised at every turn and tried to follow Lou's explanations while imagining what it would be like to live there. This was the first of Lou's houses I had been to, and I was flattered that he wanted my approval, but the small spaces and intersecting walls evoked a loneliness and withdrawal from the outer world, despite the windows at the back. My love of Frank Lloyd Wright's expansive rooms wouldn't let me like this packed assemblage of elemental ones. They made me uneasy, reluctant even to open a cupboard door. I held Lou's hand, not wanting to say that I had reservations about the house. We could live in Chestnut Hill, but not there! I thought on the walk back to the train.

A model of the Adele Levy Memorial Playground, Riverside Park, New York City, which Lou was designing with Isamu Noguchi.

On the morning of January 12, Lou and I took a train to New York City. The winter's day was surprisingly mild as we taxied, windows ajar, across the Queensboro Bridge for a meeting at Isamu Noguchi's studio in Long Island City. The two of them were going to spend the day working on the Levy Memorial Playground, which they were designing together. Noguchi greeted Lou with a bow and a warm embrace and led us into the studio, where a crew was noisily working on an installation. Noguchi seemed oblivious to the hammering and banging and took my hand to introduce me to a lovely woman, whom I joined on the sidelines to silently watch as the two men set to work, tossing their ideas onto a stubborn roll of drawings on a makeshift board. There was an aspect of performance about it—the artists at work, observed by their young female companions—but the two of them obviously enjoyed playing in each other's worlds and designing a magical place for the delight of children.

Although the playground was never built, Lou's collaboration with Noguchi was important. It released him from the rigidity of lines and corners and the geometries of designing buildings, and engaged him with the ground and its contours. It got him thinking about earth as a primal material. I believe it was Noguchi who really showed Lou the possibilities of Plasticine as a modeling material, and that it could be even more direct than a sketch for exploring and developing a site.

The easy joys of that time came crashing down in the spring when I made the heavy discovery that I was pregnant. I had gone to New York City to see my doctor, and she had delivered the news. Knowing that I was not married, she gravely offered to help with procuring an illegal abortion if that was the course I wished to pursue. I rode the train back to Philadelphia in fear and trembling.

I called Lou from the station. He was in the midst of things but arranged to meet me at a restaurant tucked away in the Old City that would still be open, as he hadn't had supper. Something in my voice must have told him not to delay, and he met my taxi in the narrow cobblestone street, which seemed deserted when it pulled away. I wanted to remain there in the darkness, to confide in him, empty my terror, and be filled with his hope and acceptance. But when I told him that I was pregnant, he staggered and uttered a plaintive "Not again," followed by a stunning silence.

That spring and early summer in Philadelphia spiraled between bewilderment and deep despair. I would return to my apartment to weep inconsolably. I knew this had indeed happened to Lou once before, with Anne Tyng, but I dared to think I was different, and that our shared dreams of living together and of "our little ones" were real, even though what had happened was not in the way we might have planned.

I wanted to turn to my family for help but was afraid. My sister Nancy was in town one day with her husband, their younger daughter, and her nanny, Gisella, who guessed my secret. The others did not. When Bob drove me to see his latest work—Grand's Restaurant, with its giant teacup sign, of which he was very proud—he suddenly asked me if I were pregnant. Horribly ashamed, I confessed that I was. He asked me if Lou was the father, and I said he was. Bob's response was another version of "Not again," but his tone conveyed a mix of irony and outrage. Eight years before he had helped Anne when she went to Rome to give birth to Alexandra. Now, I felt, he loathed Lou, but he kept himself from expressing any judgment.

I finally confessed my troubles to my brother, Abbott, whom I trusted and adored. He flew in from Chicago immediately with the singular mission of persuading Lou to divorce his wife. On the day he arrived, he went to meet Lou at the office. I never learned what passed between them, but it must have been a terrible scene, as he returned to my apartment enraged at Lou's resistance to his demands. I despaired.

In my ideal world, I had imagined Lou and Abbott, fellow artists, would be like brothers. But I ought to have known that the situation would touch on an unbearable memory that would ignite in Abbott a smoldering fury. During his wartime service in the Pacific, he had learned that his beloved fiancée had run off with a louche adventure writer and planned to become the seducer's third wife. Years later, Abbott's own devoted wife, children, and success still had not extinguished his bitterness over that betrayal.

Abbott was like a man possessed. He shocked me with the indecent and cruel suggestion that I marry Bob. I could only imagine one of Bob's wicked ripostes over such a macabre scenario. Then he went to see Esther, knocking on the door of the house on Chester Avenue and demanding that she divorce her cheating husband. I learned later that Sue Ann was in the house and overheard his righteous invective, which must have been awful. Finding no satisfaction there either, Abbott saved his parting shot for me with a hateful letter demanding that I have an abortion to avoid shaming our family.

My brother Willy was on his way from California to Paris on business and asked me to meet him in New York City. Was this to cushion the furious letter from his wife that vowed to cut me off from their family? But Willy was calm and kind, with not a word of censure, for which I loved him. With four daughters, he knew how to listen and temper his advice about the difficulty of raising and supporting a child, "especially if it's a boy," and he thought it best to give mine up for adoption, which could be arranged, if I agreed.

I did not want to be forced to make either choice offered by my brothers, and I sought out my sister that night at her midtown apartment. I should have known from the start that Eddie would be the only one in my family who knew, from her own life, my kind of helplessness. She said she would support me in whatever I decided and promised to use her every wile and resourcefulness to help me find a way out of my wreck.

In June, Lou agreed to confide in a "wise friend," but like the rabbi in one of Lou's favorite jokes, who, when challenged about his pronouncement that "life is a fountain," shrugs and says, "So it isn't a fountain," the friend reportedly listened sympathetically but offered no solution.

Lou seemed paralyzed, wanting two things at once. On the one hand he said he wanted to be with me and even that at times both he and Esther had considered divorce—but when it came down to it, he was also deeply connected to her and seemed unable to change his life. He would almost have rather taken himself out of the equation entirely and gone to live in a monastery than make any kind of decision for which he would be held accountable.

In August Lou went with me to meet a Jungian therapist I had consulted when I lived in Manhattan. The therapist was singularly unhelpful, vehemently denouncing Lou as a coward with shrieks of scorn. We then went to Eddie's apartment, where a lawyer friend had drawn up a paternity affidavit that Lou signed willingly. That meeting somehow had a calming effect. Eddie did not tell us at the time, but if I chose to keep "it" and Lou deserted me, she had already plucked a husband for hire from her Gotham crowd, who would marry me for five minutes to make my child legitimate. In spite of her worldliness, even Eddie was not able to imagine that I could have a child out of wedlock and raise it as a single mother under my own name. It was simply beyond the experience of our family, where relationships outside of marriage were never even whispered about and divorce was looked upon as a moral failure. No doubt my family members talked to each other up and down the phone lines about my situation—it must have been shocking to them, that the innocent little sister and maiden aunt had fallen so far and so fast—yet not one of them contemplated the possibility of taking me in, or of helping raise "that man's child." They were all too afraid of compromising our family's good name.

By summer's end, I could no longer conceal my pregnancy, and my situation was dire: How or where could I escape? Should I relinquish my child? I knew that Anne had gone abroad to bear Alex, dared to keep her and to return, despite being a clergyman's daughter in even worse times of back-alley abortions, shotgun weddings, and "fallen women" melodramas. That her unplanned pregnancy jeopardized the rise of her career I only learned later, but just knowing of her courage mattered to me, and gave me strength.

Continued hateful and threatening letters from the family and Lou's tilt between willful inaction and passive bewilderment tormented me that hot summer, until, casting aside all pride, I wrote two letters to the friends I had made at Yale: Mariette Russell in Porto Santo Stefano, Italy, and Susannah Jones in Long Ridge, Connecticut. I was desperate for their advice but dreaded it might be contrary to what my heart and the child within me were insistently telling me. They responded by return mail to Philadelphia.

SEPTEMBER 8, 1962

Dearest Harriet,
. . . I was so glad to see your handwriting. I let your letter rest on
my lap over half the drive up to Florence, and only opened it when I
stopped to stroll in a lovely field to let my doggie frolic.
    The news your letter contained of your love for L.K., which I
had not fully realized and your imminent pregnancy made me wish
to cry out in joy. That your life . . . shall be centered in guiding
your child to growth and fulfillment of all its potentialities, seems
to promise a gift of incredible richness for your life. But as I read
on, I was left filled with anguish by the cruelty of your dilemma.
The thought of relinquishing a child born from wedlock with one
you so love and admire yet who remains loyal to the commitments
made to his family, shocked me profoundly. . . .
    I believe failure to live up to one's responsibilities can bear
grave consequences—and in the case of relinquishing this child,
could be followed by untold regret, reproaches and unappeased

Mariette Russell at Porto Santo Stefano, Italy, 1950s.

loneliness. You seem to fear that maternal responsibilities would act as a restriction on your future. Surely this is not the case. Freedom that remains sterile and selfish is surely a travesty upon the word's meaning. If prospective motherhood alone is to be your fate, take courage and become greater than your fate.

You had the courage to enter into a relationship—have the same courage to bear its consequences! And that courage will give you <u>genuine</u> pride which nothing in the world shall bend. And someday your child shall in turn, be proud of you. . . .

With love, Mariette

And in a later letter she wrote:

<u>Remember</u>! strong men are indifferent to others' opinions. Be grateful, <u>proud</u> of all that you have shared and experienced with a man years older than yourself who has won distinction and eminence in his field. Be worthy of him and hold your head up high. . . .

Susannah's reply also arrived in September.

Dearest Harriet,
I have your letter, which as you know has prevented me from having any thoughts but of you for 24 hours.

Before we meet and I know your feelings more fully, I just want to say that the enormity of your grief, which I can scarcely grasp, is balanced by the extraordinary prospect of your child. Whatever the circumstances, a birth is the most miraculous thing on earth, entailing preparation both physical and spiritual. Whatever is behind you, this is ahead of you, and I cannot but believe that the experience will be beyond belief.

Harriet, my heart goes out to you in a way that tells my mind that there are some situations in life where every alternative is wrong. That you have written me such a letter makes me feel your deep friendship more strongly than I have ever felt it before. If there is anything in this world that I could do to help, let me know on Wednesday. I long to do anything I can if it would make things easier . . .

As ever, Harriet,
Susannah

These letters came like lifelines in a storm, and when Susannah and her husband Charles met me in Manhattan at a restaurant near Charles's office, they had already thought out my rescue: I would join them in Long Ridge, where they had found "the Twig," a guest house on a nearby estate, which I could rent. This was followed by the bravest and most generous offer of my life—they would gladly adopt my child, if I felt I could not keep it.

The logistics of my move, once my belongings had been stored, were managed by Susannah and Charles, who welcomed me to Long Ridge that September in a memorable lawn party on their pretty suburban property. A relative played the musical saw, and there were donkey rides for the children. It was the loving attention of Susannah and Charles in their hospitable community that turned everything around, transforming my sadness into the possibility of joy in the birth of my child. After months of anguish, I felt truly blessed. The locus of my recovery was the Twig, and the tools of my liberation included a driver's license and a bargain-priced red Hillman parked in the driveway.

Charles and Susannah Jones, Milton, Massachusetts, early 1950s.

The faith of my friends gave me the strength I needed to confirm my deepest feelings: that I should bear my child without shame, and trust my own will, character, and collective talents to support us. They knew who I was and could be, leading me to my inmost resourcefulness in creating an independent and responsible life that might even return me someday to Lou's world.

I could at last respond to my mother's alarming letters, which narrated the myriad excuses she was making for my absence to grandchildren and friends as well as proposed scenarios for my future, including an incognito sojourn with her in another city—all this ladled with denunciations of Lou's inconstancy and my resistance to family ultimatums. She saved my reply sent from my hideaway at the Twig to Faraway:

OCTOBER 9, 1962

. . . Please, I beg of you, do not give either my address or telephone number to Abbott, Willy or Nancy. I cannot endure any more accusations or pleas from them. I desperately need peace these last weeks in which to prepare myself for the coming child. I will keep my child. . . . The strongest plea they have for me is to sacrifice all my feelings for love of you . . . I promise you, dearest Mother, I will not make you carry my burden. . . . But to expose my own child to an unknown fate, to place it at the mercy of chance for its love and understanding and welfare—that is even more treacherous than mindlessly inflicting even a deep embarrassment and begging protection from my family. I will scrupulously keep my secret. I believe that there is no imminent possibility of its escaping to reach a scandalous situation for the family. Many families have secrets we do not dream of or care about. There are, after all, far greater disasters that can overtake them . . . Please try to love my child . . . in the light of its own uniqueness, as you have done with the other grandchildren. We love them for themselves—not for being like their parents . . . I cannot bear to see you weep. I do want so to see you proud of me and of my child one day.

Weeks later, a letter from Bob came to remind me of the world I had left behind. It was kind, and in it he refers to a trip we made to see his Visiting Nurses Association Building in Ambler, Pennsylvania, and Eddie's plan to purchase the marriage of convenience to legitimize my child.

Dear Harriet,

This is just a note since I want to answer right away.

I am very glad you are keeping "it." And the legal ceremony sounds good to me especially for the baby's sake—though melodramatic.

And your setting sounds idyllic. I hope I shall be able to visit you there. Also, how nice to have the Jones with you.

I shall give out the official story if and when the occasion arises.

Life here is exactly the same: frustration and little glimmers of hope. I'll send you photos of Ambler soon if we aren't miss-led (play on words) first.

Good luck—love—Bob

Another letter that arrived later, saved these many years, was from Edith Braun, my adored music teacher. The "we" she refers to are Mary Curtis, founder of the Curtis Institute, and her husband, the violinist Efrem Zimbalist.

Edith Evans Braun, 1960s.

JANUARY 20, 1963

Our dear Harriet—

Your letter is exactly the kind of letter I hoped to have! It is just right! And it has made me so happy—! For now I know that you have come thru a terrific experience, and it has made you face the future with courage and strength of purpose . . . I think that, up to now, you were living in a dream world, drifting, rather than guiding your own life.

Now your feet are on the ground, you are jumping over hurdles (driving a car!) and any other problems can & will be solved.

We are proud of you, my dear! You have been tested, and have come thro' with flying colors! . . . much, much love to you . . . As always,

Edith Braun

Dearest Harriet, Now that I tell you about some of the things I did since I talked to you last Wednesday on... Monday I have nothing to add. I still distrust the phone though. I was glad to hear you about the charming house you live in and the ... ... as is your landlord. Also I am grateful for ... you. This is as ... ... for me. I love ...

McHarg and the Soldier

Let the party for Roberto Burle Marx ... Jerry ... seeing thru the drinks. Hilarious funny the impressive raspy blurbs faintly resembling English Haooo—ooh annums / Rsriiii RRRR riiii Faagáaa C## ATTT eeeezzzEW— The jerky precision ...

The party was throughly gay and all out. I think I told you that Marx came to visit me Saturday afternoon to ... my work. He was different... said he had with him a young Brazilian (also at the party) ... speaks good English ... helped us ... our thoughts and explanations. Burle Marx ... the garden or painting or sculpture though I didn't dare to comment on this... differs from these arts. I promise to write even if I had nothing to say. Now you know how that feels.

I love you Love

I will try to set the ... with ... soon. How to do it — ...

Dearest Harriet,

Now that I told you about some of the things I did since I talked
to you last Wednesday or was it Monday I have nothing to add. I
still dislike the phone though I was glad to hear from you about
the charming house you live in and the good family who is your
landlord. Also I am grateful for how good Susannah and her
husband is to you. This is as though they were taking over for me.
I have somehow to show my gratitude.

At the party for Roberto Burle Marx, [Ian] McHarg and Jerry
Cope going thru the drills. Hilariously funny the impression with
raspy blurbs faintly nose wrinkling English Haooo-ooh ammms!
Reshiii RRRRRination Faya! aaCie!! ATTTeeeezzze w— The jerky
precision of their manual of arms was gut splitting. Please excuse
the very silly drawing. It is impossible for me to make a comic
drawing. This I know ever more when I see the wonder cartoons of
George Cruikshank.

The party was thoroughly gay and all out. I enjoyed it for you
too. I think I told you that B. Marx came to visit me Saturday
afternoon to look over my work. It was difficult to sense if he got
what I said. He had with him a young Brazilian landscape architect
(also at the party) who worked somewhere in the mountains of New
York who speaks good English. He helped the both of us to convey
our thoughts and explanations.

Burle Marx sees the garden as painting and sculpture though
I didn't dare to comment on this. I did explain why I thought my
work (that is architecture) differs from these arts.

I promised to write even if I had nothing to say. Now you know
how that feels.

I love you,
Lou

I will try to get the where with all soon. How to do it—well I'll find
a way.

What might have happened had I remained in Philadelphia? Lou could not have taken me to this party or even be seen with me in public in the carefree way he had once squired me around through the streets of the city where he had become a celebrity. I knew I had lost that world, and I felt that loss all the more keenly with the arrival of this letter.

In the end, the "where with all" Lou mentioned in his postscript—the money to bring a child into the world—was provided by my mother. Lou's marginal resources were limited to office petty cash furnished in twenty-dollar bills. What I did not understand at the time was how much Lou's life and work depended on Esther's financing, and had since the beginning of their marriage. At the time, all I saw was a wall of secrecy around Lou's office that was not to be breached, and which left me in the dark.

On November 4 Lou went to India to meet with clients in Ahmedabad for a commission to design the Indian Institute of Management (IIM), modeled on the Harvard Business School. This trip really marked the beginning of Lou's international career; soon he would be involved with four major projects on the Indian subcontinent. IIM would turn out to be one of his greatest works, and over the coming years he would spend a great deal of time in that part of the world. Lou's solemn, faded message on the back of a postcard of the Taj Mahal reached me several days after our child was born.

AGRA, INDIA, TO THE TWIG, NOVEMBER 15, 1962

Dearest Harriet,
I love you.

> Lou

DOHA, QATAR, TO THE TWIG, NOVEMBER 20, 1962

Dearest Harriet,
I love you.

> Lou

Too much to talk about. Found Corbusier's Chandigarh wonderful. Telephone lines down. Tried to call you. May have luck tomorrow. It takes an appointment with the wires and hanging around to get a call thru. Last time waited for several hours. No soap. I want to know how everything is.

BY AIR MAIL

POST CARD

TAJ MAHAL AGRA
Front View

Nathaniel and me at the Twig, Long Ridge, Connecticut,
January 1963.

Nathaniel Alexander Phelps Kahn was born in the evening of November 9,
1962, in the Mt. Kisco Hospital, where the two sons of Susannah and Charles
had been born. The same doctor and nurse had cared for me in the last month
and attended the delivery, with Susannah all the while accompanying me in
this wonderful happening. Charles arrived in time, standing at the nursery
window to greet the baby on the first day of his life.

Susannah's "a birth is the most miraculous thing on earth" and "the
experience will be beyond belief" was how I felt in surrendering until the
"I" was utterly lost in the overwhelming force and order of all life and death.
In that violent nothingness came the blessing of a child. I chose his name.
Nathaniel in Hebrew means "gift of God," which he was to me.

Lou came to the Twig after his return from India, when Nathaniel was
still only a few weeks old. The disconnect between the cozy suburban setting
for our reunion and the precariousness of the situation was overwhelming,
but we were together, and we made the best of the moment. Though
Lou appeared awkward with a newborn, looking, at sixty-one, more the
grandfather than the proud new father, he was clearly moved. He had a son.

However, the day went quickly, and the reality of what I was up against set in. I could not stay indefinitely where I was, relying on the kindness of the friends who had rescued my life during the past months and welcomed Nathaniel's. I needed to find a new place and the means to support the two of us. I longed to rejoin Lou, but had left Philadelphia in such a haze of helplessness and secrecy that I realized I could not return. Not then, if ever.

Lou and Nathaniel at the Twig, December 8, 1962.

PART TWO

Exile

1963–1966

"Stopping by woods on a snowy evening." A photo I took of my new home, Wings Point, Charlotte, Vermont.

1963

During the darkest time of my pregnancy, two books had fallen into my hands like a blessing: Sylvia Crowe's *Garden Design* and Russell Page's *Education of a Gardener*. I am not sure what possessed me on November 9, but I took them with me to the hospital when I was in labor, and they were to become talismans of the great changes to my life, starting that day with the birth of my son.

The authors were contemporary English landscape architects who approached their art differently: one focusing on regional and public land planning, the other on estate and garden design. I was captivated by both sensibilities. With Nathaniel came an immediate sense of my responsibility for another life as well as the miraculous, if slow-gathering, revelation that those two books offered a professional pathway that I might follow.

Could landscape architecture be a way to find the missing piece to my identity, an answer to the insistent voices calling me toward a life in the arts? I had no plan for that future, no wherewithal to pursue it, but suddenly everything came together: my love of place, of nature, stagecraft, dramatic narrative, poetry, music, and architecture, all merged in a constellation from which I would discover my métier—landscape architecture—and earn enough, I hoped, for us to live on. One day, perhaps, I would also find a way to work directly with Lou.

When Lou came to the Twig to meet Nathaniel, I described to him my discoveries and made a plan, the first that made sense of our shipwreck, by asking him, begging even, for a landscape architect he knew who might be willing to take me on as an apprentice. There was one, and on February 1 I left our Connecticut refuge and drove north with Nathaniel to the office of Daniel Urban Kiley in the snowy depths of rural Vermont. Lou had helped launch Dan's early career, and he solicited this favor for mine just as he set off overseas—via Rome—to Dhaka, where he had recently been chosen to design the capital complex for a country then known as East Pakistan (now Bangladesh).

Dearest,

I walked and walked thru the Foro Romano in places that I had
not tread before. I saw, and everyone sees what he sees differently
from another, what seemed to be slopes that I had myself made.
The church builders who stripped the Foro of its marble for
their places of worship did a good turn for fellows like me. The
underlying masses of brick that actually did the strong arm stuff is
exposed. The effort bared of all refinement shows itself and gives
what the marble covering couldn't convey—the sweat, the dogged
determination of sheer building for the sake of erecting a place
chosen. These roofless and amputated shapes are no more useful as
enclosures. They are all really garden walls, incomparable as such,
because not only is the garden dictated by the walls but the walls
dictated by the garden.

No one can make what time can do. You were by my side
constantly as I walked and talked to you and to me about the
mysterious rapport these naked walls exuded.

When I got back to the Academie Americana where I stayed for
the night, and then after a briefly revisit to the Corso in hope that I
could buy something for you (the stores were just closing it was just
5PM) I taxied to the A.A. where I was most welcomed by Dick and
Mrs. Kimbell—directors. They gave me the very best room in the
Villa Aurelia which is their home (very lush). Dick invited (when
he heard I was coming) the fellows he could round up for cocktails.
There they were when after I washed up and went down a flight to
the living room.

Villa Aurelia is age old. Garibaldi's headquarters in the war of
independence against the French 1843, before then a palace in 1497.
Then Villa Marina. Then named Villa Aurelia in 1905 by a Miss
Dupont—of Philadelphia who married at the age of 33 a retired
English officer. They lived in the villa, did it over (helped by an
English interior man). It is in the best of taste with hangings and
furniture of the very most wonderful. The rugs are fabulous . . .

AN BORD DES LUFTHANSA-SENATOR-DIENSTES

in comparable as such because not only is the
garden dictated by the walls but the walls dictated
by the garden.

No one can make what Tine could do - you
were by my side constantly as I walked and
talked to you and to me about the mysterious rapport
these marked walls exuded.

when I got back to the Academie Americana
where I stayed for the night, and then after a
briefly revisit to the casa in hope that I ~~could~~ cried
buy something for you (the stores were just
closing (it was 5 PM,) I taxied to the A.A.

BOEING Jet

Breakfast was served at 7:30 in the bedroom. Cafe au lait, toast, jelly, oranges, bananas, etc., bath, greetings and good byes in the hall downstairs and off to Ostia with Bill (a friend of Bob's [Venturi]) and an architect fellow of the A. Ostia, in the state of ruin, releasing the mind from geometric rigidity.

We have to get off, to Cairo now and want to mail this here. Will follow with a continuance of this letter.

Love,
Lou

The gardens of the American Academy in Rome.

Part 2
Monday

Dearest H'y, Dearest En'y,
The Academy brought memories. The garden almost entirely arched
with clipped rock pines and the steps leading from the garden to
the Villino where I stayed 12 years ago. Breakfast brought home the
intimate details of Asunta bringing in the tray when I was still in
bed and now the porter who took away my shoes to shine after he set
the tray down on the adjoining bed (no body in it, ahem!) and pulled
a chair to it for me. An orange, a banana, toast, a pot of hot milk,
and a mug of coffee, some cherry jams, and pads of sweet butter.
　　Must end. Plane heading down.
　　Arriving in Pakistan.

Tuesday (continued from Dhaka)
Arrived Pakistan, 1:30am . . . to bed at 3am up at 8am. Briefed on
Capitol. Took plane, 3PM, for Dhaka, arrived night, saw site then—
pretty awful—disappointed in double talk. I don't know! The
whole's a pretzel! Is this [the] site of a capitol? Are these the men I
am to depend on for support?
　　It's now midnight, tired, let down, don't like people around much.
　　My sweetest pussy cat and my sweetheart Tommy cat I am
going to bed rather anxious for tomorrow in hope that the site will
surprise me in day light and to see what others saw in choosing it.

Wednesday morning
Just read Frost died. Like a fallen temple. Each stone, though not in
place, is yet more sacred. Rejoice in tears for such as he can be.
　　'til later—
　　The site is a no man's land completely without distinction; not
a contour, a cluster of trees, not a distant landmark. I was driven
around in a jeep crisscrossing the site and all the time thinking of
what can make it worthy of the thoughts I had before I saw it.
　　Then at lunch it dawned on me to include in the assembly group
a mosque. This somehow twisted me from the hopelessness of the
location. I was sure then that I could design something that could
be its own force and even if an inspiring location would have other

The barren site of Lou's largest commission yet, the "second capital" at Dhaka, East Pakistan.

spaces suggest themselves, it would not have been as valuable if I had not thought of the mosque.

Religion is the basis of separation from India. West Pakistan and East Pakistan are separated by India. There is talk about their essential separation from each other. The legislative assembly in Dhaka is a kind of concession by the West Pakistanis. Bengali or East Pakistan feels this and wants the best or nothing as their part of the capitol. Whatever it is for I don't really understand it.

When I presented that afternoon the idea of an axial relation of the Assembly complex and a mosque it was as though heaven descended on the authorities. They thought it was IT! I am stunned by the completeness of their approval, because they said "you have put religion in this capitol just what it needed to give the meaning it lacked." I saw the relation of meeting of people to legislate—as in itself—of religion and strengthened it with the presence of the mosque. They saw it the same way.

Until later. So long H'ie sweetie and sweetie N'ie.

Love,
Lou

I so hope that your new environment is good to you. Try hard to get acquainted with it.

The Kiley House (at right) above frozen Lake Champlain, with attached garage apartment where I lived, Charlotte, Vermont.

My new environment was Wings Point, on the shores of Lake Champlain, in the raw, drafty spaces above the garage of the house once built for Wilfred Grenfell of the Grenfell Mission in Labrador and now the office of Dan Kiley. Although Lou had succeeded in persuading his colleague to accept me as an apprentice, he had not told him of my child in tow and lack of professional skills. When I drove my red Hillman to the far end of the snow-banked road (it would be a purple vale of lilacs in May), my sister, Posie, who had accompanied us, pronounced it "Grim!" But for me it was salvation. My windows had views of the lake on one side, woods on the other, and I soon discovered that I was among good people.

Kiley was "Dan" from the moment I met him. Yet he was an enigma behind the happy Boston-Irish hustler and backwoodsman pose, unknowable except in motion, at work. I was inexperienced and unable to contribute much to ongoing operations, but the opportunity to be in the midst of such an esteemed practice was invaluable. I saw how Dan, unlike Lou, effortlessly produced simple, strong designs from an initial idea with scarcely an exploratory drawing or conversation. Like Lou, however, he was a compelling and daring man. Though Dan was afraid of flying, commuting to far-flung jobs by rail, his swift and graceful ski runs were breathtaking. He could tear into space. With Fenian instincts and a touch of Zen in his ways, when the powder was right Dan shut down the office for an afternoon on the ski slopes,

Dan Kiley and Anne Sturges Kiley, Keene, New Hampshire, 1942.

and once, when the lake froze thick, he and his men heaped cedar logs on the black ice and set them ablaze for a skating party. The revelry lasted all night, and I can still see the cliffs of Wings Point in the glinting orange light of spiraling flames under the steady whiteness of a full moon.

Dan's staff was composed of six landscape architect graduates from the University of Pennsylvania, plus two local draftsmen and a secretary. One landscape architect was an Englishman, poised for success in Edinburgh, who ordered me to scrub floors and run ammonia prints when there wasn't typing and filing for "a girl" to do. Gentle Wally, however, showed me basic drafting tricks, though I was clumsy with tools and measuring, and Philip Shipman kindly gave me plans and basic design problems, like tree alignments, to work on.

Anne Sturges Kiley, Dan's wife, rarely appeared at the office, though their house was a welcoming barn of a place where she mothered eight children and a menagerie of animals. Shy, sparing of words, she spoke with the spidery originality of an Emily Dickinson. It was Anne who cajoled a stout, beaming farm woman to come on her horse and care for Nathaniel. Our son would not remember how Mrs. Anderson fed the chickadees in winter and held him in her pillowy arms to watch at the window, but he would be enthralled ever after by winged life.

After five months of separation, Lou made a visit to Vermont, ostensibly to consult with Dan on a project. The meeting was warm but awkward, as Dan could not help feeling used by Lou in encouraging him to hire me while concealing all of the circumstances and motives that had brought me there. I learned years later of Dan's anger over Lou's ploy, yet he was kindly, providing me with shelter, instruction for my simple labors, a stipend, and even a raise and my name on his letterhead. He also kept the fiction of my identity for the rest of my time in his employ, especially during this two-day visit from Lou, his sad-joyous reunion with me and our little boy.

Sunday, May 19, was an unforgettable spring day. The maples were leafing out and the lilacs about to bloom when Dan brought Lou from the Burlington airport. After stopping to see Anne, they came to my rustic digs over the garage, which I had turned into a charming nest for myself and Nathaniel. At five months old, our son was adorable and laughed at Lou's Chaplinesque clowning. There was no time for the past year's anguish or anxiety over the future to spoil our rejoicing. We jammed our stories together, Lou showing me his notebook sketches as he described exotic scenes and characters in India, Rome, and Pakistan, while I gave him our tales, colorful as they couldn't be over the phone. One story I remember was of a young British couple Lou heard about in a village he visited. Their little boy went missing one morning, and everyone in the compound fanned out in a frantic search before his Amah discovered him sitting in the middle of a courtyard beside a giant cobra that he was spoon-feeding, like a baby brother, from his bowl of breakfast porridge, even tapping it on the head with the spoon when it wasn't cooperating. Summoned, the horrified father watched his snake charmer son dismiss the cobra for its bad manners and then, as the snake coiled away, pick up the bowl and spoon like a dutiful parent and walk out of the courtyard.

Lou did not come back to Wings Point that year. Trips to both East and West Pakistan for the capital complex and Ahmedabad for the Indian Institute of Management, along with a project for an arts center in Indiana and ongoing Salk deadlines in La Jolla, kept him busy. The joy of mothering, along with the day's work and the flow of Lou's letters to my quiet outpost, buoyed my spirits, but the pain of carrying on a life so separate was always close.

Dearest Harriet and Nathaniel,
This is a hard trip from Philadelphia to Karachi without a layover.
Though it should appear inviting to have traveled by way of
London, Frankfurt, Vienna, Istanbul, it was only barely an hour
in each place—this and a few delays due to motor trouble—then
arrived in Karachi 5 hours late to begin work almost immediately.
The authorities were waiting for us. From Tuesday night to
Thursday morning without sleep, and if you add the sleepless days
of work before the trip you know then we were hardly in a physical
frame to impress the world.

From Karachi we went to Lahore. As we got off the plane,
incidentally, we means Duncan Buell and I, the air hit us at 110° and
the humidity was that of rain. The air-conditioned hotel proved the
case for the engineering of mechanical control of air. Boy, ye jist
gotta breathe.

Lahore has magnificent architecture of the Mogul period.
Palaces, gardens (irrigated), mosques, tombs and religious school all
magnificently conceived around expansive, fountained and raised
courts. Sheer beauty even if the building elements and the surface
decoration of flowers and geometric shapes repel me.

Now we are in Dhaka in the middle of the monsoon period.
Wet. Humid. No air conditioning here but that's true all over
Dhaka. We see the governor and press. Have to repair the model
and finish some drawings to show the president of Pakistan. From
here to Karachi, Rawalpindi (1st capitol) where we show the concept
to the president of Pakistan, Ayub Khan.

Give all my love to Natalex and you may snatch a few bits for
yourself.

Lou

Feed him well so he becomes strong enough to resist taking
commissions outside his country.

The Buriganga River in Old Dhaka, East Pakistan, c. 1963. The plans Lou was developing for the capital complex responded to this watery world in a way that was modern yet rooted in the conditions and traditions of the place.

HOTEL SHAHBAGH, DHAKA, TO WINGS POINT, JULY 21, 1963

Dear Harriet,
I am beginning to feel like myself again, strong and unsluggish. This was the only time that I did not look forward to Pakistan— India. I felt the futility of vesting so much feeling and effort on this . . .

All the designs I took with me were well received (to my surprise) and I even got them to approve my drawings and to admit that they will fall within the requirements of additional payment. I talked pay pay pay until it sunk in but it had come only after I made the threat to leave. I read the signed request for the release of funds—about $100,000.00 (I wish I had it to keep—but the banks damn them and bless them too).

The Monsoon makes unbelievable skies and uncountable variety of bugs. The lizards also take to the houses. They line the walls and make a pencil scraping noise, I understand, when they swallow a bug and I suppose the birds may be expected later to properly continue to carry out the ways of ecology.

I am unable to work here on corrections to my drawings or even getting information. During the time of my absence they start to guess what is meant in the instructions I leave. They are taken either lifelessly or grossly misinterpreted. Still when I am here nothing is too good for me. They all become alive and eager to carry out to the smallest wish my instructions. Chairs are shoved under me. Tea is served constantly. The youngest and oldest defer to even my corniest remarks. I kid them about their being Mahomedans who talk about their "bearers." They even tell me how much they like Moses and how they can't see Christ because God is above the needs of the body and that a son of God is a complete misconception of God. I was invited to a religious ceremony. The reader recited passages from the Koran in Arabic and spoke also in Bengali. We were seated on a white cloth facing each other and some facing the reader. Penetrating sweets were served after the strictly formal service. It was simple, full of reverence. It left me with the feeling that the next step asks of you to worship your own way—that the formality was merely a reminder.

I realize how resistive it is to work away from the familiar environment. I cannot get the same response from my pencil. It seems to want to go home. It is hard for the Pakistanis I am working with to understand why I can't sit down and dash off a design for "merely" a house.

Sweetheart I left with hopelessness of shattered altars and dangling indecisions and worst of all a feeling of my ugliness. Though dimmed, these feelings have not left me.

By the time I finished talking to you and called my office it was too late to mail the money. The flight had been called—didn't hear it—had only five minutes to catch the plane.

Good night my only ones Harriet and Nathaniel.

With love,
Lou

Hotel Shahbagh
RAMNA, DACCA.
(East Pakistan)
(Direction : Pakistan Hotels Limited)

Ref. No. _____

Dated _____ 196

I am unable to work here on corrections to my drawings
or even getting information. During the time of my absence
they start to guess what is meant in the instructions
I leave. They are taken either lifelessly or grossly misinterpreted. Still when I am here nothing is too good for
me. They all become alive and eager to carry out to the
smallest wish my instructions. Chairs are placed under me.
Tea is served constantly. The youngest and oldest defer to
even my careless remarks. I kid them about their being
Mohomedans and talk about their 'bearers'. They even
tell me how much they like Jesus and how they can't
see Christ because God is above the needs of the body and
that a son of God is a complete misconception of God.
I was invited to a religious ceremony. The reader recited
passages from the Koran in Arabic and spoke also in Bengali.
We were seated on a white cloth facing each
other and some facing the reader. Penetrating
sweets were served after the strictly formal
service. It was simple, full of reverence.
It left me with the feeling that the
next step asks of you to worship
your own way — that the formality
was merely a reminder

Lou's early perspective sketch of the capital complex at Dhaka: the National Assembly and pyramidal mosque in a lake.

DHAKA TO WINGS POINT, JULY 22, 1963

Dearest Harriet and Natalex—

Today, Sunday, we saw the governor of East Pakistan. What had to be taken up was the question of how much land and exactly where were the boundaries of the land. When I arrived in Pakistan I found that they had shifted land around so drastically as to break the scheme up. Everything was meat politically for the engineers and the ministers but hopeless for the architect.

With the help of coaching on the politics behind the moves and who is who all around I entered rather insecurely before the governor and his retinue of advisors to explain the concepts and how vital it was to keep the land as it was originally. With the help of my model of the Assembly buildings and photographs of the site plan I argued well and left with the governor's full respect and the land fully intact and with a promise of more land if I said the word.

What helps so much is my title of professor. I am addressed as either professor or doctor and to emphasize the special meaning of the title, Kafiluddin Ahmed said nearly always "You see Mr. Governor or Mr. Minister he is no ordinary architect." "We must be guided by the professor!"

. . . Every scene before one is of full green, of damp fresh red earth and overcast threatening sky. The rain has left numerous lakes and half buried huts. We drove to see a brick-making factory in the jungle. The owner told me he lived there 10 years ago. Then there were tigers and panthers roaming about.

All my love . . .
Lou

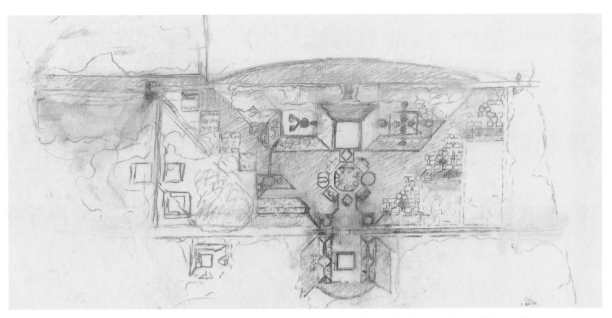

Lou's early site plan for the four-hundred-acre capital complex at Dhaka: the National Assembly and mosque in the center, with residences for government officials along the sides of the lake.

AHMEDABAD, INDIA, TO WINGS POINT, JULY 22, 1963

Dearest Sweetheart, Little Sweetheart:
When I wrote to you last, I believe, I was in Karachi—no Dhaka. Anyway from there back to Karachi to prepare for our meeting with the President of Pakistan. Kafiluddin Ahmed introduced me to the chief engineer Khatack, a softspoken cookie with a full hooked nose mustachio and thoughtful eyes framed in black arches. He spoke softly like one who doesn't want to hurt you in cutting off your head. So I also spoke softly like I was going to keep my head. He questioned the practicality of my scheme. I won him over on all points. On trip to Murree (on the way to Kashmir 150 miles farther up). I met the Cabinet and the President. He approved the scheme. The President knocked down an attempt to introduce a minaret (even if only one). He suggested an inflatable one to please the orthodox Muslims capable also of pleasing the revolutionary young Turks who believe in nothing.

Before we saw the president we met the members of the Assembly. The speaker, who is the head of the assembly and, next to the President, the most important man in Pakistan, gave me a hard time with his dome-mindedness. I could have given him a slaughter-house instead of an assembly building for Dhaka just so it had a dome. Others chimed in with him. I said I would only develop one that came as an element of the structure that answered all the problems. Gee, stop to think of it as I write, who in the world would refuse to build

115

a dome? I might at that—but at the moment, I would not concede to it as the design stood. This was in Rawalpindi (the new 1st capital of Pakistan). You know, of course, that I am doing the 2nd capital.

The agreement between architect and Pakistan is not yet satisfactory to me. I did not sign. I don't know what will happen. The feather in my cap is the President's approval. There will have to be some conceding on the two ends. I have left Pakistan without a contract under my belt.

From India to go home via Rome. I will write you again. You know by my hurried hand that I am being called for and must leave now.

All my love,
Lou

Unlike the bureaucrats and politicians of East and West Pakistan, Lou's clients in India were philanthropists—Kasturbhai Lalbhai, a textile magnate, and Vikram Sarabhai, a renowned physicist. Working with a prominent young architect, Balkrishna Doshi, they had established the Indian Institute of Management for their city of Ahmedabad, to promote the cultural and economic vitality of Gujarat, Gandhi's home state. Lou had expected to spend his time on the IIM site, but when he arrived he was whisked away into the wilderness to the north by his new friends, who wanted him also to conceive a master plan for an entirely new city, to be called Gandhinagar.

AHMEDABAD TO WINGS POINT, C. JULY 25, 1963

The plan of stay in India was changed when I met Shri Kasturbhai Lalbhai the head of the planning committee for the new capital of Gujarat. He is proposing me as the architect for the capital. I've seen the site of 16,000 acres situated on a broad river. The land is characterized by groves of mango trees great planes and deep rills that drain the land near the river.

I am being asked to plan a city and design the major buildings. As much as my work is my life, it would be little without your love.

Early this morning and at nightfall I was honored by the priest to hold the sacred incense in front of the God image of a Jain Temple. It was night when we left the candle lit spaces. The stars were diamonds. Soldiers and worshipers with lanterns led the way back to the hotel. There is no electricity.

The Temple is in the wilderness 200 miles from Ahmedabad. The windows of my room are barred to keep the leopards out.

Lou

Be sure to flatten your model to the proper scale. I noticed that the vertical dimensions are exaggerated. You will note that in my sketch that I attempted to make the waterways more distinct in shape and the lagoon to have an interesting shoreline, related to the placement of events.

You wanted a sketch—this is one I made in India on the way to the temples in the wilderness I told you about.   Lou

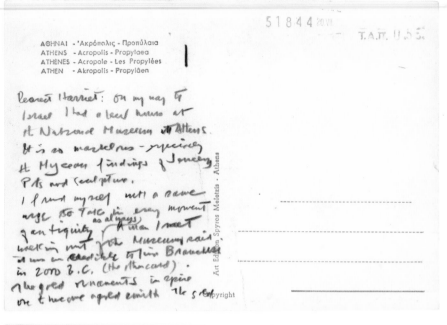

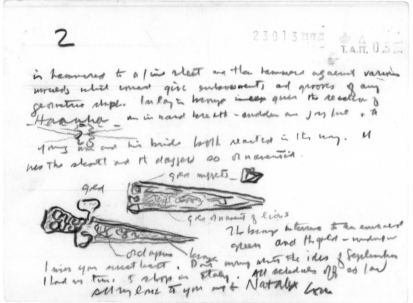

Gold / octopus / bronze / gold nuggets / gold ornament of lions / the bronze returns to
an emerald green and the gold—wonderful

On August 28 Lou flew to Israel, via Athens, to participate in a panel judging an architectural competition in Tel Aviv. I loved getting these postcards in spite of the fact that Lou ribbed me in the second one about my superstitions—referring to "The Ides of September." I expect that I had confessed a foreboding about another fall coming on with us being still apart.

ATHENS TO FARAWAY, LINCOLNVILLE, MAINE, C. AUGUST 29, 1963

1

Dearest Harriet:
On my way to Israel I had a few hours at the National Museum in Athens. It is so marvelous—especially the Mycenae findings of jewelry, pots and sculpture. I found myself with the same urge to take in every moment of antiquity as always. A man I met walking out of the museum said it was incredible to him: Brancusi in 2000 B.C. (the other card). The gold ornaments inspire one to become a goldsmith. The gold

2

is hammered to a fine sheet and then hammered against various molds which could give embossments and grooves of any geometric shape. Inlay in bronze gives the reaction of—Haaaha—an inward breath—sudden and joyful. A young man and his bride both reacted in this way. It was the sheath and the dagger so ornamented.

I miss you sweetheart. Don't worry about The ides of September. I had no time to shop in Italy. All schedules off so far.

All my love to you and to Natalex

Lou

Dearest:

This morning the Jurors (except Sir Halford) met for a quick glance of the entries. There are one hundred fifty Drawings and Models. My first impression tells me to reject nearly all. I may not take it stay as long as I thought. There is some talk about [circling] this week end the latest.

The people are wonderful. They are kind and anxious to serve. They seem so happy and healthy. The cities are growing maybe not beautifully but not shabbily either. The [noise] and gardens and flower balconies give an even flow of harmony that makes the architectural [monstrosities] stand aside for it. [Flights of] people seem relaxed have time to talk relate themselves to others and there seems to be work for all.

I went to-day to a Yemenite Village. The men were working on the making of Jewelry – very fine work – the most ancient looking man I ever saw. He sat at his bench over his work, his pate was covered with a skull cap which covered his abundant black curly hair. His side burns were trained to long curled locks which hung down to his shoulders. A pipe about 8 feet long in his mouth constantly and smoke came out yet or not his mouth. He exhaled it all. He never looked up as we watched. I asked him if he had old old pieces of jewelry — he just had fragments from which he re composed new pieces.

To night we have dinner with the mayor of TEV AVIV-Jaffa. They are calling for me now. Will mail this as is and write you later.
Dearest and little dearest Nathaniel I bid you both good night. Will write tis morning since will be back too late —
Love Lou

Dearest:

This morning the Jurors (except Sir [William] Holford) met for a quick glance of the entries. There are one hundred fifty drawings and models. My first impression told me to reject nearly all. I may not have to stay as long as I thought. There is some talk about finishing this weekend the latest.

The people are wonderful. They are kind and anxious to serve. They seem so happy and healthy. The cities are growing, maybe not beautifully, but not shabbily either. The walls and gardens and flower balconies give an even flow of harmony that makes the architectural nonentities stand aside for the foliage and for the whole. People seem relaxed, more time to talk, relate themselves to others, and there seems to be work for all.

I went today to a Yemenite village. The men work mostly on the making of jewelry—very fine work—the most ancient looking man I ever saw. He sat at his bench over his work. His pate was covered with a skull cap which covered his abundant black curly hair. His sideburns were trained to long curled locks which hung down to his shoulders. A pipe, about 8 feet long, was constantly in his mouth. No smoke came out of it or out of his mouth. He inhaled it all. He never looked up as we watched. I asked him if he had an old piece of jewelry—he just had fragments from which he composed new pieces.

Tonight we have dinner with the mayor of Tel Aviv. They are calling for me now. Will mail this as is and write to you later.

Dearest and little dearest Nathaniel I bid you both good night. Will write in morning since will be back too late.

Love,
Lou

Thursday, Midnight
Dearest Harriet,
We have just finished the judgment of the competition. . . . We have worked constantly every morning and afternoon until late (with a siesta break in the afternoon after an early lunch). In the evening, went to dinner and to bed. But tonight, we had a good strong party . . . so strong that I had the time to show the party slides of my recent work.

It's nice to hear the sea outside. Tomorrow, the Prime Minister, the press. Saturday, Haifa. Sunday, Jerusalem. Then Monday, Rome and the next day America!

This morning I looked again at our little boy. I have the set of pictures with me and the note you sent . . . I love you my darling (even more than the Rebeccas I haven't met here yet. They are hiding from me or maybe they don't exist). This is to rib you on the Ides of September and in the hope that it will cure you of the faith of tea leaf readers.

With all my love,
Lou

PHILADELPHIA TO FARAWAY, SEPTEMBER 14, 1963

Dearest Harriet,

I have been back now since Wednesday from Rome. I was hoping you would write a word from Faraway or sneak a call to me somehow. I am so accustomed to ringing you up and now it is so frustrating. When are you coming back? I am planning a visit to Rochester and want to see you soon before I again go away to Dhaka. When I was still in Israel I got several telegrams urging me to continue on to Pakistan before I returned to U.S. I was so sick of travel and so far away from distressing problems in the office that I did not heed their request. Though now I have to think seriously about signing my contract and starting serious negotiations for the building of the capital.

Please sweetheart write me a little note about your plans about returning to Charlotte and how Nathaniel likes Maine and how your mother is and how she is like a mother should be to you.

. . . when in Israel, I found some Assyrian beads of stone and Phoenician glass which are about 3000 to 4000 years old. So I bought them for you. I felt like sending them on to Faraway and then thought better to bring the gifts to you. I could find nothing that hit me for Nathaniel. I'll talk it over with you and the next time I'll be specific about it.

With all my love, my darling,
Lou

Saturday, after dinner

Sweetie:

. . . In Rome I stayed at the Academy—not at the Villa—in one of the studios. The Kimbells are away. Berthe Marti (friend of Bob Venturi and teacher at Bryn Mawr) is living in a fabulous Villa on the Gianicolo. Villa Doria Pamphili next to the Via Aurelia Antica and bound by Via della Nocetta and Via Vitellia. She drove me thru the place and I learned much about Roman Gardens of which this one is unbelievably wonderful.

She said the Roman doesn't really like natural landscape. The deliberate garden is characteristic. In any case it is fabulous. Now the Count wants to sell the place. He offered it to Rome and to the Belgian Embassy. Rome wants to pay too little and it may go into bad hands. What a shame if it does. Dearest, I miss you. Pardon the small talk and the not too well told tales.

Love,
Lou

Lou's pastel of the Large Baths at Hadrian's Villa, Tivoli, 1951.

Sunday 15 Sept.

The quiet ruin reveals again the spirit out
of which it once stood as a proud structure. Now
it is free of its bonds

To of this spirit is a building being built now
more wonderful than when it once be completed. Its
spirit is young and anxious to become it sees. It too
is free and need not answer.

The building standing complete has its spaces
locked in unbending structure. Its bonds are
the dictates of use. The spirit is engaged and
must answer.

The quiet ruin now freed from use welcomes
wild growth to play joyously around it and is
like a father who delights in the little one
tugging at its clothes

The ancient building still vigorous in use has the light
of Eternity.

Dearest;
This time in Rome I came upon the Forum and Caracalla from a different angle
I always walked from the Academy taking usually the same path. Always the
ruins were like new and for this reason was satisfied not to explore too often new
places. Being driven this time and in the fading light of the dying day showed
me angles new and the ruins made me think what I wrote above.
I promised to write every day when away. You know I aren't an writer. I have
now written 3 letters in 2 days because I miss you and just feel like writing.
Did you go to the Island? Does Nathaniel seem to like it? Has he been good
like his daddy?
Love Lou

Sunday 15 Sept.

The quiet ruin reveals again the spirit out
of which it once stood as a proud structure. Now
it is free of its bonds.
Too of this spirit is a building being built now
more wonderful than when it will be completed. Its
spirit is young and anxious to become itself. It too
is free and need not answer.
The building standing complete has its spaces
locked in unbending structure. Its bonds are
the duties of use. The spirit is engaged and
must answer.
The quiet ruin now freed from use welcomes
wild growth to play joyously around it and is
like a father who delights in the little one
tugging at its clothes.
The ancient building still vigorous in use has the light
of eternity.

Dearest:

This time in Rome I came upon the Forum and Caracalla from a
different angle. I always walked from the Academy taking usually
the same path. Always the ruins were like new and for this reason
was satisfied not to explore too often new places. Being driven this
time and in the fading light of the closing day showed me angles
new and the ruins made me think of what I wrote above.

I promised to write every day when away. You knew I couldn't
and wouldn't. I have now written 3 letters in 2 days because I miss
you and just feel like writing.

Did you go to the Island? Does Nathaniel seem to like it? Has
he been good like his daddy?

Love,
Lou

125

Lou with his friend and Penn colleague Robert Le Ricolais, a French engineer and pioneer of space-frame structures.

Dearest Harriet:

Tomorrow night after school I leave for San Diego.

I gave my usual opening lecture at Penn yesterday and was prepared for it by Robert Le Ricolais at his hostel. Took him out to dinner at the Faculty Club before the talk. Received two more telegrams from Dhaka urging me to bring the construction drawings for the first steps in construction. I haven't, as yet, started on my final plans and I am beginning to feel worried. Because I feel so well it helps me not to get deeply upset with the slowness of things there.

When in Israel I slept out on the Veranda outside my room facing the sea under the full moon. The sound of the surf was like a mother's song. And also the siesta, which is customary in Israel during August, became so welcome. All contributed to my feeling rested now and needing less food and feeling calmer too.

My love hearing not a word and reading not a word from you is not good. I know you must have your hands full with the baby but still just the littlest sign that you are healthy and happy would mean so much.

I heard that the Florida new school went to I. M. Pei. Rather sorry John Johansen and Dan didn't succeed. You know I went down there too. I had a feeling that the Board was not for me. The director wrote me a nice letter and I believe he was entirely sincere. Being in competition is not a comfortable feeling.

Am anxious to hear if some of your friends in Maine are still there. It must be getting depopulated with the weather I imagine (as it is already here) getting chilly.

I love you my dear and my little dear.

Lou

At the end of August I took Nathaniel to Maine for the first time. I had not been back for two years, and, rereading Lou's letters to me there, I remember how I avoided calling him, hoping he would pick up the phone and call *me*. But the fear of speaking to my mother, or worse my brother Abbott, was apparently too much for him.

Faraway was empty now. Wanting to avoid any conflict, my mother had invited me to bring Nathaniel after the rest of the family had left. She was practical and reserved, but also forgiving and generous, suggesting I "pay no mind" to gossipy villagers and offering to help with her limited resources. She welcomed my advice about her garden, showing confidence in my growing skills, and tried not to question my future plans or my abiding love for a man she did not trust to make them happen.

My mother was about to return to Chicago for the winter, and we set about closing the house as we had done at the end of so many summers past. We chatted as I stowed books in the library, leafing through a favorite, Bernard Boutet de Monvel's *Jeanne d'Arc*, and I carried silver to the third-floor hideaway, passing the familiar posters of *Theatre Arts* covers with century-old celebrities: Isadora Duncan, Ellen Terry, and Sarah Bernhardt. It struck me, as I descended the back stairs, that as much as these mythical women had been my childhood heroines, I had overlooked my mother's own quiet courage. She was caring to so many, lending support through trials such as mine, while sparing us the kinds of judgments she exacted of herself. Having been born in 1883, my mother was of another era and had not considered a professional career for herself. But I felt that her vision of a woman's life was evolving, and that she now hoped a career would be possible for me, even as a single mother. I returned to Wings Point with a renewed determination to learn as much as I could about landscape architecture, albeit as an apprentice with a small salary.

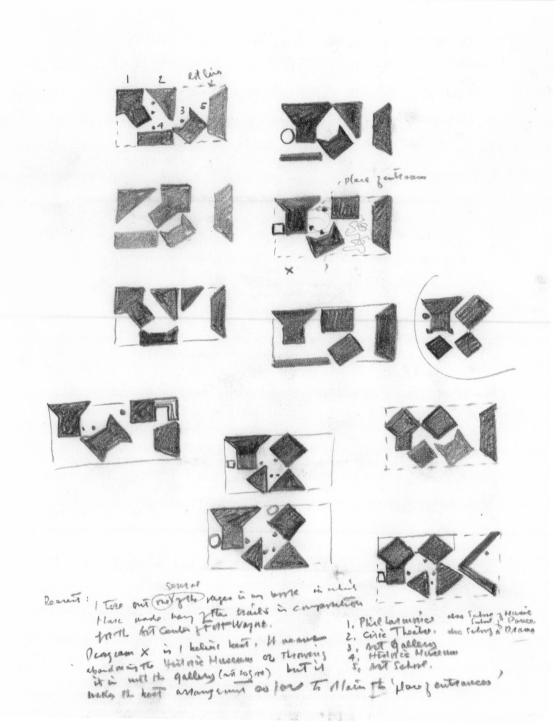

1. Philharmonic 2. Civic Theater 3. Art Gallery 4. Historic Museum 5. Art School,
also School of Music, School of Dance, also School of Drama

Dearest:

I tore out several of the one pages in my book in which I have
made many of these trials in composition for the Art Center of
Fort Wayne. Diagram X is I believe best. It means abandoning the
Historic Museum or throwing it in with the Gallery (not so good)
but it makes the best arrangement so far to obtain the "place of
entrances."

The day before my thirty-fifth birthday, Lou sent me a bulky envelope with
sketches crystallizing his ideas for an arts complex in Fort Wayne, Indiana.
The program was ambitious, calling for performance spaces as well as for a
museum and administrative offices. Rather than jamming all these functions
together, Lou developed a scheme composed of multiple buildings. It was a
village of the arts, where each discipline would have its own voice but would
also speak to all the others. Lou loved the spaces between buildings as much as
the buildings themselves, and he endlessly played with these spaces on paper
and in his head, often changing scales to imagine what a composition would
look like from the ground, from the air, and even from space.

"A city is a place where a small boy wandering through it can find what he
wants to do for the rest of his life," Lou was fond of saying. The first page of
this letter might as well be a physical expression of that idea. You can imagine
moving among these buildings, with the endless interest of angle and light
and shadow, encountering the allure of different arts—music, theater, ballet,
dance, sculpture, painting—and being drawn more or less by them according
to your natural inclinations. While this might have been a beautiful way to
experience the arts, in the end only one building would be built: a performing
arts hall.

In the next pages Lou developed his ideas for the hall, thinking mainly
of its use for music, although he had met with the prominent Broadway set
designer Jo Mielziner, who advised him on how to make the auditorium
and backstage spaces work for theater as well. In a talk to students, Lou
said, "I am building a theater in Fort Wayne, Indiana, and having observed
theaters, I came to the conclusion that one must regard the auditorium and
the stage as a violin, a sensitive instrument where one should be able to hear
even a whisper without any amplification. The lobbies and all other adjunct
spaces may be compared to the violin case. The violin and its case are
completely different."

Organ chamber above the conductor / Construction shaped to the demands of the acoustical principles

This little diagram may lead me to a shape of room made from the demands of the acoustics and seating capacity and above all I should like to make a stark concert chamber pinched as balconies and recesses for people which contribute to the quality of the sound—as though you entered a musical instrument.

Chamber for spot lighting

main structural beams of the auditorium which span from wall to wall and are shaped for acoustic purposes.

The space[s] between the roof members and the main members are tied structurally to economize with structure

Ft. Wayne Philharmonic Hall
The classical place

Stage area / band shell / Orchestra / Balcony

Orchestra pit / Balconies 1st and 2nd

The above sketch is the image I have of a classical example of a music hall. The balconies interfere with the total sense of the room. These are however necessary because the capacity of 2500 is too great to obtain [in] a volume not too large.

100 × 100 is the most the dimensions should be. (I am told). There are however many more factors.

Probable scheme for the civic theater seating 500.
Stage / orchestra / Stairs / Balcony / Balcony

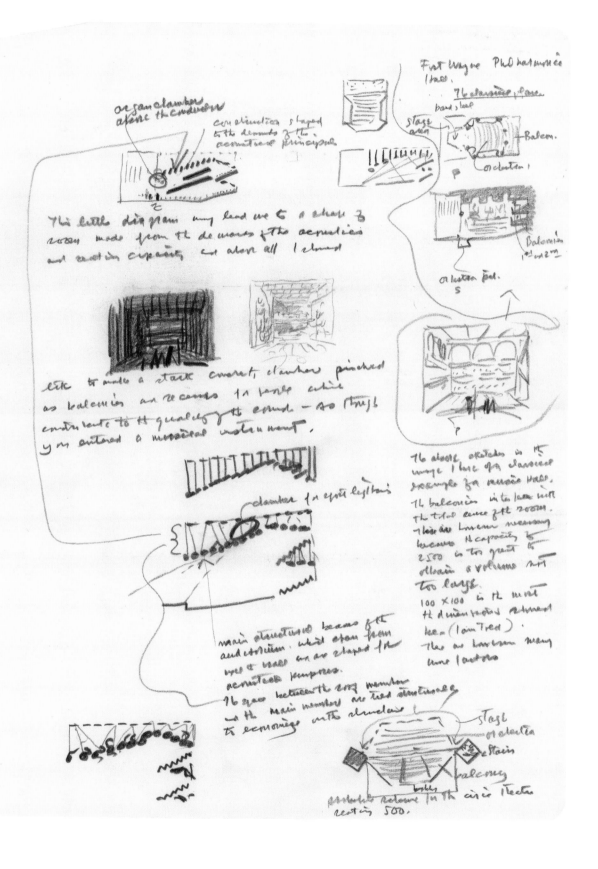

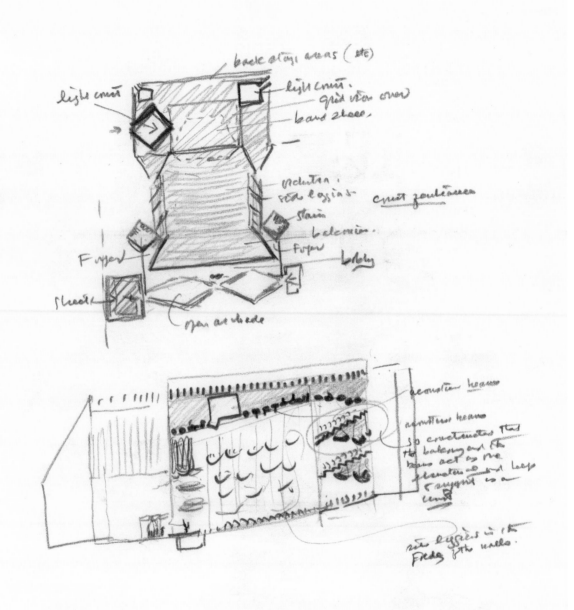

Hassan
I made the sketch just before I was required to begin to move. It is hurried in its ... I have attempted to express the idea ... the lightcrusts are a new idea I once ... embodiment in the synagogue ... and is some yet finds at ... finished ... design it ... and my my attitude of the ...

Sorry about not meeting the 30 I promised you. Had no ... in time in case you ...

[TOP: plan] *light court / back stage areas (etc.) / light court / gridiron over / band shell orchestra / side loggias / stairs / court of entrances / balconies / foyer*
Court of entrances

[BOTTOM: section] *lobby / open arcade / street / foyer*
acoustical beams / acoustical beams / so constructed that the balcony and the beams act as one structure and help to support as a unit.
side loggias in the folding of the walls.

Harriet,
I made the sketch just before I will deposit in box to mail. It is hurried in the first attempt to express the idea. The light courts are a new idea I have introduced in the synagogue and in some of the Indian buildings. Will send you sketches of this soon.

Lou

Sorry about not sending the 30 I promised you. I had no dough in till. Will call you Sunday.

KARACHI, WEST PAKISTAN, TO WINGS POINT, DECEMBER 3, 1963

Dearest:
I am leaving momentarily for America. Everything went well finally until the last few hours here when the Minister of Finance reversed the decisions of the other Ministers who had looked over my contract conditions and now wants more restrictions. It is humiliating and tiring. I had not a moment to myself. It was contract and sleep. I must say though that is in a way fun as long as I had time to negotiate but now I must leave again without a signed contract. The details read like a maze.

I read two stories before going to bed: "The Two Hussars" and "A Happy Married Life" by Tolstoy. Now I appreciate them as works of art with the realization that art is a life because it comes from life. His beings are word beings yet implant in the mind a presence free from the words.

I am sad, my sweet dears, because I see the image of the Assembly Building as though it were a reality and I feel the helplessness of my financial situation. I could give in and take a gander. The building may turn out well and hopefully break even. I could refuse the terms and never see the work of a dream. What should I do?

With all my love,
Lou

Lou was well aware of the price of dreams. He knew what the Dhaka project would take out of him, that it might bankrupt him, but how could he deny it? Once the Assembly Building was a reality in his mind, he had to go for it, whatever the cost. But I do wonder if he was aware of the human cost of his work at that time. I had experienced the dazzling autumn beauty of Vermont woodlands amid tasks and pleasures in workdays and mothering. But at nightfall, when the workers departed and my boy slept, I was alone at Wings Point to contemplate the moods of the lake close by, in the early darkness that spoke not of capital plans but of the simple joys I desired, and with winter snows again on the way.

The view from my window at Wings Point.

Dearest,

I arrived here Christmas day. The holiday is observed reminiscent of English ways. They anticipate the fun of days off from school and work and expect gifts but feel nothing of course of the meaning of this day that overwhelmed us as kids and remained with us as grown ups. How beautiful is the reliving thru children these days of innocent and bright images and shrilly joys. When at the Academy during Xmas of '51 mountain shepherds were called in to play the wooden flute while we sat around in the festooned room sipping "Ye blude reed wine."

My first time in Europe, everlastingly full of joyful memories, Xmas was also in Rome. I was awakened by my colleague to attend mass in the ultra matins of four in the morning. He was a great fixer and somehow obtained the rare passes to St. Peters. The Pope sprinkled the multitude. I was elated to have felt the drops on me. The first light of the coming day is the promise of life. As we left the cathedral with the night barely gone it seemed like we were rewarded with a day within a day.

One Christmas came to me as the most wonderful. It was the afternoon before that symbolic day when I brought the branches of holly to you. My feelings were life full. I felt love for you intermingled with thoughts of Bob whom I loved as a friend. The image of you then I described in my first letter to you. This has never left me having come from me untouched unconsidered. When I imagine you this moment it is as I thought of you then.

In the early days with Sue I recall Christmas, glad in going from shop to shop selecting unusual decorations for the tree. I brushed off insinuations of indiscriminate spending since we lived on meager income. Then as now Xmas and the American holidays were the signposts of courage and confidence. On those days the string of disappointments were forgotten.

Home sweet home in the days of school my people liked Christmas too though we kids reveled in it free from the recollections of old world oppression and prejudice which they could not altogether forget. I lived for everybody. I excused all pain caused me. I felt only friendship. Never have I known home again as then.

When I brought the holly to you I dared not believe that you could love me. I know now because you also never forgot that day that it became symbolic of our home.

Nathaniel came of our love. He is now the most precious, the most beautiful.

Lou

Nathaniel with his red sled at Wings Point, Charlotte, Vermont.

1964

In Vermont I discovered a different way of living. Dan's world was a kind of utopia, an openhearted commune focused on a single artist's work and family. It was self-sustaining and so like a colony of dedicated New England transcendentalists that I felt I was living in another century. Even the shattering news of the Kennedy assassination in November seemed unreal and distant. It was difficult to absorb the magnitude of the tragedy, although I heard from Lou of people crying in the streets and how Philadelphia came to a dead stop. America was shaken and changing, but it was hard to feel that at Wings Point.

Nathaniel was thriving. We fed the birds in the snow, and he was fascinated by the morning frost on our windowpanes. Light shows and wind showers played across the snow-clad mountains beyond the frozen lake and cedar and spruce woods. Mothering was a joy, and I rarely went out at night, although once in Burlington after a concert by Arthur Rubinstein of works that I loved, I attended a midnight reception for him in a neighboring mansion. Stepping from snowdrifts into candlelit rooms with massive flower bouquets, a festive board, and the ebullient pianist framed by a gorgeous Odilon Redon screen, I was reminded of how far I now was from a world I once knew.

Yet behind Dan's backwoods setup was in fact an ambitious man conceiving landscapes that were very much engaged with the contemporary scene. I was fortunate to be in the office as he was reexamining the Miller House gardens in Columbus, Indiana, and began work on the Oakland Museum in Oakland, California. I saw how he used water to create drama and movement and how plant material could define space and create alluring perspectival effects. I admired, too, how Dan anticipated the play of time, designing his landscapes to set the stage for current happenings but also imagining how they would mature to inspire future ones.

Unlike Lou, however, Dan had no use for my "good eye." He was his own critic and saw no real value in training me. I think it may have annoyed him that I made a cozy home for myself and my son in the crude space over the garage and that I had become part of his office family, replacing my own lost one, while he was paying for my keep without much gratitude or acknowledgment from Lou.

Rereading the following letters, I feel the distance that was opening between Lou and me. We were drifting like the snows, now that we had no shared experience to rely on. I was a refugee in Dan's utopia, without connection to the urban world that was Lou's lifeblood—although he did try to connect through his experiences in our once-shared city and in the far-flung places where his buildings were beginning to rise.

AHMEDABAD, INDIA, TO WINGS POINT, CHARLOTTE, VERMONT, JANUARY 2, 1964

Dearest:
Couldn't resist whetting your feminine appetite with this picture. How strong they must have been. Maybe Nathaniel will be a strong artist.

Love,
Lou

London-Paris-Geneva-Cairo-Bombay-Ahmedabad

TEHRAN, IRAN, TO WINGS POINT, JANUARY 11, 1964

Dearest Harriet and Nathaniel,
Imprisoned in airport terminal.

All my love,
Lou

138

Dearest,

On the way in by street car there was an incident between the white and black man.

After I paid my fare, I noticed the car was not particularly full. I went back and was about to take a seat when I realized that the young boy occupying it had his legs across it. Nothing crossed my mind to have him move but went on to the next seat and the same thing was there and so with the next still. Those fellows terribly arrogant. I still didn't bother to disturb their unbearable attitudes and settled on a seat nearby next to a very nice lady.

I noticed, since I kept looking in their direction, (though I was seeming absorbed in the magazine enclosed), that an elderly lady following me tried the same thing I did and the boys (grown up strong ones about 17–18 years) didn't move from their insulting poses. Then on the heels of the lady came a young burly Negro who tried the first seat and immediately decided on the next only to find resistance to his taking that seat. The guy just wouldn't budge! The Negro took hold of his legs and gave them a quick and effective jerk to the side and sat down at the moment of which the young white one lunged out to hit him but the young Negro was like lightning—striking the boy a crack on the nose, the blood coming freely. This started an exchange of movie violence between the two—the Negro having with easy calm the better of the fight by far. Some whites broke it up not his friends. The colored boy just sat down as though he had just finished reciting Tennyson. The other was ushered out of the car, flustered, incensed and cursing back. The boy who was in the fight, explaining that he couldn't move because his bag was with him, so and so and so, making remarks.

This upset the entire car. The women yelled. Its small space gave little room to the fighters so they swayed from wall to wall causing more alarm. The victor's manner was that of a worthy man. Everyone felt he was justified. I can't still get over the terrible arrogance. It depressed me so that now approaching night I keep thinking about man's hatreds as being the most distinguishable difference between man and beast. I believe an animal feels devotion and love—a kind of love, but knows no hate, nor displays the ugliness of arrogance.

This upset the entire car. The women yelled the small space gave little room to the fighters so they swayed from wall to wall causing more alarm. The victor's manner was that of a worthy man everyone felt he was justified. I can't still get over the terrible arrogance. It depressed me so that now approaching night I keep thinking about man's hatreds as being the most distinguishable difference between man and beast. I believe an animal feels devotion or love — a kind place. but knows no hate. nor displays the ugliness of arrogance

I cut my own hair in the back just now. It was getting a bit 'colonial'. For a moment I thought of sending you a lock of it but was afraid to assume that our love is still the unquestioned bond that feels no fault and that each little part of one is sacred and uncontestable. each cell of the million million individuals and a lock of hair at the center of love. Now were I to receive just a hair of your beautiful head I would love it as if were all of you. Could you then trust that I love you the same way. If so I send it of you. I'll be very good.

Love Lou

I cut my own hair in the back just now. It was getting a bit "colonial." For a moment I thought of sending you a lock of it but was afraid to assume that our love is still the unquestioned bond that feels no fault and that each little part of one is sacred and uncriticizable, each cell of the million-million individual and then a lock of hair is also the center of love. Now were I to receive just a hair of your beautiful head (not as many as I sent you), I would love it as [if] it were all of you. Could you then sweetheart think of me the same way. "If so I send it glad. If no I'll be very sad."

Love,
Lou

By April, the winter was lifting and I could look forward to visitors: Mariette, from Italy, and Susannah with her boys for joyous reunions. Then, to my distress, my mother's Maine caretaker showed up at Wings Point, not only unbidden but transformed from the gentle man I thought I knew to a lecher, thinking me an easy target. I immediately dismissed him, but that he even dared to ferret out my retreat made me aware that hiding from my former life had only fueled rumors, and that the perception others might have of me as a wanton woman might trail me—as it did—for years to come.

Nathaniel with me, Susannah, Tim, and Amos Jones at Wings Point.

ROME TO WINGS POINT, APRIL 30, 1964

Dearest:

Made a hit with my plans of the Indian Institute of Management.
I believe they need more study but they do have the springy look of
life and the firm colors of decision.

They want me to design the city of Gandhinagar the capital of
Gujarat. I had to disagree with a term they demand—of 60 days/
year of stay in India for the 3 years of the contract. This may decide
against me. 60 days away from the 360 every year with school with
all the other days that belong to others. I must refuse though the
project is fabulous. I will get no dollars only rupees. I can't spend
them except to buy things in India including tickets of travel (with
rupees) and pay for living.

I miss you dearest Harriet. The memory of the beautiful
moments with you never leaves me.

Love,

Lou

Lou had been developing plans for the Indian Institute of Management in
Ahmedabad since he first traveled to view the site in November 1962, the
month Nathaniel was born. The project meant a great deal to him; he had
always wanted to design a school, and this was an entire campus, with a
library, classrooms, dormitories, dining halls, offices, and faculty housing.
Lou felt at home in Ahmedabad and had become close with Balkrishna Doshi,

Lou's early perspective of the dormitories for the Indian Institute of Management, Ahmedabad, India.

Lou's later perspective hints at the remarkable variety of buildings and spaces at the Indian Institute of Management, all composed of local brick.

the associated architect on the project, who had worked with Le Corbusier and saw Lou as a great teacher—a yogi even—who could help India discover new directions in architecture. Lou's friends there hoped he would spend more time in Ahmedabad, and perhaps to entice him, they offered additional projects, including the master plan for Gandhinagar, a project Lou realized would be financially ruinous to accept.

There was one job Lou was up for that he did not tell me about. Perhaps it was because he didn't want to jinx it, or perhaps it was because he knew I would be jealous—after all, the client was the most beautiful woman in the world.

After the death of President Kennedy, a committee was assembled to select an architect to design a library in his honor. Lou was on the short list, along with Ludwig Mies van der Rohe, Alvar Aalto, and I. M. Pei, which was a tough position for him; not only was he up against the best but he never did well in competitions, though he had won them for his drawings in his youth. But if ever there were a competition Lou wanted to win, this was it.

Years later the men in his office were still talking about the day the client came to visit and how they had all tried to make the fifth-floor office at 1501 Walnut Street presentable. Lou had moved there the previous year to accommodate the work in India and Pakistan, and the place was still unfinished: the drywall was spotted with dabs of spackle, there were no rugs on the floor, and drawings were piled high on doors mounted on sawhorses. Lou dashed out at the last minute and bought ashtrays, placing them around strategically as a sign of sophistication, but there was only so much that could be done.

At the appointed hour, the elevator door opened and out stepped Jackie Kennedy. She was gorgeous. Since there was no proper conference room, Lou conducted her into his small private office and closed the door. The men kept their heads down and strained their ears to hear. One quipped, "I wonder how long it will take him?"

Lou told me later the story of what happened next: Jackie sat across from him at his oak-board table. She talked about how she wanted to build a place that would allow future generations to know Jack and what he stood for. Lou then talked about the spirit of architecture. He did his best to seduce with his poetry, but he was distracted by sirens growing louder and louder. He got up and looked down from the window. Police cars were blocking the street, and a fire truck arrived on the scene. A large crowd had gathered, and people were pointing upward at Lou's building. "Mrs. Kennedy," Lou said, turning from the window, "I'm terribly sorry, but I believe my building must be on fire." And Jackie looked at him and smiled, covering her mouth with the back of her hand. "Mr. Kahn," she said, "I don't think there's a fire, I just think it might be me."

Mrs. Kennedy Here to See Architect

Mrs. John F. Kennedy came to Philadelphia this afternoon to consult with Architect Louis I. Kahn on plans for the John F. Kennedy Library which is to be built on a site near Harvard University.

The wife of the late President flew here from New York where last night she attended a dinner with the President and Mrs. Johnson.

Word of her arrival spread fast in center city. Crowds gathered in the vicinity of Kahn's office at 1501 Walnut st.

Several Architects Considered

Mrs. Kennedy and William Walton, an artist and friend of the family who is helping in the decision on plans for the library, consulted with Kahn in his fifth floor office.

So far several architects have been under consideration for the job. The decision as to who will design the building has not yet been made.

Kahn, 63, is internationally known for such works as the Richards Medical Research Building at the University of Pennsylvania.

One of his current projects is the Salk Center for Biological Studies at La Jolla, Calif.

No Decision on Plans

After meeting with Kahn about three-quarters of an hour, Mrs. Kennedy left the office at 3:13 P. M.

Accompanied by Walton, Kahn and a secret service man, she got into a black limousine and headed west on Walnut st.

Continued on Page 36, Col. 4

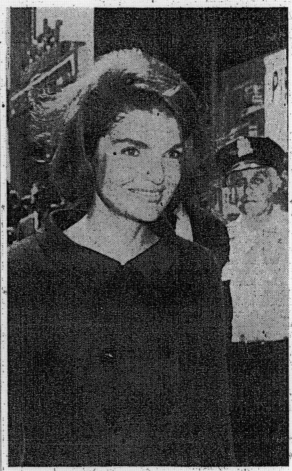

MRS. JACQUELINE KENNEDY, widow of President John F. Kennedy, leaves the office of architect Louis I. Kahn at 1501 Walnut st. this afternoon.

The *Evening Bulletin*'s June 17, 1964, report of Jackie Kennedy's visit to Lou's office.

One day in midsummer, Dan took me aside and said almost casually that it was time that I think about moving on. I might have anticipated this, but it was a blow. I was very much enjoying the camaraderie of the office, and I was picking up skills; but of course, since I was unable to draft, there really wasn't much use for me. I was suddenly afraid and humiliated, shorn of all conviction that I would ever amount to anything. I don't recall the frightened message I cabled Lou in India, but he replied with a telegram—followed by a letter shortly thereafter.

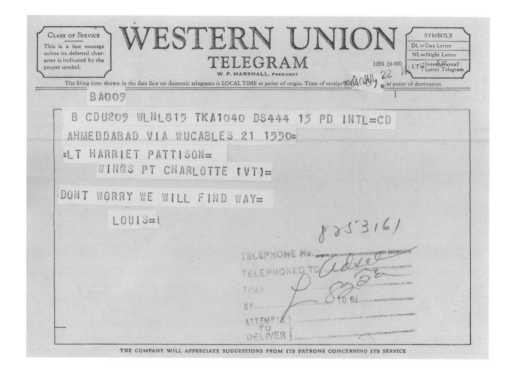

Dearest Harriet and Nathaniel,

At last on way home from India. Never wanted to come back more.

Have to stop in London for a day to see Sir Robert Matthew on the Presidents House.

Heard that [Tony] Walmsley is going to stay a bit longer in Pakistan to finish his work before joining my office. I hope to see him in London. Understand he is also in camera with Sir Robert discussing the landscaping of the Secretariat part of the Capital in Islamabad.

I am shocked about Dan K. My beautiful Harriet, only don't worry. Got your telegram. Don't feel blue.

You'll be wonderful with gardens.

Love,
Lou

Will send you $ on arrival can't trust mail over seas. Did you receive $ via Pakistan?

I tore open Lou's letter, hoping for a solution, and remember feeling that his phrase, "You'll be wonderful with gardens," wasn't very encouraging. But I had realized that if ever I had a hope of supporting myself and my child, I would need to go back to school for a professional degree in landscape architecture. The hierarchy of Dan's office had taught me that much. I retreated to Maine and quickly wrote for applications to the two schools I knew had good programs—the University of Pennsylvania, where most of Dan's men had come from, and Harvard, where Dan himself had gone. On the phone, I asked Lou to put in a good word for me with the two department heads, which he agreed to do, but he seemed reluctant. I angrily demanded help for myself, and I remember wondering in exasperation why he was so tentative when it came to his professional colleagues. Was he afraid to stand up for me? Did he think I had little talent, or was he just uncomfortable? What did he expect me to do?

Dearest Harriet
      This is what I wrote Sasaki. —

I am grateful that you regard my recommendation of Harriet Pattison
as a student in your School of Landscape Architecture.
Following your suggestion I asked her to write to you. She called me to-day
to tell me she had written immediately but as yet not received a
reply.
Those days with the Kennedys are constantly on my mind. They are
unusually great people. I feel so undeservedly rewarded just to have
known them those moments.. Lou —

When you were trying to steer the call the way you wanted I heard
an angry blast of cool words — God Damn it! What a
temper! I told Louise that she is to accept a call from Maine if the
person asks for me personally. The only one I don't confide in is my
book keeper who is a bit thick and the zenith of dullness. She makes
no mistakes with Figures but hasn't the slightest sense of the meaning
of it. If you happen to catch her ask for Louise Badgley or try later.
      You will notice, Harriet, that my letter was calm and not gushing with
persuasion. I will try also if the chance presents itself to meet
him either in Boston or Washington. That is if it proves necessary.
Don't worry sweet heart.
      All my love   Harriet   and   Nathaniel.
                  Lou   X   X

In September —
I planned to meet Sir Robert
Mathew in London or Rome. But it
seems better to wait and attend
the meeting in Rawalpindi in
October. Now I must write
more telegrams to make this
change. It means of course
That I will stay more time in
U.S. before school starts.
Since my glasses I cannot
write straight across the invisible
line.

Dearest Harriet,

This is what I wrote [Hideo] Sasaki—

"I am grateful that you regard my recommendation of Harriet Pattison as a student in your school of Landscape Architecture.

Following your suggestion I asked her to write to you. She called me today to tell me she had written immediately but as yet not received a reply.

Those days with the Kennedys are constantly on my mind. They are unusually great people. I feel so undeservingly rewarded just to have known them those moments. Lou"

When you were trying to steer the call the way you wanted I heard an angry slash of words—God Damn it! What a temper!

I told Louise that she is to accept a call from Maine if the person asks for me personally. The only one I don't confide in is my book keeper who is a bit thick and the zenith of dullness. She makes no mistakes with figures but hasn't the slightest sense of the meaning of 1. If you happen to catch her, ask for Louise Badgley or try later.

You will notice, Harriet, that my letter was calm and not gushing with personal coy. I will try also if the chance presents itself to meet him either in Boston or Washington. That is if it proves necessary.

Don't worry sweetheart.

All my love Harriet and Nathaniel.

Lou

In September—I planned to meet Sir Robert Matthew in London or Rome. But it seems better to wait and attend the meeting in Rawalpindi in October. Now I must write more telegrams to make that change. It means, of course, that I will stay more time in U.S. before school starts.

Since my glasses, I cannot write straight across the invisible line.

What a faint-hearted letter Lou wrote to the head of Harvard's School of Design. Was he of two minds in writing Sasaki? Going to Harvard might have freed each of us for other lives. It was at this time that I even challenged Lou to let me go, and he didn't directly resist. Perhaps he wanted a roll of the dice to determine the outcome? As it happened, I did not get into Harvard, and an acceptance to Penn sealed my fate. I would return to Philadelphia.

I found an apartment on Wolcott Drive in the suburban neighborhood of Chestnut Hill—not far from the Esherick House—and a wonderful young woman from Ireland to take care of Nathaniel during the day. Roseanne Grabowski was newly married and would have children of her own, but she was full of love for Nathaniel and had only the kindest thoughts, without judgment, for me. However, not everyone was so charitable, and in the mid-1960s a woman with a child and no wedding ring was cause for gossip and even suspicion. In the leafy lanes and culs-de-sac of Chestnut Hill I hoped I could maintain a quiet anonymity, but I soon found myself developing a kind of affectless outer shell to protect myself.

The eighteenth-century neighborhoods where I had once lived in downtown Philadelphia felt like forbidden territory now, and the places I had shared with Lou no longer charmed me. I ventured into town only for

Cherokee Apartments in Chestnut Hill, Philadelphia.

150

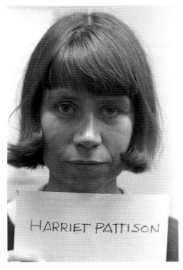

My University of Pennsylvania
student ID "mug shot," caught
between the backwoods and
graduate studies, September 1964.

classes at Penn or to visit loyal friends like Edith Braun. I joined the ranks
(if not the routines) of suburban mothers at Cherokee, an apartment complex
designed by Oscar Stonorov, who had been a partner of Lou's in the 1940s.
Stonorov's two-story brick buildings had small rooms, high strip windows,
and common entrances—mine was shared by a nosy couple next door and a
kindly researcher of bats upstairs.

Although the buildings were dreary, the grounds, designed by a landscape
architect destined for eminence, Cornelia Hahn Oberlander, redeemed the
development with fine plantings and specimens saved from the grand estate
that had once been there, like the glorious Atlas cedar at one end of my
street. Among Cherokee's residents was an Italian couple, the Giurgolas, who
befriended me. Aldo was a younger colleague of Lou's, and Adelaide was his
vivacious wife, who drove a red Mustang with Roman gusto. Their lovely
daughter, Paola, often came to play with Nathaniel and sang songs to him.

I was excited to be at Penn and formally learning the tools and techniques
of the landscape architect, but going back to school at thirty-five was not easy.
I was tormented by fears of failure, feeling that this was my final chance to
succeed. What I'd garnered from Wings Point was procedural, while here
I was to explore an art with uses for my talents. The landscape department
also enforced a bruising regime that would make a three-year degree hard-
earned, with withering all-night assignments too often completed in my tiny
linoleum-floored bedroom, boxed in between a narrow bed and a man-sized
drafting board that Lou gave me.

Lou at the Hayden Hall blackboard drawing with both hands, which he would sometimes do at the drafting board as well.

Lou was a powerful presence at Penn when I began classes in the landscape program. It was wonderful to be near each other again, and I would sit in on his architectural juries in Hayden Hall, which went on for many hours, often into the night. Sometimes I would join him for supper afterward at a nearby restaurant, La Terrasse, or he would take me along for drinks at his friend Robert Le Ricolais's apartment.

I was thrilled when one weekend Lou showed me his new project in West Pakistan. We studied the site photographs on a broad table in the office's fourth-floor storage room by a bank of windows where there was good light. As Lou described what he had seen, the vast plain framed by the mountains, it was almost like a summons: he needed landscape skills for this commission.

Islamabad would be a new capital city, built to administer both sides of a divided Pakistan; the British withdrawal of 1947 had left the Muslim republic separated by India's thousand-mile wedge into Urdu-speaking West Pakistan, with its capital of Karachi, and Bengali-speaking East Pakistan, with Dhaka as its capital. The new city would be the ruling seat of Ayub Khan, the Sandhurst-trained military dictator who, after seizing the nation's presidency in 1958, wanted the best the design world had to offer. The Greek planner Constantinos Doxiadis had laid out the street grid, and now an international collection of architects was supposed to take on various precincts, under the leadership of Sir Robert Matthew, a polished bureaucrat and chief municipal architect for the city of London. The arrangement was a postcolonial mess, and Lou sensed in it not only a need for a unifying voice but also an

The planned site for Islamabad, West Pakistan's new capital, against the backdrop of the Himalayan foothills.

An early study model of the Islamabad site, with the president's house, Lou's assignment, at the center. Working with Plasticine felt like sculpting the ground itself.

opportunity to expand his role. Initially assigned only the president's house (which was more of a palace), Lou extended his drawings and models well beyond that, stepping into other architects' territories and developing a comprehensive layout for the whole site, including a plaza for gatherings, a viewing stadium, and a large assembly building for the parliament.

Suddenly I remembered Edinburgh, where I had been a student briefly after leaving Yale. I imagined how the Scottish city, which I adored, must have grown in a similarly stark landscape, with first only the castle on a peak dominating the wilderness to the Firth of Forth, then the medieval city growing around it, and later, across the river gorge, the exquisite Georgian precinct taking shape—the geography and layout holding all centuries and crags together. I was struck by the unfathomable opportunity Lou might have of drawing up a city and its infrastructure, all at once, out of the rough and beautiful landscape of Islamabad.

STATE GUEST HOUSE, RAWALPINDI, WEST PAKISTAN, TO
726 WOLCOTT DR., PHILADELPHIA, OCTOBER 7, 1964

Dearest Harriet and Nathaniel,
I caught the plane by route V.I.P. It took off at 10. I got to New York via National, a car was waiting by the runway it shooed me to BOAC as they took in the gang plank.

I feel like I've been away for ages. Monday the meetings started, Wednesday, I am packing for the early flight next morning to Dhaka, via Lahore-Delhi-Dhaka. The [Islamabad] drawings withstood varied reactions from the dome minded, minaret obsessed, and tile-full souls, on the one hand—the square foot area doctrinarians on the other.

The argument for traditional is the people want it: "our problem is psychological." The argument for cost control is raised by fattest ministers—finance, commerce: "The people are poor." I want so much to give them the most there is in me. The clay and paper models they read as clay and paper. I begin to distrust myself. I talk of how it will all look and feel like when built. They and I are both left in despair. One dome I would promise them could save the day. A dome under an assembly, reception, banquet hall, court room would make it impossible to hear in. I like domes too. Where a dome?

With it all I left the meetings with the feeling that they believe I will not disappoint them. It is late Sweethearts, excuse your old man if he knocks off. Tired but sure.

Love,
Lou

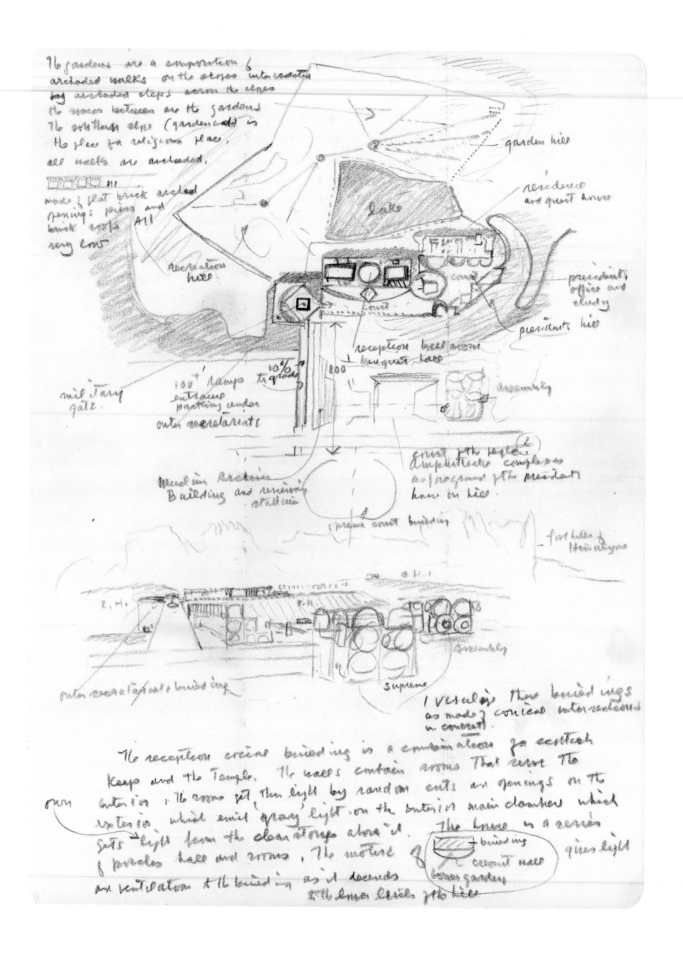

The gardens are a composition of arcaded walks on the slopes intersected by arcaded steps across the slopes. The spaces between are the gardens. The southern slope (gardens, etc.) is the place of a religious place. All walls are arcaded, made of flat brick arched openings, piers and brick roofs. All very low.

[TOP: site plan] *recreation hill / lake / garden hill / residence and guest house / president's office and study / president's hill / court / reception, ballroom, banquet hall / court / assembly / court of the people (?), amphitheater complexes as foreground of the president's house on hill / supreme court building / Muslim Archives Building and reviewing stadium / 800' / 10% to grade / 100' ramp / entrance, parking under / outer secretariat / military gate*

[BOTTOM: perspective] *outer secretariat building / Supreme [Court] / Assembly*

r.h. [recreation hill] / p.h. [president's hill] / g.h. [garden hill] / foothills of Himalayas

I visualize these buildings as made of conical intersections in concrete. The reception social building is a combination of a Scottish keep and the Temple. The walls contain rooms that serve the interior. The rooms get their light by random cuts and openings on the exterior which emits "gray" light on the interior main chamber which gets [its] own light from the clerestories above it. The house is a series of porches, halls, and rooms. The motif of building–crescent wall–lower garden gives light and ventilation to the building as it descends to the lower levels of the hill.

BOMBAY, INDIA, TO WOLCOTT DR., DECEMBER 21, 1964

Dear Harriet and Nathaniel:

The construction of my school in India has started. The workmanship is nothing short of horrible. The brick is irregular and laid with abandon not in keeping with the thought I had given this design. All day today and also yesterday I have been racking my brain to find the answer to the correction of the entire first story construction. I am mad and the terrible tempered Mr. Bang with everyone around.

I miss you both very much and hope you manage Xmas without feeling too sorry about my stupid absence.

Love,
Lou

Merry Xmas and Happy New Year.
Hope you got the four checks I sent you from England.

The sample arch at the Indian Institute of Management, Ahmedabad, India.

A construction crew at the Indian Institute of Management, Ahmedabad, India, 1965.

Lou's eye was like a laser beam. He would run it over an edge or surface, assessing the quality of the material and the workmanship. It was as if sloppiness or lack of care hurt him physically, and he would have walls torn down if they had been done poorly. But he was also practical and a true teacher, and he knew that the problem with the brickwork in Ahmedabad would not be solved by an outburst from "Mr. Bang"—an ill-tempered character from the funny papers that Lou enjoyed. Needing to demonstrate specifically how he wanted the bricks laid and the joints finished with a score from the trowel, he instructed the workers to build a sample arch while he stood by, showing them each step of the way exactly how he wanted things done. The arch is there to this day, and the brickwork at IIM after that was beautiful.

AHMEDABAD TO WOLCOTT DR., DECEMBER 22, 1964

My dear Harriet,
I heard that [I. M.] Pei was selected [for the Kennedy Library].

I had the same feeling after every competition I lost—of pride and self-doubt. I lost every competition I ever entered.

When I heard the news I was in worry about the walls they had erected in my absence and in the process of correcting the work. It seems that every work has been the overcoming of adversity— always also a new angle of it. Yet this adversity seems to build in its way. I remain undaunted by it. I sense in the building group of the Management School I am building, there is the touch of the incredible. I believe this must be the way of art. The incredible that seeks existence.

Soon I shall be back—though I feel for the first time here since work has started that I should not leave. To make the work well done I really should remain.

Do you think Nathaniel will take over where I left off?

Love,
Lou

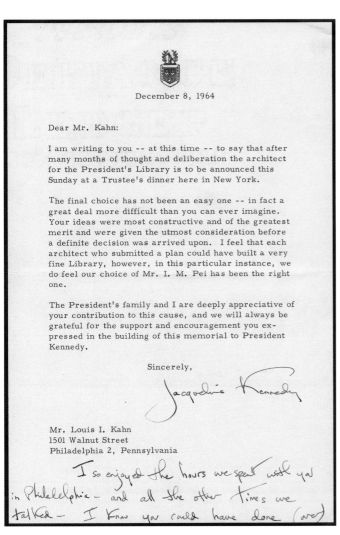

December 8, 1964

Dear Mr. Kahn:

I am writing to you -- at this time -- to say that after
many months of thought and deliberation the architect
for the President's Library is to be announced this
Sunday at a Trustee's dinner here in New York.

The final choice has not been an easy one -- in fact a
great deal more difficult than you can ever imagine.
Your ideas were most constructive and of the greatest
merit and were given the utmost consideration before
a definite decision was arrived upon. I feel that each
architect who submitted a plan could have built a very
fine Library, however, in this particular instance, we
do feel our choice of Mr. I. M. Pei has been the right
one.

The President's family and I are deeply appreciative of
your contribution to this cause, and we will always be
grateful for the support and encouragement you expressed in the building of this memorial to President
Kennedy.

Sincerely,

Jacqueline Kennedy

Mr. Louis I. Kahn
1501 Walnut Street
Philadelphia 2, Pennsylvania

I so enjoyed the hours we spent with you
in Philadelphia - and all the other times we
talked - I know you could have done (over)

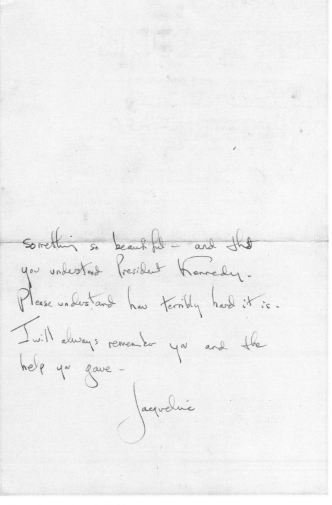

something so beautiful - and that
you understood President Kennedy.
Please understand how terribly hard it is.
I will always remember you and the
help you gave -

Jacqueline

Jacqueline Kennedy's letter to Lou, December 8, 1964.

An illustration by Ivan Bilibin for "The White Duck," from an old book of Russian fairy tales Lou brought back from his trip to Russia in May.

1965

Although Lou was not surprised that the Kennedy Library commission went to someone else, he was sorry to have missed the chance to work with powerful, courageous young people he admired, and he knew that a high-profile project like that would have helped immeasurably toward his desire to build on the large urban scale in America. But beyond bids for recognition or the desire to win was a lone, ambitious quest for transcendent ideals Lou believed in and sought, like a knight seeking the grail.

People with power and vision—like the Kennedys or Jonas Salk—could help Lou, while committees and bureaucrats failed him, especially in Philadelphia, where he freely gave of his ideas for decades without tangible results. But Lou just kept moving, finding champions overseas, and by this year he had not one but three city-scale plans underway on the Indian subcontinent.

Where did it come from, Lou's resilience, his belief that tomorrow would be better, giving him fervor to carry on in a career so full of disappointments? I was beginning to realize the perils of the design professions firsthand. To win you had to be a risk taker, a gambler, and Lou was always willing to bet it all on himself and his architecture.

When I entered Penn, I naively thought it would be like an art school. Instead, I discovered a kind of factory environment under the charismatic leadership of Ian McHarg, a tall, craggy Scot with bristling mustaches and thundering delivery honed by combat command throughout the Mediterranean in World War II. McHarg was dogmatic and fiery; I can still hear the fuming outrage in his voice as he cut down a student with "Gardens, mon? When yuv got a bloody aquifer problem!"

McHarg had restarted Penn's defunct Beaux-Arts-based landscape department in 1954 and reenergized it with the earth sciences, combining the emerging study of ecology and the dying one of geography. He offered a prescriptive approach to landscape that fit the unrest and activism of the time, when everyone was reading Jane Jacobs's *The Death and Life of Great American Cities* and Rachel Carson's *Silent Spring*. We were all awakening to the realization that consumerism and big business, enabled by technology, was plundering and despoiling the planet. To a design profession that had lost its footing with the waning patronage of wealthy families and philanthropists,

McHarg's system also offered a new way of engaging with clients, and soon many adopted his approach and methods of presentation.

I appreciated McHarg's ideals, but there was a clinical, anti-artistic quality to it that I instinctively reacted against. It seemed to be sweeping aside generations of designers, including my hero, the great visionary Frederick Law Olmsted, and more recent garden designers, many of them women, who had given shape to the American landscape. And while measuring, mapping, layering, and analyzing of regional plans in eye-grabbing colors and graphics was a useful tool for understanding natural resources and capabilities, it often led to disappointing design solutions.

I was drawn to the landscapes I had loved from the past and from my travels and ones in books that Lou admired and gave to me: J. C. Shepherd and Geoffrey Jellicoe's watercolors in *Italian Gardens of the Renaissance*, Steen Eiler Rasmussen's delicate inks in *Experiencing Architecture*, and Claude Lorrain's soft chalk and pencil sketches. And so, when we were given the assignment to render a work of architecture we admired, I took out my Winsor & Newton paints and brushes and did a sepia watercolor of Alvar Aalto's Säynätsalo Town Hall. My stubborn challenge to the bold, primary-

My drawing of Alvar Aalto's Säynätsalo Town Hall.

colored diagrams favored by the department drew captious judgments, but Sir Peter Shepheard, the distinguished landscape architect and professor, appreciated the technique as he later would my designs. His kind words and encouragement have lingered with me always, and I have continued to use "old-fashioned" techniques of presenting garden designs and master plans throughout my life.

The most interesting assignment in the first year was a joint studio with architects that took us on an overnight bus trip to study the site of the Cleveland Museum of Art. The architecture students were to propose a building addition, while the landscape students were to prepare designs for the surrounding park. Rather than an environmental study or minimalist solution, I submitted a romantic landscape plan to complement the museum's art world with a public outdoor theater, rambles, overlooks, and a water course as a unifying element, inviting winter skating and summer boating in a scheme that I had to defend in my first jury. I dreaded the sleepless preparations for those presentations—called "charettes" in the design professions—and the presentation rituals themselves, which left me tongue-tied and struck me as murderous tribunals.

Two of Nathaniel's early memories are of seeing me at night, in a pool of yellow light, poring over drawings on my drafting board, and of being lifted by Roseanne to the window to wave as I drove off to school in the Hillman. Sometimes I came home with Lou, formally suited and bow-tied, for a few hours of being a family. Delighting in my domestic role, I would cook an elaborate dinner and decorate the house with spring flowers or fall leaves, while father and son played on the floor or out on the patio or in the pine grove, before I lighted candles and mixed Lou's martini in a frozen glass.

Although I made a few friends in class—Leslie Mesnick, Niall Hyde, and Richard Penton spring to mind—Penn's demanding schedule left little time for socializing. I was one of four women, outnumbered and taught by men in a martial regime. Being a single mother also provoked demonstrable spite in one or two young bullies who didn't have children waiting for them to come home.

There were a few welcome breaks: a lecture by the exuberant Brazilian landscape architect Roberto Burle Marx, who rhapsodized about "moonlight in the garden," and field trips to New Jersey's Pine Barrens to study self-sustaining native plant communities and to a New York City playground where Nathaniel boldly told its famous designer, M. Paul Friedberg, that a small boy wouldn't play there "because it wasn't any fun."

I was captivated by Dr. George Tatum's illustrated lectures on the history of garden art and reveled in learning how to represent and sculpt

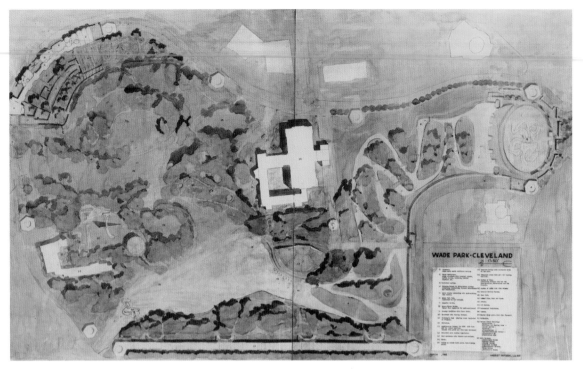

My first-year studio project, a plan for Wade Park at the Cleveland Museum of Art.

land with linear-contour graphics. I struggled, under Tony Walmsley's patient overview, to better understand building materials and the design of structures, but the class I enjoyed most was given by Penn's venerable professor of botany and horticulture Dr. John Fogg, whose knowledge of plants was legion—too voluminous to record. Dr. Fogg was always furlongs ahead of students on Penn's fine and extensive arboretum rounds despite his substantial age and girth, pausing in admiration of the least green specimen at his feet. I was an avid pupil and indulged in the sheer love of recognizing, naming, and describing the shapes and colors and varieties of trees and shrubs that are a primary material for the landscape architect. There were familiar species I already knew, and also a host of exotic plants that fascinated me and that I learned one could use appropriately and creatively at every scale.

I recorded notes and sketches from Dr. Fogg's lectures in two red sketchbooks Lou gave me, like his own. By a twist of fate, Lou borrowed the second one, half filled, for his own thoughts and drawings. That is how my horticultural notes found their way into a publication of his papers, convincing some that Lou was an avid botanist in addition to his other gifts. No one seemed to notice how the script differed from the master's hand.

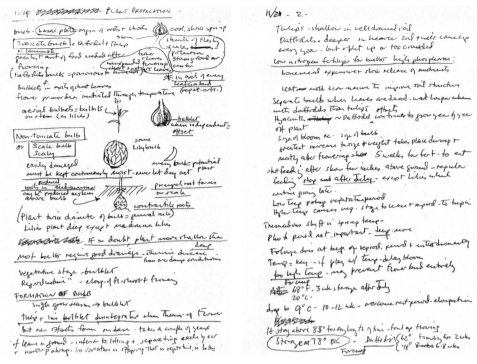

Two pages of my notes from one of Dr. Fogg's botanical lectures.

KARACHI, WEST PAKISTAN, TO 726 WOLCOTT DR., PHILADELPHIA,
FEBRUARY 2, 1965

Dearest ones,

The flights by Lufthansa and Kuwait Airlines were good. I had each
time 3 seats to myself which provided a bed. Still when I arrived in
Karachi at 5am I was tired. First thing Kafiluddin took me to his
house. Rehana served me fresh orange juice after greeting me most
profusely. The other children were all on deck to see the professor.
I stayed for breakfast. Rehana and Roxana went off to college
dressed in parochial school regulars and Kafil took me to his office.
He is the Chief engineer of Pakistan who was awarded a special title
by President Ayub Khan S.Q.E.

Some while back I sent [Jack] McAllister to Pakistan to negotiate
a change in contract since so much work has developed since the
signing of the initial contract of January 1, 1964. Now he showed
me what they are ready to offer. It is so out of line that I will not
sign. The difficulties mount. All seems to be traded on one-sided
advantages. I left his office at noon to take a few winks at the hotel
(very comfortable Intercontinental chain). I was called and given
transport back to his house for lunch after which I showed him

photographs of the changes in the model of the overall site plan. He always withholds favorable reaction. This is the way of oriental trade—to show no emotion about what you want. We are so different but not more interacting nor revealing of man's deeper nature which reveals the sharper edges of our protective instincts. The body movements of the women are of the same strata of the survival sense.

And now, my wonderful one, about you. Leaving you, before lodging enfolded in you, or leaving Nathaniel without his beauty of innocence and faith enveloping me, is the feeling of having forgotten an amulet always with you.

To love as we do is the coming of morning, the mountain stream in the resolute course born of the many courses and now only itself ready for name.

I am now on my way to Dhaka. What I will see and hear, ugliness and complaint, I am not looking forward to, but I hope everything will be better than I expect. In any case, I will adjust and find a direction to the vector that is always going off course.

I love you my darling. Be strong so you can give strength to my boy and to me. Give all to your work when you work. Don't ever worry about knowing things. To love what you are doing and give thought to what you are making will bring all the means.

Love,
Lou

Lou in his office, surrounded by staff, working on the site model for the capital complex in Dhaka, East Pakistan. The National Assembly is at the center.

In reassuring me, perhaps Lou was also steadying himself, as the challenges of his dual projects in East and West Pakistan were testing his love for what he was doing to the limit. Progress on the capital complex in Dhaka was painfully slow. Lou's office had worked throughout 1963 without a contract, and the one signed in January 1964 was inadequate, necessitating the sending of Jack McAllister, a young architect who was overseeing work at the Salk Institute, to try to straighten things out. Piles were being driven for the foundations of the National Assembly Building at last, but everything had to be done by hand, and construction drawings were incomplete. At least Lou had total design control of the Dhaka project, with people from his office on the ground and support from the distinguished Bengali architect Muzharul Islam and the deputy head of public works, Kafiluddin Ahmed.

In Islamabad, however, Lou didn't have control, and his ongoing attempt to take over the design for the core of the new city was causing friction. A note on file from Sir Robert Matthew, leader of the team, addressed to "My dear Louis," hints at the problem: "Now it appears you have really put the cat among the pigeons. . . . Meantime it would greatly ease matters if you concentrated on the President's house and gave us all time to recover." As the following three letters mailed to me in one envelope from Rawalpindi, where the international design team was meeting, indicate, Lou paid no attention to Sir Robert's plea for him to stay in his lane. He was continuing to pester the "pigeons."

STATE GUEST HOUSE, RAWALPINDI, WEST PAKISTAN, TO
WOLCOTT DR., APRIL 1, 1965

Tuesday [March 30th]
Dearest Harriet,
This is my second day here. The first I draped myself over chair, table, or seat in front of me to catch the many lost winks. Work is orderly in Rawalpindi. Everything goes by agenda typed out as to time limit and subjects discussed. I am now about to visit the site. It is 4 pm. The meeting this morning was the discussion on roads and landscaping, Derek Lovejoy, England and Walmsley holding forth. The work is good but not even close to potentialities of the site. Everything is very well presented. The Lovejoy's typed out statements are letter perfect after-storm clear. They have deferred the showing of my ideas for tomorrow. Sir Matthew saw and liked (I believe but jealously I detected) the scheme. He referred to it constantly today as a warning to the discussions that it may change

169

matters tomorrow. Lovejoy kept asking that it be shown "straight away" as he put it feeling that what we were saying in regard to the area I was on, was redundant. I felt very ready to get it over with but no, the agenda was the agenda. Time marches on even in the opposite direction. I am being called to board the transport to the site. My designs are based on memory of conditions. I hope I find them as I remembered them last time. I must go now will continue later—

I'm back for a few minutes. Saw site again. Found I have made some mistakes which I will edge out of tomorrow. It's good sometimes to have a nebulous presentation that lends itself to change.

I picked up a copy of "My Autobiography" [by] Charles Chaplin. It's great. I read it feeling myself in it. The poverty of his young days, his natural talents and values—I have taken slices out of the book in reading starting every time, between dozings, anywhere. It is sheer inspiration to live.

I hope I can hold strictly to the time I have given to the trip which means I will be back Sunday night. If you get the mail before I arrive it will be a Pakistani miracle.

Love to Nathaniel and to you Sweetheart,

Lou

Wednesday afternoon, March 31
Sweetie,
The conquering hero has conquered nothing. I entered a den of snakes full of the venom of professional conduct, good when applied to the other man and not to one's self.

It seems that I had an unorthodox meeting in February when Sir Robert Matthew was not present. He is the planning coordinator. At this meeting, I promised the study of the area adjoining mine in order to bring it in better unity with my area. I told you about it and how worried I was about the effect of the study on Ponti-Rossellis ([Alberto] Rosselli, son in law of [Gio] Ponti), partners in Mediocrity Inc., Ltd., sealed and delivered in gold printing raised on white the finest Tiffany Inc. also gold on white guaranteed not to tarnish.

It was hell, and is still to be, on the defensive. Sir Robert (I didn't know) really considers me as a danger to his smooth mesmerizing of the Pakistani, "is no famous man" in Architecture, but though is smart enough to sense that what they have now is unworthy of being noted as Architecture.

Sure they want domes, arches, but who doesn't?

I spent two days of hell defending without words but with disdainful quiet, my intention. Not in sense meant for any other purpose than to better the architectural quality of the other man's work. Rosselli is one [of] those "fainting spell" aesthetes who feels everything. He assembles from all cliché corners a concoction of ups and downs, ins and outs, pierced and unpierced, wrapped in brise-soleil for unity. Unity is a screen behind which all decision, decision, decisions are quieted from the eye.

Sir Robert is gunning for my hide. He wants to hang me up as Exhibit A: the un-team man of Rawalpindi. He has himself changed his previous work after he has seen mine, realizing its precious nothingness. Rosselli is so blinded by the blaze of his "R-chi-tec-chur" that to be re-inspired means to be charred to a crisp already being in the full fire of inspiration. Nothing can get thru him except a poker.

Am I bitter? No, disgusted with the successful colleagues of mine.

But I know that the teacher in me sometimes is hard to take and can assume the atmosphere of the didactic.

Today the President's Design Committee met with the architects. They expressed their dislike of all the buildings so far built. To a man they reacted unfavorably against the "boxes of concrete." Now to offset this most un-exemplary architecture they want a sprinkling of domes and arches.

The model for Islamabad that Lou presented in March, imposing his organizational ideas on the site. The president's house is at the back, and Lou's proposed assembly building and monument square—which he had not been asked to do—are to the right. Rosselli's building is at the left, and Sir Robert Matthew's is beyond the edge of the picture to the right.

Telephone No.
5463

STATE GUEST HOUSE
THE MALL
RAWALPINDI

3

Wednesday Night
March 31

Sir Robert spoke up in defence of 'creativity' "The creative spirit must not be squeeched" How true and how true also that it applies to the very few. Rosell is sitting next to me also chimed in about the creative pains. They said that the committee can expect no domes. The committee answered by telling Rosell what they thought about the results of his creative pains and that they hoped it did not continue to plague them as well as it does him. He made some remark which sounded like "They know not what they do".

Sir Galahad Louis Lancelot Merlin Kahn then spoke. Spake he thus, and then some, by Galahad!

"Domes are valid now as they were when they first appeared. Arches are equally valid now as ever before. Their logical use the Dome is dependent on the true order of the spaces which they crown. By now means should be used for exterior effect applied to an order which does not include their essentialness in service.

I believe I can explain, if given time, to present the meaning the arch the dome to-day. As an example I showed that a Dome is not the proper element for a place of assembly. The echoes would make confusion. But take the same assembly framed to take around

[sketch]

space / ceiling assembly / assembly / space

— as one vaulted structure which again is crowned by a dome enclosing another space where sound is not important but of another required use best over the auditorium. This way the dome is visible on the out side, sound is achieve; but a valid and beautiful one — if however it belongs to a whole family of architecture order

dome / ×—space / ceiling assembly / ×—space / assembly

172

Wednesday Night, March 31

Sir Robert spoke up in defense of "creativity." "The creative spirit
must not be squelched." How true and how true also that it applies
to the very few. Rosselli sitting next to me also chimed in about the
creative pains. They said that the committee can expect no domes.
The committee answered by telling Rosselli what they thought
about the results of his creative pains and that they hoped it didn't
continue to plague them as well as it does him. He made some
remark which sounded like "They know not what they do."

Sir Galahad Louis Lancelot Merlin Kahn then spoke. "Spake he
thus, and then some, by Galahad!"

"Domes are valid now as they were when they first appeared.
Arches are equally valid now as ever before. The logical use of
the dome is dependent on the total order of the spaces which they
crown. By [no] means should [they] be used for exterior effect
applied to an order which does not include their essentialness
in service."

I believe I can explain, if given time, to present the meaning
of the arch, the dome, today. As an example I showed that a dome
is not the proper element for a place of assembly. The echoes
would make confusion. But take the same assembly framed to take
sound, as one overhead structure which again is crowned by a
dome enclosing another space, where sound is not important but of
another required use best over the auditorium. This way the dome
is visible on the outside. Sure it is a choice but a valid and beautiful
one if however it belongs to a whole family of architectural order.

. . . The President's Committee were satisfied with my say and
asked Sir Robert if what I said agreed with him. He answered much
in my favor. The meeting broke up with a feeling of hope (by the
Muslims) that things were going to be beautiful from now on. . . .
Tomorrow is the last meeting. I dread it because I have the feeling
that I will be assigned a more restrained position, which is now
hard for me to take. What I brought this time had little value and
consequently [I] could not talk with a sense of belief.

With all my love—good night,
Lou

In May, Lou was sent to Russia as a goodwill ambassador by the US Department of State to accompany a show of contemporary American design being put on in St. Petersburg (then Leningrad). Lou hadn't been back to the land of his birth since 1928, and he was excited about the trip—it would be a much-needed break and also a chance to spend time with his friend Vincent Scully, professor of art history and architecture at Yale, who was going on the trip as well. It occurs to me now that what Lou saw in Russia helped spark a breakthrough idea for Islamabad—although Lou himself might not have realized it.

HOTEL ASTORIA, MOSCOW, TO WOLCOTT DR., MAY 23–27, 1965

гости́ница «Асто́рия» Gostìnìtza "Astoria" (Hotel Astoria) built by John Jacob, 1912—not as good as some of the real old ones, one of which I stayed in (not supposed to) in Moscow.

After my visit with Sir Robert in London I was able to leave on an earlier plane to Paris which I hoped to do. There is no fun coming in to Paris at night. I love to walk to Notre Dame. I called on no one although I know a few people there now. I had my usual bread and Camembert and wine in a little cafe that seems always to look different overlooking the south façade. There are so many lovely things to buy in shops of the little streets off the river. I walked till dark [and] settled in a cafe near Notre Dame. My innocent choice of practically the least expensive thing on the menu seemed to drag with it enough hidden charges after I nodded yes to the suggestion of a salad and coffee to amount to six dollars. All alone to eat for 6 dollars is a pig's paradise. It was time to walk back to the hotel. On my way I took several small streets discovering delightful hidden away places. One of these secondary streets was tin packed with people—young people shouting forth here and there with the Russian revolutionary songs. People everywhere draped even on cornices and low roofs drinking beer. I continued in the general direction of the hotel. Dropped into bed. Asked to be awakened at 5:30 . . .

It is a long flight from Paris to Moscow. The temperature was around 40°. The Intourist [agency] knew nothing of my arrival. Had to wait around until they found a hotel. When I got to Moscow proper finally the hotel had nothing but a bad room without toilet or bath. We tried all we could, that is the representative of the Embassy, and I. When I went up to my room I liked it right away. Though the bath room was far down the corridor it began not to matter to me.

Vincent Scully, who came a day before I did, was put up in the "Ukraina" which is a new Stalin-built tower building. Vincent and I walked around town and particularly spent our time around the Red Square and the Kremlin. It is truly overwhelming—Italian in hand but Russian in spirit. On my return to Moscow I will go inside these buildings.

And now Harriet, sweetheart, I am in Leningrad since Monday and this is Thursday. It is a marvelous city. Unforgettable. Vincent came to Leningrad with me, stayed until Wednesday morning. He is off on a trip south and will return to Leningrad on the day I am to leave, possibly the 6th of June.

I met Isaac Stern in the hotel Monday night. He gave me two tickets to his concert. Vincent and I went. The music was superb. The hall he played was used by royalty, beautifully conceived. Isaac Stern and I hit it off right away. He is friendly and completely in sympathy with those around him.

Today I was introduced to the head of the Union of Architects at a reception given by him. He is going to arrange a meeting of the architects and students. It is the first day where the Soviets showed their hospitality to me and it was warm and welcoming. Even though everything is extremely interesting, Vincent and I felt all the while like leaving because let down by no sign of reception over what we saw. Felt sad and lonely.

All my love to you and Nathaniel,

Lou

Saturday

Dear Harriet,

Today the Union of architects arranged a tour of Leningrad. The architect responsible for restoration of monuments and his wife who speaks a fine English conducted this tour. I became more conscious of the value of the buildings thru their explanations. The adaptations from the Dutch and the Italian is intermingled with an architecture, which the architects from Europe working in Leningrad found in parts of Russia built mostly in wood. It is Baroque turned Russian, incorporating at times, the onion domes indigenous to Russia and the other parts of Europe like Bavaria, Romania, which, in turn, is derived from Byzantium. Without having made sketches I feel that I can draw generally what a Russian building of those times could look like. . . .

I inquired about the possibility of a visit to Kizhi an island on Lake Ladoga north of Leningrad adjoining Finland. Intourist tells me that they have no representation there and is the reason why it is not open for tourists. We will continue to try because it is the one remaining example of the source from which stem the combined European and indigenous Russians it inspired.

Tomorrow, I start at 10 in the morning for Pushkin Pavlovsk. I will be accompanied by architects S. N. Davidov, N. D. Kremchershaja, and W. J. Popov. Pushkin is the new name given to the Versailles of Russia . . . or the Tzars Palace. You go there by special boat that skims along the water on the end of a vault carrying the house of the passengers.

On my way back, I will be introduced to the new areas of massive industrial housing construction in what is called the Moscovskiin Raion.

Sweetie I hope you miss me and give my love to Nathaniel.

Love,

Lou

Lou was impressed with the way the European architects who built in St. Petersburg (Leningrad) had been true to their essential spirit in the design of their Baroque municipal buildings, while also channeling a "Russian-ness" into their work—even incorporating domes. Lou's imagination was captivated, and I believe this trip helped him solve the "dome problem" in

Islamabad. The European team there had ruled out domes as being too overtly Islamic, yet the Pakistani clients wanted domes. In Russia, Lou was seeing all kinds of domes, and the possibilities of the form opened up for him.

Always looking for the source, Lou especially wanted to go to Kizhi Island, with its fairy-tale wooden churches of layered volumes and onion domes that are quintessentially Russian. The churches on Kizhi (as with other wooden Russian churches) are monumental buildings: complete in themselves, belonging where they are, but also evoking an architectural journey across time, continents, cultures, and religions, from the ancient world through Byzantium and the Middle East, even to a remote island in tzarist Russia, and carrying all the while one form—the dome—along the way.

Двадцатиодноглавая Преображенская церковь въ Кижахъ
Олонецк. губ. Петрозаводск. уѣзда.—Начало 18-го вѣка.
(Фот. И. Я. Билибина).

The Church of the Transfiguration on Kizhi Island, built in 1715 entirely of wood without nails, from a pair of volumes on Russian churches that Lou brought back from his trip to Russia.

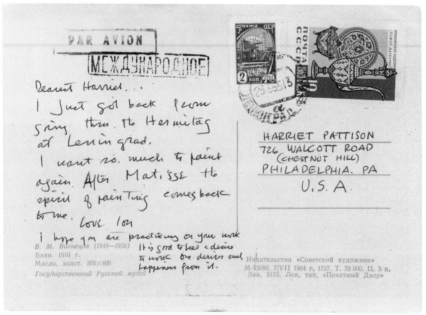

LENINGRAD TO WOLCOTT DR., MAY 29, 1965

Dearest Harriet,

I just got back from going thru the Hermitage at Leningrad.

    I want so much to paint again. After Matisse, the spirit of painting comes back to me.

Love,

Lou

I hope you are practicing on your work. It is good to feel a desire to work. One derives such happiness from it.

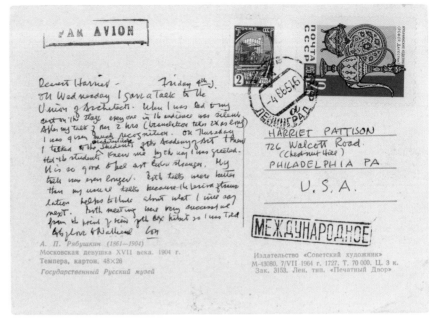

А. П. Рябушкин. (1861—1904)
Московская девушка XVII века. 1904 г.
Темпера, картон. 48×26

Государственный Русский музей

Издательство «Советский художник»
М-43080. 7/VII 1964 г. 1727. Т. 70 000. Ц. 3 к.
Зак. 3153. Лен. тип. «Печатный Двор»

MOSCOW TO WOLCOTT DR., JUNE 4, 1965

Friday, 4th J.

Dearest Harriet,

On Wednesday I gave a talk to the Union of Architects. When I was led to my seat on the stage every one in the audience was silent. After my talk of over 2 hours (translation takes 2x as long) I was given much recognition.

On Thursday I talked to the architecture students of the Academy of Art. I found that the students knew me by the way I was greeted. It is so good to feel not like a stranger. My talk was even longer. Both talks were better than my usual talks because the period of translation helps to think about what I will say next.

Both meetings were very successful from the point of view of the exhibit, so I was told.

Lots of love to Nathaniel,

Lou

И. И. Левитан (1860—1900)
Сумерки. Луна. 1899 г.
Масло, холст. 49,5×61,3
Государственный Русский музей

Издательство «Советский художник»
М-43080. 7/VII 1964 г. 1727. Т. 70 000. Ц. 3 к.
Зак. 3153. Лен. тип. «Печатный Двор»

MOSCOW TO WOLCOTT DR., JUNE 4, 1965

Harriet,
I send you this card as a sequel to the other one marked Friday, 4th.
I thought both cards are very Russian. There are many paintings in
the Russian Museum like these.

Lou

Dearest Harriet,

I keep thinking about you and Nathaniel. I imagine by this time he has the run of the place and found his favorite haunts. How does the family take to him. How can they resist him!

On Friday I went to Washington to see Sir Robert Matthew about the plan of Islamabad and its gardens. My visit important, but brief. Found enough time on my hands before taking the plane to California that I attended the luncheon of the A.I.A. and there heard [Lewis] Mumford. Before the talk I met Ada Louise Huxtable of the N.Y. Times and next to her Wolf von Eckardt, art historian who wrote some stuff about me in the Encyclopedia of Modern Architecture and in other places. . . . I was pleased to hear him on the subject of Jacqueline Kennedy. He had met her only a few days ago. He related her as saying on the subject of "Louie Kahn," "He is the one man I could put my arms around." Nice to hear and even to disbelieve, and coming from him, as a gross exaggeration.

Mumford speech was good on the subject of the destruction of the city. . . . The students heard I was there. They got me to talk to them in the 15 minutes I had left before leaving for California.

I arrived Friday night, stayed over Saturday (the Salk buildings are good), left Sunday morning, arrived Sunday afternoon and today, Monday, is my first day of solid work since I came back from Russia. I am very far behind. I will have to leave on the 5th or 6th of July but it looks bad about finishing by then.

Keep well you darling two and think about your daddy-O once in a while. Maine must be terrific. Oh for a free undutiful time with the rocks and the sea.

I bought several books in San Diego. One, Thomas Moore illustrated with unrelated old engravings, I believe the poetry good . . . One—The Fairy Book—a collection of well known fairy tales published 1880, illustrated with play card like pictures, bold and kind of incredible. And one on Gothic Architecture showing elements of its style in England and a book on the buildings (engraving illustrations) of Oxford, Eng. The Fairy book is naturally for the three of us with Nathaniel as custodian and owner. The Thomas Moore is for you, and exclusively, since my ventures in poetry exhausts itself after the first 7 stanzas. The poem of Lalla Rookh (an Indian poem of Kashmir) is very long.

Love,
Lou

Dearest:

I wanted that you call me while in Maine. Come back soon Sweetheart with our wonderful son. I am completely swamped getting ready for Islamabad and India. Working on the garden of the Presidents Estate I find little to feed the great gaps reserved for thoughts on landscaping. The square is getting better, more locked in its boundaries. The house remains undone but with belief that it will find its repose (the most important in the mind of the Pakistanis).

So far, all in all, nothing is settled with only a little over a week before I leave. The pressure from India and Pakistan is so great that I cannot postpone leaving later than 7th of July.

Get lots of sun and rest, save the good it gives enough to give me a little. Only back a little while, I have completely forgotten

PHILADELPHIA TO FARAWAY, JUNE 26, 1965

about my Russian experience. It was really not so significant—looking back.

Have you had a chance to think about the gardens on the hills? Try to drop me a little note or call me some evening. Tell me when you plan to return. Want so much to see you before I leave again.

Love,
Lou

I opened this letter in the rain after fetching it from the mailbox at Faraway, the drops making the ink run. I *had* been thinking about the "gardens on the hills," and I returned to Philadelphia to be with Lou while he was scrambling to prepare his upcoming presentations. As I remember it, Dhaka had taken a back seat, and most of Lou's energy was focused on Islamabad and the development of a new idea for the assembly building on the plaza below the president's house.

I proposed making use of the steep terrain and abundant mountain waters held in surrounding reflecting ponds to create a series of cascading water gardens. The water would flow down the escarpment in stepped levels, running through gardens and meandering streamways, to connect and unify all parts of the master plan. It would be a fabric of light, movement, and sound like the Shalimar gardens in Lahore, or the gardens designed by André Le Nôtre for Louis XIV. Perhaps the delight of water gardens would calm the restless soul of Ayub Khan—then slipping toward battle with India over Kashmir—as they had once done for another autocrat at Versailles.

Lou's model of the Islamabad project from May 1965, showing the assembly building with a dome.

PIA Great people to Fly with

Printed at PIA Press

A panoramic view of the remains of SALBAN VIHARA an ancient
Buddhist monastery in East Pakistan.

on way to Karachi.
via (Frankfurt Geneva
Beirut Teheran

Dearest,
This is typical of the land
soaked in water now during
the monsoon. A good plan —
the monks worked into the
boundary wall with the religious
buildings in the center.
It is good to feel I miss the two
of you so. Hope you receive the airmail
envelope
Love Lou —

Harriet Pattison
726 Walcott Road
(Chestnut Hill)
Philadelphia Pa.
U.S.A.

On way to Karachi via Frankfurt, Geneva, Beirut, Tehran
Dearest,
This is typical of the land soaked in water now during the
monsoon. A good plan—the monks worked into the boundary wall
with the religious buildings in the center.

It is good to feel I miss the two of you so. Hope you received the
airport envelope.

Love,
Lou

HOTEL METROPOLE, KARACHI, TO WOLCOTT DR., JULY 18, 1965

Friday night, July 16
Dearest Harriet,
This time last week I left for Europe, I've gone thru so much
during this time.

When I arrived Kafiluddin was not on hand to greet me as
usual—this meant trouble. I learned that the last Parliament lit
into him for not pushing the building of the 2nd capitol [at Dhaka].
The word got around in the assembly that the delay was due to
the inability of the architect to supply details of construction.
This is serious. When the main constituted body of a nation puts
things on record in criticism, then heads must roll. The minister
in charge of this government bureau usually replaces the director
(Kafiluddin) and maybe his architect. The long faces rehashing
what might have been done was very hard to bear for the first few
days. I slept little worried much. The air ominous. They were
comparing Dhaka with Islamabad. I arrived Sunday night in Dhaka.
Tuesday night I left for Karachi and the next morning Rawalpindi.
Kafiluddin accompanied me. All the ministers were in Rawalpindi.
On the plane I stilled his sadness by pointing out to him that even
if it all took longer, from the politicians' point of view, he had what
Islamabad does not have—Architecture. I advised him that his
best stand in seeing the ministers was to tell them why the work
has not been dramatic—that he had to put up with an artist but he
believed in what ultimately would prove of greater value than the
momentary enjoyment of praise of speed. I further explained the
greater meaning this has in view of the present disappointment over
the architecture in Islamabad (near Rawalpindi and the site of the 1st

capital Doxiadis, Ponti, etc., and now LIK) which has brought about the forming of a ministers committee on design determined to dress the present buildings with applied silhouettes, domes and minarets. They hate the buildings as they are. He saw the meaning of what I said very well—his mind, always political, turned this meaning into his own and so far having seen some of the ministers and their secretaries has repaired the situation for himself to a great extent.

At a party at the home of the chairman of the Capital Development Authority I met one secretary who expressed what a good impression everyone has of my work and I appear to him to be easy on Kafiluddin mainly because he showed so much patience in dealing with an artist. The next day Kafil. reported to me that he had a very encouraging meeting with him. Yesterday I met Foreign Minister [Zulfikar Ali] Bhutto (This is all to show that Kafil. and I are friends and it gives me an opportunity to explain my work.)

I had my meeting today with the "Design Committee of Islam Architecture or Bust." They liked what I presented though they saw little of Islam except the Dome. It seems to me it will take time. I told them to forget speed if they want a thoughtful work.

Tomorrow I see the minister of works (initially responsible) who is not going to be easy on me. I may also see the President. So let's hope sweethearts mine that I come back in one piece.

Someone gave me [a] photographic album to look thru of the sculpture erotica of Indian temples. What fun these carvers had making the body do the impossible.

Love,
Lou

On July 18 Lou inspected the subterranean brick vaults of the National Assembly Building in Dhaka. The building still had not risen above ground level, and the slow delivery of construction documents had pushed everything to the breaking point. Summoned to explain himself in Rawalpindi, Lou found his excuses to government ministers accepted, and his ideas for Islamabad— which he'd risked losing everything to develop—seemed to be gaining favor.

With echoes of Kizhi Island, Lou's final scheme for Islamabad's assembly building had indeed delivered the dome the client wanted—but in an utterly unique way. Gathering all in its round and grounded mass, with porches and openings that made it porous and mysteriously inviting, Lou's entire building was in fact one big dome. Soaring to over a hundred and fifty feet, the interior was to be of marble and might have evoked something of the awe of Lou's favorite building in Rome, the Pantheon. Lou continued to develop the plan throughout the fall, and before the end of the year he was invited to a reception for Ayub Khan at the White House, given by President Lyndon Johnson. At that moment it looked as if the boldest gamble of Lou's career was about to pay off—he was going to be the architect of the capitals of both East and West Pakistan.

But in the meantime, a great pillar in the architectural pantheon had fallen: Lou wrote to me in Maine about Le Corbusier's death. I knew how deep the loss was for Lou when he said, "Who will I design for now?"

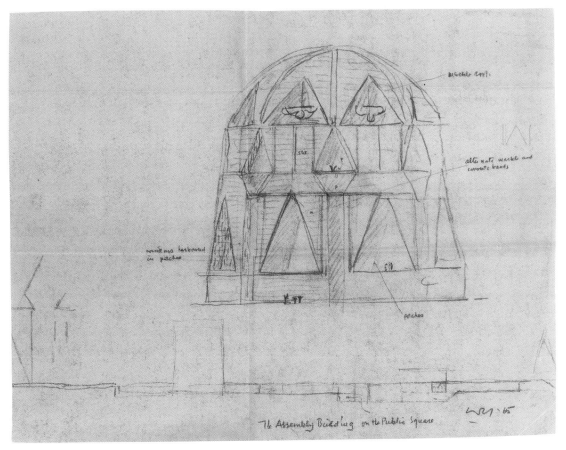

Lou gave me this annotated sepia print of his final design for the assembly building in Islamabad. Like the National Assembly in Dhaka, it projects a unique geometric monumentality.

The Assembly Building on the Public Square

Windows harbored in porches / [marble] roof / alternate marble and concrete bands / porches

[handwritten draft]

Yesterday Le Corbusier died. Death felt like a great door that fell between here and somewhere. Everything that led the spirit in one to make is from there that the combined treasury of all minds cannot sense, yet every mind alone seeks its meerest lumen to live to give life and give one life to express it.

Yesterday something died in me in the loss of its someday when I could have met Le Corbusier with the feeling of the right to give him my reverence.

Dearest Sweethearts
You — my fine feathered Eva could spare not a feather to scratch "une note" and you my very wee and loved one full of innocent and destructive projects together could not get up enough enthusiasm to buzz me!!!! But alas I excuse you for you (meaning me) who writes but sparingly too should lay off.
Posted and illustrated in the bar where I have lunch occasionally is a profound truth.
Once a King always a King once a Knight is enough
Lou Lou

PHILADELPHIA TO FARAWAY, AUGUST 29, 1965

Yesterday Le Corbusier died. Death felt like a great door that fell
between here and somewhere. Everything that led the spirit in one
"to make" is from there that the combined treasury of all minds
cannot sense, yet every mind alone seeks its merest lumen to live to
give life and give one life to express it. Yesterday something died in
me in the loss of its someday when I could have met Le Corbusier
with the feeling of the right to give him my reverence.

Dearest Sweethearts,
You—my fine feathered Eva could spare not a feather to scratch
"une note" and you my very wee and loved one full of innocent and
destructive projects together could not get up enough enthusiasm to
buzz me!!!!! But, alas, I excuse you for you (meaning me) who writes
but sparingly too should lay off.

Posted and illustrated in the bar where I have lunch occasionally is a
profound truth. Once a king always a king once a knight is enough.

Love,
Lou

188

Dearest,

I was ready to go to Paris to see my teacher off. I thought and told the State Department's Cultural Activities should arrange things for a few to [attend]. At present, I can't afford anything. They thought it a good idea but later I got a call explaining there are no funds for this "sort of thing." Think of the clumsiness of it all.

I am sad at heart about my teacher, secretly as he was so to me. I miss telling you about how I feel. Nathaniel should also be so favored in the course of his life to find a teacher to guide him.

Lou

Nathaniel offers a snapdragon to the photographer, his uncle Willy, in the garden I designed at Faraway.

Lou on the construction site of the National Assembly in Dhaka, wearing a jacket we had made from tweed I'd bought in Edinburgh. "Just the stuff I should always wear," he wrote me later.

1966

Dearest Harriet and Nathaniel:

I am now back to Karachi, staying overnight at the Midway
(airport) Hotel to continue to Dhaka.

In Rawalpindi, I presented my latest version of the Presidents
Estate. I could tell at the first meeting that some decisions were
made before my coming. The last and third meeting with the
design committee of the "Islamic Touch" was today. After the
meeting I was told that what I presented was not what they expected
and I am now ex-architect of the Presidents Estate. The hell
of it is that they detected what I felt about my own design—no
conviction. For this lack, which I thought I could overcome in time,
I cannot blame them. The example is tremendous in shaking me
up and exposing me. Criticisms for not working harder if I wanted
to consent and for not quitting when the "Islamic Touch" was
announced as the sign of Pakistan Architecture. My design was
weak. I can't stomach it now it having none of [the] love that I see in
it now that it cannot be.

What has happened may have an effect on Dhaka. This would
hurt much more because there are good things about it.

When I was so, so politely told, I felt like [Gustave] Dore's
drawing of the lover cut in two by the hiding husband's sword
in sight of his lady. After each of the several meetings I felt on
trial. On those nights I slept only in spurts out of accumulated
exhaustion stored up at home and the gnawing feeling of failure and
not a chink to escape from.

Please sweetie have faith in your "old boy" but tell him when
his confidence is isolated from his being and his faith. It was clear
to them (I really believe) that I had nothing to offer. I believe
they have Ed Stone in mind to do the Presidents Estate. He is
unquestionably the man who can please them. He has already done

so by a building in Rawalpindi that makes a mosque and minaret the structure for an atomic reactor laboratory.

The "boys" from England have been so good as to warn me that I was game. If only they would have informed me before I left for Rawalpindi.

Love,
Lou

EN ROUTE TO DHAKA, EAST PAKISTAN, TO WOLCOTT DR.,
JANUARY 13, 1966

Dearest Harriet,
I feel that I have lost my mastery and doubt even if I ever had it. What I now sense they wanted, though never expressed by them, really offers the best opportunity. All the symbols I was looking for could be expressed in a single building, just the President's house for Pakistan. I constantly thought only about the modesty of our White House, but what they aspire to is monumentality The Palace, and why not? I looked to the Assembly Building for strength not the House.

Am in the air toward Dhaka. I expect little friendship there. We are so far behind.

Love,
Lou

MILLBURNE, RICHMOND, VIRGINIA, TO WOLCOTT DR.,
JANUARY 25, 1966

Dearest Harriet,
. . . What happened to me in Islamabad could have brought on the resignations they feel. Somehow I have mixed feeling of utter disappointment in myself mixed with a feeling of relief. I never really loved that project nor did I understand it. As I mentioned to them, I never felt the presence of a leader from whom I could have gathered my will to serve him with all the out-pouring capable in me.

Dhaka has the same loneliness as its atmosphere . . .

Try to explain it all to Nathaniel. It is good for the soul to bring complex things to the mind of a child. It could make a poet out of a worrisome adult.

Lou

192

Pouring the concrete walls of the National Assembly in Dhaka by hand, five feet at a time.

Lou's postmortem of his involvement with Islamabad is fascinating in the light of later events in that part of the world. He chides himself for wanting to design an assembly building—a place for the voices of the people—instead of focusing on the president's house and making *that* a symbol for the democratic ideals he wanted to inspire. But by attempting to design the dual capitals of Pakistan, West and East, Lou's instinct was to make a unity out of a duality, to knit together two halves of an impossible country. He was trying to do architecturally what couldn't be done politically. The will of the people for unity was not there, and no dictator could force it, as would soon become clear.

Luckily, Lou had not lost the Dhaka project in the midst of all the confusion. His capital complex in East Pakistan was taking shape, with the vast National Assembly Building like a mandala at its center—rising steadily through the manual labor of thousands of workers carrying buckets of concrete on their heads. This building was truly built by the people, for the people, and it would become a symbol for the democratic ideals and "human agreement" Lou deeply believed in.

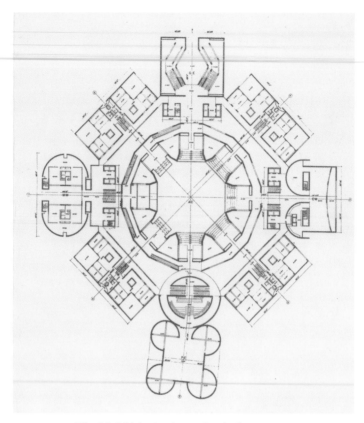

The MoMA invitation to Lou's show, 1966.

The intricate plan of the National Assembly Building in Dhaka illustrated the invitation to *The Architecture of Louis I. Kahn*, a comprehensive exhibition that opened at the Museum of Modern Art in April. Lou was now recognized as a major modern architect, and the work he had completed in the seven years since we met, on display in drawings, models, and photographs, was astonishing.

I attended the preview, invited to dine at a table of strangers—professional, rich, or vaguely connected to Lou—straining to hear the toasts in his honor while he was far away on a dais with his wife, Esther, as well as Philip Johnson and other notables. I remember thinking that as much as Lou was now embraced by the in crowd, he would never be one of them. He was a man apart, with a heart for the people and dreams of a finer world, like Charlie Chaplin's Tramp with his animal grace and baggy trousers. I still have a remnant sash of the Liberty silk Lou gave me for the dress I wore on that evening of celebration, and of my inclusion as a beginning professional with a connection, like many others, to the Architect of the Hour.

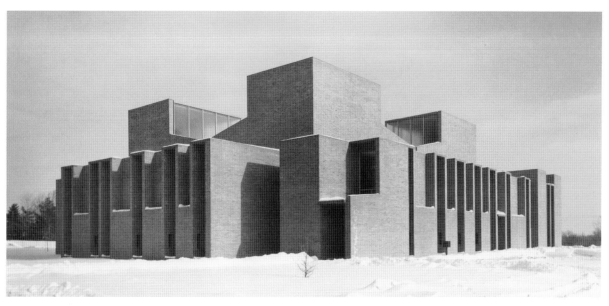

The First Unitarian Church, Rochester, New York, 1959–62.

The sanctuary of the First Unitarian Church.

Eleanor Donnelley Erdman Hall, Bryn Mawr College, Bryn Mawr, Pennsylvania, 1960–65.

With its plan of interlocking squares, slate-clad walls, and casement windows, Erdman Hall has the feel of a medieval castle.

One of the serene interior courts in Erdman Hall.

The Salk Institute for Biological Studies, La Jolla, California, 1959–65. Lou had considered planting trees between the wings of the laboratories, but Mexican architect Luis Barragán suggested that the space was a plaza, "a façade to the sky." Lou instantly knew this was right, and he detailed it in travertine with the single rill of water running down the center toward the Pacific.

One of the 18 dormitory units during construction of the Indian Institute of Management,
Ahmedabad, India.

Dearest Harriet and Nathaniel.

This time in India had its reward in seeing the buildings I designed.
They are good architecture. Maybe the houses fall short. I know
why—the strictness of the budget (which I had exceeded by 50%
but still not enough to make architecture).

But I had mean days otherwise. I think or rather I know that the
Capital Project [Gandhinagar] is not for me. This disappoints so
much. I wanted above all things to build a town.

Politics has moved in. Men already in—a planner and a few half-
baked architects—the planner has yet not been put into the oven.
All the ideas I gave them on my first visit are on the plan in the
wrong place and otherwise misinterpreted. It's sickening!

Mr. Kasturbhai, whom I depended on, is being now disregarded.
He will therefore resign from the chairmanship of the board. So if
he does, it's all over.

Tonight I was invited to Manorama Sarabhai House (it was
built by Le Corbusier). Wonderful house with great Indian Village
objects around. It is set in a truly great garden. She was married to
the eldest Sarabhai. He died. She is of the Kasturbhai family. They
were scheming to get me in as the planner. I talked about the plans
I had, [my] vision of the path of water in the town, drawn from the
river upstream. Water is the fire-place of India.

I must forget it.
It is hard.
It would have been ruinous financially.
It would have revived my dormant spirit.
A source of strength and Might.
It would have made me generous.
But somehow I feel that my energy can have
its outlet for the sheer need of an outlet.
Love to Nathaniel and to the one I miss so much.

Lou

Lou traveled to Dhaka in July, visiting with Gus Langford, who had moved
there to oversee the concrete work on the National Assembly building. Gus
and his brother Fred had designed the formwork for the Salk Institute and
together they devised an ingenious construction system for the Dhaka project.

Dearest,

At Twilight, twixt sunset and night, some people from the Embassy, my engineers, Gus and Maris Langford, and I were sitting in Langford's garden having our before-dinner drink. The monsoon sunsets are unbelievable. This one will always be remembered for its alternate cloud streaks of gold and red covering the entire sky with little black animal shaped clouds spotted here and there cutting across this flag-like sky. The garden is entirely enclosed by banana trees, neem, and acacia. Before we knew it, it was night and the sky covered with stars. Then someone spotted Echo [satellite], unique in its appearance on high because of its speed and movement. It was visible because the sun was, for it, still out though for us sitting there it had set. We all followed its way across the sky until it disappeared on its orbiting way.

Now that reminds me of what we must point out to our little boy about these diamonds in the sky. Echo, we all knew, was not a star because it didn't twinkle. You see the twinkling little fellows are the stars because they make their own fire like our own sun, which is also a star. The planets do not twinkle because they get their light by reflection from our sun. Of course there must be countless planets around the billions upon billions of stars which of course are too small or rather their light relatively too faint to be seen by even the most powerful telescope. So Venus Mercury Mars with all the brightness shine with a steady light untwinkling.

Now you go out there, in my most inexcusable absence from you two beautiful beings, on the first starry night and point out the stars from the planets. I, in turn, promise to learn more about the skies than this measly bit and even buy a globe of the stars, which I always wanted someday to buy.

My love for books dates way back, wanting now to hold them, the old ones. To fill the still lingering feeling for them when they were completely inaccessible to me, outside of course, the library. To own a book—how marvelous it all seemed to me. The strange thing about the desire was, though I had none or only a few, I loved those who had them, not envied nor hated. My feelings were aspiring ones without jealousy. I see this trait in Nathaniel. It will show him to be patient and determined and not possessive . . .

I long so to see you my little boy and little girl.

With all my love,
Lou

Fred Langford (center) with (to his left and right) officials from the public works department and members of the local construction crew on the site of the National Assembly building. Before them are the components of the construction system devised by the Langford brothers and made locally: the reusable teakwood forms, mixing containers, carriers, clamps, ties, and jacks that allowed the vast building to be made literally by hand from the ground up.

Lou's entry in my notebook, c. July 1966:

On Saturday Harriet, Nathaniel and I decided to visit the Zoo.
It was all for Nathaniel. Before closing time, we took in the last
performance of the Children's Zoo. The little area is flanked by
cages. The mummies and daddies and the children are grouped
around and slightly above the area. A female [guide] began her spiel
introducing the little farm animals and pacing them around to
be petted. She was comely, blonde and likeable. Holding a striped
skunk and explaining, she faltered and seemed to be sick. Quietly
she turned the show over to another. . . . Nathaniel was sitting on
my lap. The blonde leaving affected him. He hardly listened to
the substitute. He kept asking about the other—what happened is
she all right—will she come back. The show went on. They passed
around quite a number of other animals including a snake. Nothing
could keep him from his concern about the first girl. At the end of
the show we spotted her. I took him over to her. She said she was
well now. I told her about Nathaniel's concern. She was happy and
caressed him. He feels so much the plight of others. It is good to
have such a wonderful son.

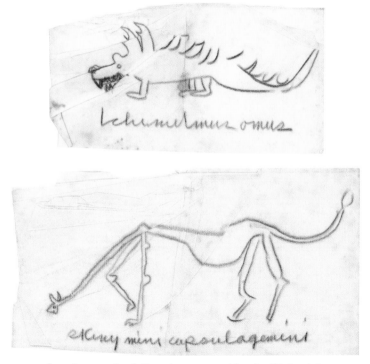

Imaginary animals Lou drew on napkins for Nathaniel.

Looking for frogs with Nathaniel, 1966.

PHILADELPHIA TO FARAWAY, AUGUST 6, 1966

Dearest Harriet,
This morning I missed not calling you first thing. The day starts well that way! . . .

My eyes still hurt but they itch so they are getting much better. I try not to use the patch.

Things must be great in Faraway, Nathaniel in his bigger world. Get into the sun Sweetheart. Get hold of your best spirit. Try to think a little about your coming adventure in work. Look at everything as if it would belong to you. You need, as everyone, to observe and draw values to yourself.

Send me as you promised little sketches of your bridge bathhouse and boat house. I will try to find the time to make a few suggestions. I miss you sweetheart . . . Regards to anyone who might even remotely regards me.

Love to you and Nathaniel,
Lou

I was relieved to get this letter, bearing the news that Lou's latest eye surgery had gone well. He'd had cataracts removed some years earlier and the memory of that scare was still fresh. I had noticed one day how the blue in his eyes seemed translucent and the glitter was gone. I finally dared mention it and Lou shrugged, but on one walk, when he asked me to compare distances with what he saw, I persisted. He then told me that he had cataracts and needed to have the lenses in his eyes removed. Such surgery was not routine then, and the possibility of blindness silenced both of us. Difficulty with his eyes had persisted, but as with any other physical ailment, Lou just shrugged it off and kept moving.

Dearest Harriet

Are these the buildings that I will soon build? The internal   Sunday.
spaces have the faces of their shapes. Then what you will see is outside
the mould of them.

I am thinking of the Capital of Gujarat Ghandi nagar on the Sabramati
My knowledge of the nature of the Assembly could lead to a lighter order of
brick and concrete in which concrete plays a greater role. The filtering
of the banks and promontories of the river could give fantastic base out
then for access to the river.

Sunday.

Dearest Harriet,

Are these the buildings that I will soon build? The internal spaces have the forces of their shapes, then what you will see, is outside the mold of them.

I am thinking of the Capital of Gujarat, Gandhinagar on the Sabarmati. My knowledge of the nature of the Assembly could lead to a higher order of brick and concrete in which concrete plays a greater role. The firming of the banks and promontories of the river could give a fantastic base cut thru for access to the river.

. . . Had no thought of drawing these little things until I sat down to write. I feel good that [this] unknown urges the spontaneous.

I truly dislike writing to you about my little happenings. I already told you all over the phone and now after my tiny plane trip to Harrisburg I am working to recapture the good ideas I had in the abstract.

I like to read those every little bits about the family, you and Nathaniel, and I know from this that it is just those little bits that you want from me. You write so well about what happens around you. Unless I can find a strain of invention to bundle together what happened, what happened flows thru a sieve.

I am hoping for Olivetti's check to deposit money but I will anyway by some other means so your check can be honored. Don't worry sweetheart.

With all my love,

Lou

An unbuilt project for Lou was just as important as one under construction—in some ways more so. Nothing was fixed, and he was free to dream and explore, and no one could tell him no. Although he'd turned the Gandhinagar project down, Lou kept working on it, as he did with many unbuilt projects, even those he'd been fired from. Gandhinagar allowed Lou to discover with his pencil ideas about cities and landscapes and even India itself, channeling inspirations he'd had there. Looking at these drawings now, I am tantalized—wondering what those forms, more fluid and free than much of Lou's work, would have been like had they been built.

PHILADELPHIA TO FARAWAY, AUGUST 18, 1966

Wed.

Dearest Harriet,

I went into your favorite little book shop on 17th St. Couldn't resist this card on which to jot a few words to you. FIRST: Why? don't you send me the drawing!? You lazy lazy lazy. (I got off on the wrong start on such a beautiful card) But secretly I do excuse you for you are enjoying Maine so and to supply Nathaniel with all his personal needs must be a Maineful. SO must I tell you that I am working hard. Boy its great! To work hard and see emergence! Well, I <u>am</u> trapped. It's a habit by now. But I am not all habit. For instance I love you. That's not a habit. That's a prevalence. Morning!!! all the evidence and accusations but with all intentions there <u>is</u> a limit. After all, Maine is Maine where it is and I am where I am. I am suing for an extension. Legal advice as always is helpless.

Love to "H'ie" and Nathaniel,
Lou

208

PHILADELPHIA TO FARAWAY, C. AUGUST 18, 1966

Sunday.

Dearest Harriet and Nathaniel:

You must be having a good time and I am glad it is so. Maybe
you could nick off a bit of it to send me the original drawings for
printing. I promise to send them right back to you.

 Times are very tough having not yet received any payment from
O [Olivetti]. Corporations go thru organized motions and we have
to wait our turn.

Love,
Lou

Tuesday, afternoon

Dearest Harriet

This is your chance to brush up on your
Italian. Maybe you can tell me what it says.

The days are long without you
near.
The Photo was made in Italy
Do you recognize the material of the coat
I am wearing. Just the stuff I stored
always near.

I promised to call you this afternoon
which I shall do.

Have a great time with Nathaniel
and the family and remember the
guests

I am working as usual

poor me How my, my you sit all weeks of hard day's work away.

love Guy

Monday afternoon

Dearest Harriet,

This is your chance to brush up on your Italian. Maybe you can tell me what it says. The days are long without you near.

The photo was made in Italy.

Do you recognize the material of the coat I am wearing? Just the stuff I should always wear.

I promised to call you this afternoon, which I shall do.

Have a great time with Nathaniel and the family and of course the guests.

I am working, as usual. Poor me. How may anyone actually work so hard and be so lonely!

Love,

Lou

What was it about the downward-curving line of diminishing script to Lou's name at the ending of this letter that brought tears to my eyes on reading it so many years later? Then I remembered the last pages of Antoine de Saint-Exupéry's *The Little Prince*, where the exquisite spirit whom the author/aviator had encountered in the Sahara gently falls to the sand, and disappears from the planet in a similar descending line.

PART THREE

A Slice of the Sun

1967–1970

Lou speaking in Paris, late 1960s.

1967

Lou's dream, as told to me, May 20, 1967:

> I was presenting a model of a scheme for Washington. It was a
> magnificent pier, with great banks of steps rising (Renaissance,
> off axis) and many governmental buildings, a truly marvelous
> complex, at the top. Around me was a gathering of my colleagues,
> all architects and influential people. They greeted my proposals
> with silence, which indicated a general disapproval. Not one
> architect who might have encouraged its acceptance by explaining
> it or redirecting it, came to champion my cause. They had been
> eager to greet the work but on seeing it, to the man, they kept a
> shocked, numb silence uttering not a word in its defense or praise.
> They withdrew just after President Johnson came to view it. He too
> showed his disfavor of it and I was left to try to prove its worth to
> this man. If the others, far more sensitive, could not see its merit,
> how could I persuade him? I felt my lips trembling uncontrollably
> as if I should not be able to stifle my sobbing and Johnson smiled at
> me trying to tell me gently they couldn't use the plan. There were
> tears in his eyes. He slowly but firmly departed down the stairs
> backwards (of my office) trying to smile at me, and I was left alone,
> miserable.

Lou's dream as told to me, May 23, 1967:

> Here they come up the stairs in their bear (bare?) skins with their
> watches. What chance do you have against all those dead people
> with your authentic time?

Lou had vivid dreams, and after a visit from Bob Venturi, he had these two,
which he told me and I wrote down. In spite of the celebration of his work at
MoMA and the broad acknowledgment of its worth, Lou was burdened with
anxieties over lost projects like Islamabad and doubts about his persuasive
powers in public talks. He worried that architecture was moving away from the
deep spiritual search for form, truth, and essence that he cared so much about.

Lou had been trained in the Beaux-Arts tradition and had come of age during the ascendency of the International style. He used elements of both, but reacted against them, going back to the very beginnings of architecture, restoring a sense of timelessness and monumentality to the profession. His buildings are mysterious, spatial, solid, and *built*. He believed in "the institutions of man" and an architecture that would serve the needs of people, elevating their lives. His was a heroic vision of modernism, and suddenly it was thrown into question.

Pop art had become the rage, and its wry sensibilities and catchy imagery had found their way into architecture through the quicksilver mind of Bob Venturi. Lou's early champion Vincent Scully called the playful house Bob built for his mother in Chestnut Hill (around the corner from Lou's Esherick House) the "biggest small building of the second half of the 20th century," and Bob's book *Complexity and Contradiction in Architecture*, published in 1966, celebrated the ad hoc eclecticism of "Main Street" along with the decorated facades of Baroque and Mannerist buildings, not the brooding volumes of ancient ruins. Bob's ideas marked the rise of a new sensibility for an unstable time, and his "gentle manifesto" was in direct contradiction to the heroic mode.

MILAN TO 726 WOLCOTT DR., PHILADELPHIA, JANUARY [22], 1967

Hi Sweetie and little sweetie,
Miss you very much. Hotels are not homes.

Got lots from reading T. Jefferson—to keep up my spirits—in the feeling of the greatness of his beliefs and persistence in seeing them take root.

Don't know still the outcome of my visit to Olivetti. Roberto O. [Olivetti] and many of the good architects and others too came to a dinner given for me yesterday (Saturday). I spoke at the Academia Polytechnic in the afternoon. All my expenses are being paid. Quite a treat.

I have had to travel by train a great deal since planes don't fly in bad weather. Now must go to Paris by train from Milan. I will arrive late at night. This will delay my return until Tuesday.

Love,
Lou

Lou's Olivetti-Underwood Factory, Harrisburg, Pennsylvania, 1966–70.

At the end of May I graduated from Penn with a master's degree in landscape architecture. Nathaniel was my family at the ceremony. We moved that summer to a little house in Chestnut Hill, in the towering, beautiful woods above Wissahickon Creek. The house was at the end of a long drive on the grounds of a residence owned by Dr. Francis Adler, a renowned ophthalmologist and early client of Lou. The Adlers befriended us, and Dr. Adler, five years Lou's senior, soon became Nathaniel's grandfather of choice.

In that house on Towanda Street, we discovered how magnificent the spring in the mid-Atlantic woodlands can be. There were no surviving American chestnuts on the hill, but every other native tree and shrub put forth exquisite color and scent in dramatic succession through the season until summer. There were birds, chipmunks, and raccoons, and a red barn with a horse weather vane on its roof. The house had a porch in the treetops. It felt like our lives had settled into belonging to a somewhere that we could call home. Nathaniel made it a place of origin and gave me a role connected to his growing circle of friends and his school. I too made new friends, including Sarah Baltzell, who lived with her family on a neighboring street in a rambling mansion with a black-and-white marble floor and enormous mirrors reflecting each other to infinity. One unforgettable evening at the Baltzells' stands out; I met charming strangers in candlelit rooms, and then Lou walked in to make the scene ever more alight with dazzling repartee and gallant toasts, keeping all the guests there long past midnight. I felt that I was living a dream as Lou's true partner, with a place at the table. Sarah remembered for many years how our joy seemed to cast a rapturous spell over all.

Lou's plans for the Mikveh Israel Synagogue, to be built a block from Independence Hall and the Liberty Bell in Philadelphia's historic district, had stalled repeatedly over weak fund-raising to meet its $2.25 million price tag. Lou loved the project, which he had begun in 1963, and to keep it alive he returned to it at times, reworking details. When I was in my final semester at Penn, Lou asked me to design a garden walkway linking the synagogue with Independence Mall and its surroundings to show his clients. It felt wonderful to be useful to his work in this way.

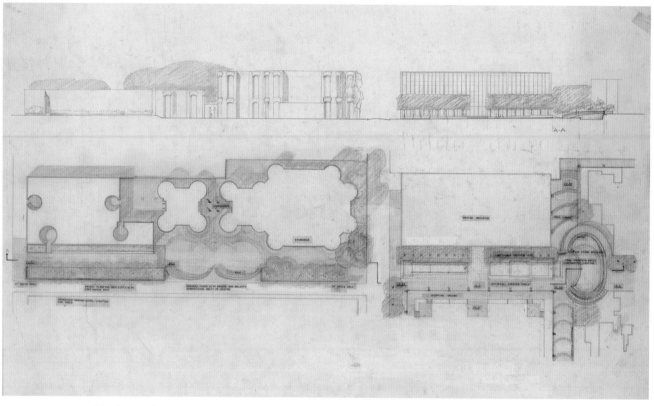

My design drawing for the surroundings of the Mikveh Israel Synagogue featured magnolias, a watercourse, and paving to complement the building's brick exterior and to prepare congregants for the mystery that would unfold within.

Lou's sketch of the sanctuary for the Mikveh Israel Synagogue; its smooth concrete interior would have vibrated with silvery light. That it was never built is a great loss for Philadelphia and beyond.

Dearest,

. . . When I arrived in Karachi (West Pakistan) I was given a letter
from Kafiluddin Ahmed requesting that I stay over in Karachi
that morning and a day before leaving for Dhaka (East Pakistan).
He is the chief engineer of Pakistan and I stayed. My engineer
went on to Dhaka. I was put up at the InterContinental Hotel in
a suite of rooms costing 350 rupees a day (7 rupees to the dollar)
by Commodore Dass who is the leading official of the Pakistan
International Airlines. The reason—he wanted to talk over . . . the
terminal building of the new Dhaka airport.

The program for the day started at 10:30 a.m. (giving me a good
sleep after a few sleepless nights traveling and arriving in Karachi
3 a.m.) to talk to Kafil first and then at 11:30 to Commodore Dass
about the building. Then lunch at Kafiluddin's house where Rehana
was waiting for me. I was greeted very warmly indeed. After lunch,
prepared especially by Rehana, I was asked to rest since the family
rests after lunch; Kafil saying his prayers then rest. I stretched
out on an unmade bed, Hyder's (son), and fell asleep (really) while
Rehana sat in a chair beside me as though sitting vigil. Their
customs will always be fascinating to me. When I got up after a
short rest I asked her if I snored. She said no but that I slept with
my mouth open.

She told me about her loneliness after her little sister passed
away. From the story I was told by her father Kafil, I deduce that
she was given a wrong injection. She was doing very well. Then
the doctor, to make sure of no recurrence of a complaint of the
throat, gave her an injection before discharge and she immediately
collapsed. (What else could it be?) Rehana raised this child from
the beginning (her mother being sick in the head).

After nap, Kafiluddin said he was going to [the] grave of his little
girl and proposed to take me along. We drove thru town and some
interesting sections, especially a Portuguese area (Vasco da Gama)
and near it he pointed out the cemetery and the grave. He built a
little mosque within which was made a depressed area lined with
marble about 6′ long and 3′ wide where the little one (who always
called me professor, who was five when she died) lies buried. Men
were around undoing garlands of flowers for the petals to be strewn

over the grave. He gave me a basket of stems and kept one for himself, containing a different flower. He and I then intermittently spread and mingled their two colors and scent. Garlands later woven in loose nets were laid over the entire length of the grave until the whole measured space was brim full. Two Sufi (priests) then prayed in enchanting tones from the Koran introducing phrases with introductory humming sounds of mmmmmm---- nnnnn----

After prayers we left. Kafil explaining accepting the fates as God has preordained. He asked me what my religion believes about death.

Only a tried old tradition which no longer was under question, as compared with a philosophic thought, could sooth the feeling of "why to me."

That night we—Rehana, Hyder, Kafiluddin and I were invited to have dinner with the Commodore and his wife. It was very pleasant, extremely good food at the KLM retreat near the airport. The Commodore had to meet later that night some dignitaries from Nigeria. That plane was late, very late. It wasn't until 2 o'clock in the morning that it felt like the graceful solution to go back to the hotel and leave him there with his duties. Kafil, Rehana, and Hyder had left earlier and Mrs. Dass and I left in the car to the P.I.A. office in town to arrange my passage that morning at 7AM for return to Dhaka and then was driven to the Hotel for a few hours of sleep.

I arrived in Dhaka yesterday. I have been inspecting the work. It is not excellent but I am thinking of ways to adjust.

The hotel is comfortable (the InterContinental of Dhaka) and I am writing to you at 1AM. I am sleepy and full of love for you. My handwriting is miserable because of one or the other. Having trouble getting into Warsaw but will still try.

Love,
Lou
to Har.ri.et
and
Nath.an.i.el
coca doodil do

In April, Lou was selected by the American Jewish Committee, representing thirty groups nationwide, to design a memorial for the six million Jews murdered in the Holocaust, to be located on New York City's waterfront at Battery Park. Committee members suggested Lou visit the Warsaw Ghetto for historic perspective, which Lou accomplished by a convoluted rerouting of his ticket from Pakistan to Philadelphia through Tehran, Moscow, Warsaw, and London.

Lou's watercolor of the Old Jewish Cemetery in Prague, which he'd seen on his European tour, 1928–29.

Dearest:

I am on my way back via Moscow, Warsaw, London.

I arrived in Karachi last night from Dhaka, was put up in the
Intercontinental Hotel—up bright and early to catch the Moscow
flight leaving 8:30AM. Then while I was having breakfast we were
told that the flight will go at 10:00. Then it became 2PM, then
4PM, then 6PM. And now I am sitting at the airport waiting. It is
well after 6—they just announced it will be 7PM. The way of going
to Warsaw, London via Moscow is like moving backwards. Since I
don't have a visa for Warsaw I was advised to arrive at the airport in
Warsaw in transit. A transit passenger can get a visa for a short stay
if he is waiting for a connecting flight (London). I tried everything
involving the embassies in Dhaka, Karachi, and Russia to make sure
I get to Warsaw. . . . I wanted intermittently [to] give up the whole
struggle but something always pulled me back to trying.

Now we are in the plane, waiting again. It is beginning to get
dark. We will see very little below. The hostess is announcing our
departure. It looks like we're off . . .

2

I am in my room now in transit to Warsaw in an old hotel near the
[Moscow] airport. The room has no bath, no toilet, but is clean
and seems like I'll have a nights sleep here. Tomorrow at 10AM I
fly to Warsaw. When the flight from Karachi was to have begun
at 8:30AM instead of 7:00PM, I was to have arrived in W. 12
midnight. Now at least I will get to Warsaw during the day. The
problem of getting into Russia without a visa (which I couldn't
obtain because of the weekend lull) was not particularly difficult.
I just had to make numerous explanations. After all I got in at
midnight and very few people were around. I will mail this little
note of so little interest in the morning and go to bed now . . .

The work in Pakistan is very faulty. My representatives are doing
little to fight for what the plans show or imply. I am heartbroken
about it all. Maybe photos of it could be enough but that's faint
support. I am going back with renewed determination not to let
everything go down the drain. My determination to go to Warsaw
at tremendous odds contrasting with American service may prove
worthwhile even if only to convey my concern about the problem.

With all my love to you and to Nathaniel.

Lou

3

Had to add that I have just had breakfast in the airport. Caviar, boiled eggs, mineral water and tea (in a glass). It is awfully good to eat at a table covered with spotless white. Though the airport falls short of greatness architecturally it has a directness in its logic of circulation. The sound of Russian is like speaking underwater with escaping breath and at times it appears above the surface as though it were eating air. There are little flags on the table of various countries. The American flag is absent. What a pity! How little they know Americans but again—America is changing.

Soon I will have to register. I know not what that could possibly mean, Passport, etc., etc. But I do feel I will be able to get off in Warsaw. I could not, however, go into town when I was in Moscow. I stayed in this quaint place, awfully good really.

Will have lots to tell you. . . .

Lou

The sketch on the other side is an early study of the library in Exeter. I did not know I was using so precious a page for only you. HA, HA!

Around this time, Lou was struggling to write an introduction for a book on eighteenth-century visionary French architects. He admired their drawings and their architectural dreams, most of them unbuilt. In the end, Lou came up with just twelve lines—a kind of haiku to these champions of monumental architecture ending with, "Ledoux is, Boullée is, thus architecture is."

The unbuilt design for the National Library by Étienne-Louis Boullée, from *Visionary Architects*, 1967.

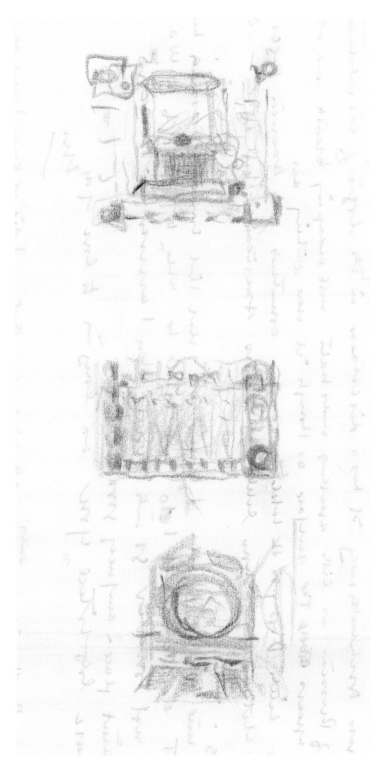

Lou's sketches on the reverse of the letter, exploring ideas for the library at Phillips Exeter Academy, Exeter, New Hampshire.

Dearest

So:— I've written you from Russia now on my to Warsaw after a good breakfast of cold chicken caviar white wine pumpernickel cake apricot preserve bread and tomatoes I can settle down to a few words.

I have but to hurdle the visa problem in Poland. I assume as I was told that a visa may be obtained at the airport. If not all will go to naught. in going this round about way to see the ghetto and the monument to its end. I don't have to see it to find an expression though I am completely barren of ideas or even a deeply felt urge to express. I feel a flop as an expressionist — steps that rise to nowhere? a single stone. The wall of stone surrounding with but a single small opening inside a continuous stone seat inscription all around — PROPORTION, A WALLED PLACE

A WALLED PLACE
PROPORTION!! CONVERGING TO A SMALL
PROPORTION!!! CONVERGING
~ - a small opening.

Proportion is this psychic meeting that cannot go nearer or farther

Maybe Warsaw will tell me what is proportion and lead me not to the pitfalls of appropriateness.

All my love

EN ROUTE MOSCOW—WARSAW TO FARAWAY, JULY 23, 1967

Dearest,

So—I've written you from Russia, now on way to Warsaw after a good breakfast of cold chicken, caviar, white wine, pumpernickel cake, apricot preserves, bread and tomatoes, I can settle down to a few words.

I have but to hurdle the visa problem in Poland, I assume, as I was told that a visa may be obtained at the airport. If not all will go to naught in going this roundabout way to see the Ghetto and the monument to its end. I don't have to see it to find an expression though I am completely barren of ideas or even a deeply felt urge to express. I feel a flop as an expressionist—steps that rise to nowhere? A single stone. The wall of stone surrounding with but a single small opening, inside a continuous stone seat inscription all around—

PROPORTION! A WALLED PLACE. A WALLED PLACE PROPORTION!! CONVERGING TO A SMALL OPENING PROPORTION!!!, CONVERGING to a small opening.

proportion is this psychic meeting that cannot go nearer or farther.

Maybe Warsaw will tell me what is proportion and lead me not to the pitfalls of appropriateness.

All my love,
Lou

EN ROUTE PARIS–LONDON TO FARAWAY, JULY 24, 1967

Monday on flight
Dearest Harriet and Nathaniel,
I arrived in Paris from Warsaw at 10:30 p.m. too late to catch a flight to London. I decided, instead of going into Paris which meant all the rigmarole of customs and passport control, to stay at the airport hotel. It has really an interesting plan.

Cost is $13 per night with of course many mysterious charges added. From a $20 bill I at first got only 3 Francs back. I questioned the change and up came 30 additional francs. It took so long for the mechanical calculator to get the right done that I almost lost my connection, 7:40 a.m. to London.

I wrote you a quicky at the airport just for the stamps. We are nearing land in flight. I imagine you get all this mail in one lump on your return from California. I hope it was good to have gone to the wedding and especially to come back to Nathaniel.

Love,
Lou

While Lou was reflecting on proportion and the "pitfalls of appropriateness" in Warsaw, I was attending Bob Venturi and Denise Scott Brown's New Age wedding at Denise's house in Venice Beach, California. The countercultural scene might have been a bit much for Denise's sophisticated mother from South Africa, as it was for mine, who attended as well—but to me the hippie neighbors and psychedelic Volkswagen bus as a getaway car seemed right on target, knowing Bob's penchant for the bizarre. By coincidence, their wedding took place in the same week as my niece's garden nuptials, a few miles but light years apart in Brentwood. I felt terribly vulnerable on both occasions, and in Brentwood my brother Abbott was relentless in trying to persuade me to leave the man he demonized as a rake and a fabulist, telling me to "start over." I was glad to leave California and return to Maine and Nathaniel.

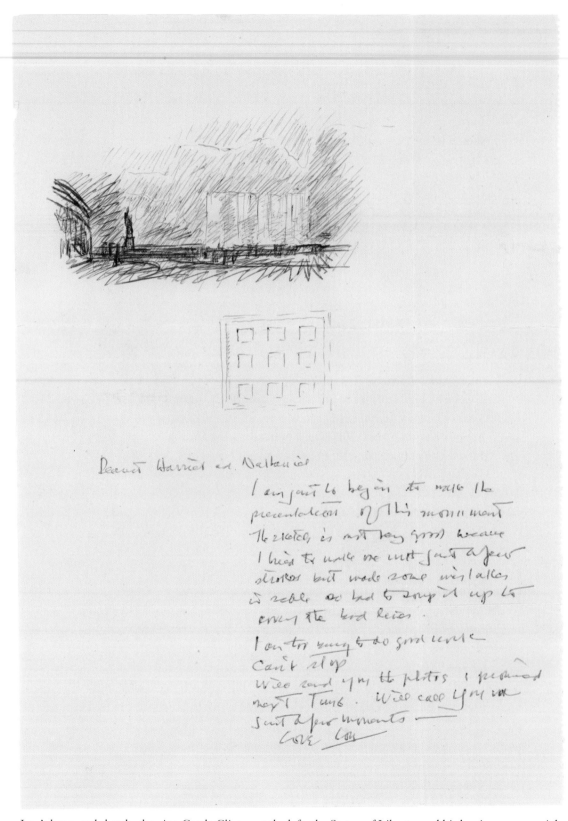

Lou's letter and sketch, showing Castle Clinton at the left, the Statue of Liberty, and his luminous memorial.

Dearest Harriet and Nathaniel,
I am just to begin to make the presentation of this monument. The sketch is not very good because I tried to make one with just a few strokes but made some mistakes in scale so had to soup it up to cover the bad lines.

I am too busy to do good work.

Can't stop.

Will send you the photos I promised next time. Will call you in just a few moments—

Love,
Lou

"Monumentality is enigmatic. It cannot be intentionally created," Lou wrote in a 1944 essay, and now he was trying to conjure it with the poetics of minimalism. Inspired by Warsaw, books I'd given him, and most of all the Manhattan site next to Castle Clinton's bastion, with views of the Statue of Liberty and Ellis Island across the water—icons of the immigrant experience and hope—Lou conceived a memorial radically different from those given over to torment and despair.

From the letter he'd written me from Warsaw, I assumed the memorial would be built of stone. Lou loved stone, keeping pieces on his desk that he shifted like chess moves, and his mastery of concrete, which he called "liquid stone," was proverbial. So I hardly believed it when he said he wanted his memorial "stones" to be made of glass.

Lou went to the Corning Company in upstate New York to see if it was possible to cast monumental pieces of semi-opaque straw-colored glass, but this proved to be too expensive and difficult to control. So Lou resorted to large glass blocks, to be assembled into ten-foot piers, sixteen of them arranged at equal intervals on a square plinth and choreographed by light. These soon became nine, three on each side, to contain a central, hollowed pier bearing inscriptions. There was an expressed desire to record all six million names, but the impossibility of this—being equal to printing the shocking number of names in the New York City telephone directory—allowed Lou to suggest what he most truly felt: that the spatial experience of the hollow glass chamber at the memorial's core might honor the immeasurable value of an individual human life.

Who else had the audacity to use glass in this daring and expressive manner? Formed in fire but with stolid translucence and the cool shock of ice, this vision

TOP: Lou's perspective of the Memorial to the Six Million Jewish Martyrs in daylight.

BOTTOM: Lou's perspective of the memorial at night, illuminated by torchières.

Lou used this model of the memorial to study proportions and imagine the changing light—
from the sun, the moon, the rippling water, and the torches at nightfall. To me, the glass
piers were a Cycladic congregation, or a kind of spectral Stonehenge.

was haunting and extraordinary. Yet the memorial proved too abstract, too
pagan, and perhaps not dark enough for its supporters, who forced revisions
even after Lou contributed a large model to exhibit at MoMA to raise public
awareness and launch a fund drive. It failed to unite a divided patronage, which
ultimately abandoned this luminous work, building instead a traditional and
"appropriate" museum on the site. But for a generation of sculptors and land
artists like Donald Judd, Richard Serra, Mark di Suvero, and James Turrell,
Lou's work on this and other projects continued to resonate through their own
transformative careers.

Dearest Harriet

It was good to talk to you Sunday
morning. Trying to overcome the difficulty
of concentrating on the buildings and
worrying also about the money problems.
I am beyond talking about financing - its
just plain everyday money.

I tried to write down what we talked
about - work, and the spirit, the source of
inspiration, the self caught in space ——
Soon I will send it to you my love.
Lov

Dearest Harriet,

It was good to talk to you Sunday morning. Trying to overcome the difficulty of concentrating on buildings and worrying also about the money problems. I am beyond talking about financing—it's just plain everyday money.

I tried to write down what we talked about—work, another spirit, the source of inspiration, that self cannot inspire—

Soon I will send it to you my love.

Lou

Dearest,

Set out for Corning today. They had arranged a meeting with the department heads. When I got to the airport the flight was cancelled. Now I am going Tuesday after Labor Day.

I keep thinking about Abbott. I can't help liking him for his concern. He must associate you with love that holds him to your family of youth. How much I know the feeling of this even now the only true feeling of indestructible "family." I just have to respect his feeling of love. Ideal. Everlasting.

Even though you want to refute his attitude you show your regard. I know it as you speak with lostness and desire for the deep affinity for the same haunting beauty of family and position. For all this I love you—for whatever may be your way. I know its motivation to just sheer good.

Lou

Bob Venturi and Denise Scott Brown on the balcony of his "Mother's House" in Chestnut Hill, Philadelphia.

PHILADELPHIA TO FARAWAY, SEPTEMBER 8, 1967

Harriet dear,

Sorry nothing to say. Just hope you get this in time for your needs. Yesterday I intended to send you the money but just plumb forgot.

Got an invitation from David Crane honoring Denise and Bob. Not going feel funny about whole thing. Will speak to you tonight, sweetie. Hope Nathaniel is better now.

It is wonderful to be as engaged as I am but the demands of time, at specific times, hurts.

On my way now to meeting of monument committees. I have no new ideas except that the central block must be a key block of inscription hoping it will take the mind from 9 and make it 1.

Love,
Lou

I imagine the invitation from city planner David Crane to a party celebrating Bob and Denise could have made Lou "feel funny" for several reasons. Perhaps it was that Bob and I had once been devoted friends, and that Denise, Bob, and I were of another generation, or that Bob's filial respect had eroded as he learned more about Lou's personal life and grew confident of his own, unique talents. This had set a distance between them, although Lou continued to feel great affection for Bob. Perhaps most of all, it was that while Bob's life had become integrated with his marriage to Denise, Lou's life remained divided and secretive.

Respectability—which Bob so brilliantly mocked in his work but now embraced in his personal life—seemed lost to me. I was with a man I loved, I had a child I adored and a path toward a career, but these had cost me the acceptance of "society." I felt caught between two eras, and even two parts of myself. While I didn't regret my choices, I longed for acceptance and a domestic life. My cottage in the woods on Towanda Street was hardly the bohemian home of "a single mother." With family antiques and some I had collected over the years, a piano, a playroom, and specimen plants I'd planted in a garden, it made a cozy extension of the world I had grown up in. Lou loved it and my hope persisted that someday soon he would move there to be with us. But that promising fantasy was dealt a sudden blow when Lou reluctantly confessed to me that Esther had bought a house in Society Hill, not far from his office, that he was renovating it with his men, and that he was planning to move there in the fall.

As much as this hurt, at the same time I felt drawn closer to Lou because he had been truthful with me and allowed me to see the complexities of his life more fully. A new ritual began. After an evening or weekend of closeness at Towanda Street, I would drive Lou into town, with Nathaniel sleeping in the back seat, to the home he shared with Esther. It was there under the streetlight at the end of Clinton Street that the conflict in Lou's soul was laid bare, as he sadly parted from us and walked down the block, disappearing into the darkened town house. Nathaniel and I would then drive home in silence.

Lou and I were photographed separately at a wedding we attended together, summer 1967.

George Patton (left) with me, John Moss, and Ken Arnold in George's office at 1501 Walnut Street, Philadelphia.

1968

My professional career began in the fall of 1967, when Lou encouraged a friend since their shared days at the American Academy in Rome, George Patton, to add me to the three-man staff of his landscape architecture firm, just then relocating to the third floor of Lou's building at 1501 Walnut Street.

Only eight years my senior, George already had a distinguished practice, was vice president of the American Society of Landscape Architects (ASLA), and taught at Penn. Originally from North Carolina, George was charming, with a wry sense of humor, speaking with a slight southern drawl from the side of his mouth. Although he could occasionally be sarcastic in his critiques, he was encouraging and generous, and I couldn't have been luckier to have him as a boss and mentor for the next critical years when I was on trial, based on Lou's belief in my "good eye" and as-yet-untested design skills.

Focused neither on the singular vision of an artist like Dan Kiley nor on the ecological crusades of Ian McHarg, George's firm was committed to serving the needs of architects and to landscape design informed by a deep knowledge of plant material and classic gardens. This practical, even humble, philosophy was reflected in the businesslike decor of the carpeted, air-conditioned, glass-partitioned office, equipped with potted plants at windows and green night cloths on drafting tables. The office was a cooperative environment, and the men welcomed me into their midst. George's loyal clerk of the works, the birdlike Ken Arnold, was a master of surveys, detailing, plant specifications, and sitework. An amateur organist, he whistled cheerful Sunday tunes and cared for a widowed mother in New Jersey. Her delicious cookies domesticated the scene, as did Nathaniel's visits, which George—married but childless—kindly indulged with a desk, access to tree stamps, paper, markers, and use of the magical copy machine. Bob Kesnick, a muscular, sardonic young guy who could build anything, consulted "Nat" about wooden jungle gyms and drank coffee endlessly. John Moss, southern and boyishly handsome, turned out flawless work at high speed and entertained us with stories of risqué Philadelphia nightlife. John and I became fast friends, although he could be mercurial, drinking and smoking with abandon. He was openly gay at a time when it was daring and even dangerous to be so, and his escapades, although fascinating to hear about, worried me for

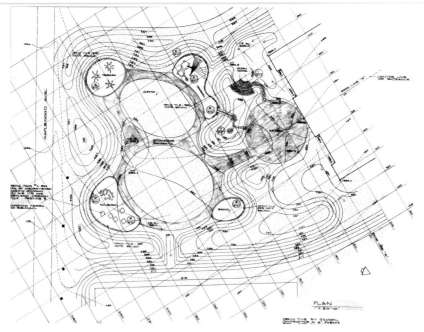

My grading plan for a playground in Wayne, Pennsylvania.

The playground design included natural equipment for imaginative play in varied terrain, enlivened with tree and shrub "islands," water, and sand pockets.

his safety (John later moved to Rome, opening the first—highly successful—gay bar there).

Within a few months, a young German landscape architect on a visa, Heidi Shleigel, came aboard. Heidi was blond, disciplined, talented, and lovely, lending a gracious, stylish air to the office, like the fragrant bouquets she placed on the desk of Adele, George's savvy secretary, to charm our ascetic surroundings.

My first assignment, creating a PR brochure for the ASLA, was something of a nonstarter; though George deemed it well written, I had included extensive material on the historic role of women like Beatrix Farrand and Gertrude Jekyll in the field—for an organization that was then almost exclusively male. Next, George assigned me an elementary school playground, as one who had been marginally involved with the Noguchi-Kahn experiment and who also had a child critic in residence. This yielded positive results, along with another design for a small estate around the corner from the house I had recently moved to on Towanda Street. There I was able to indulge the love of plants that I shared with George—a superb gardener—and my romantic taste for Italian gardens and water features. Both designs were quickly sent out for bids and were soon under construction, convincing George that I did have something to offer as a designer.

SECTION THROUGH GARDEN
SCALE: 1/8" = 1'

This presentation drawing of the Richard Brown Garden, in Chestnut Hill, was one of the first I made in George's office. The design featured walls, with steps leading past perennial borders to a distant fountain and a surprise vista of the Wissahickon Gorge.

The stone walls, step levels, perennial borders, and fountain at the Brown Garden.

Dearest Harriet Darling—

That was a fine breakfast this morning. The oatmeal simmering all
night was the mostest by the mostest. Everything that's made with the
least is not always best. What takes longer may often be the best if the
best is not too often. Oatmeal—the "what's time" kind—has a home
spun effect on a man. He longs for the crackling fire and the tugging
wind and the joyous cry of welcome. The quick-as-a-trick kind—
with all the imprint of the captivating package—is just delicious.

The other day a man came to the shop to show me, as he termed
it, a modern stained glass technique. I asked if he be the artist. No
but I am close friend of the artist acting as his agent. Right away
of course I knew he had nothing but I was curious. He unwrapped
the thing and held it away from me against the light and damn it
all it was quite beautiful. I reached closer for it and saw globs of
glass protruding from the surface of the deep colors crossed by
nervous lines a la Pollock. "How is this done?" "By epoxy plastic
cement these chunks of glass adhere to the glass." I looked in the
back. It was a clear plate glass surface and I realized that the whole
damned thing was phony. The colored glass was pasted on plastic,

the black divisions and markings was paint and the globs not fused.
The whole thing a chewing gum art. It was so disgusting. He
said "What do you think of it?" He glowed with the love of art. It
reminds me, I said, of two beautiful women. One with a beautiful
voice the other wired with background music of Galli-Curci.
He left thanking me for the frank criticism. A real lick-splittlish
peddling jerk. I have little pity for men who sell what others make
with their hands.

With all my love,
Lou

Lou thought of himself as a craftsman and cared as much for how something
was done as for the idea behind it. Perhaps he took after his father, Leopold,
who was a maker of stained glass and once smashed a piece of his work to
prove its authenticity to a skeptical buyer.

Lou and Nathaniel on our back porch at Towanda Street.

In April a prominent Venetian, Giuseppe Mazzariol, came to Philadelphia
to invite Lou to exhibit his work (and his craftsmanship) at the Venice
Biennale—which was including architecture in its celebration of the arts
for the first time in 1968. Even more stunning was Mazzariol's offer of a
commission to design a great gathering hall, the Palazzo dei Congressi, at
the Giardini della Biennale. Lou readily accepted both offers, and within a
month was en route to Venice—at a time when revolution was in the air and
demonstrations and riots were sweeping through Europe, as they had in the
United States.

Carlo Scarpa with Lou and Carles Vallhonrat in Asolo.　　　Lou and Giuseppe Mazzariol in Venice.

EN ROUTE ROME–VENICE TO TOWANDA ST., MAY 24, 1968

Dearest,

. . . We don't feel the Paris uprising too much in America but here
everything is affected. Tourists everywhere have to re-route their
flight around Paris because the services at the airport in Paris are dead.
DeGaulle is in a tight spot. Money changers (the scum of the earth) are
putting their gambling instincts on the German Mark dividing $'s £'s
and Fr's. I hope they go completely broke and die of heartbreak. I hate
the work that sells money. Money must be earned to have meaning.

I always think of "how can I change the world" never realizing
that the world is inaccessible except thru a single person.

Lots and lots of love to you and Nathaniel

Lou

VENICE TO TOWANDA ST., MAY 24, 1968

Dearest,

I arrived in Venice in the rain—water everywhere top to bottom. It
felt like being in a watercolor.

The next day—today the sun made Venice the storybook Venice.

What a place! What a site for the buildings! The reception
was all heart. I have a great deal to do on the Biennale. It is very
important that I exhibit with thought. I have so far no thought
and everything must be ready by the 19th. [Carlo] Scarpa, the
Italian architect in Venice, is up to his nose with details. He has an
insurmountable problem. I must do it all myself, my part. But—it
will be so worthwhile.

Love,
Lou

VENEZIA
Basilica di S. Marco - Martirio di S. Marco. (Mosaico del sec. XIII)
Basilique de S. Marc - Martyre de S. Marc (Mosaïque du XIII siècle)
Basilica of S. Mark - Martyrdom of S. Mark (Mosaic of the XIII. century)
Basilika S. Marcus - Martyrium des heiligen Markus (Mosaik des XIII. Jahrhunderts)

Dearest,
I arrived in Venice in the rain - water
everywhere top to bottom. It was
like being in a water color
The next day - today the sun made
Venice the storybook Venice.
What a place! What a site for the buildings! The reception was excellent.
I have a great deal to do on the Biennale
it is very important that I exhibit well
thought. I leave 20/or 26 thought. and
everything must be ready by the 19th. Scarpa
the Italian architect in Venice is up to his
nose. most details. It has an insurmountable
problem. I must do it all myself my part.
But Venice is so wonderful while
LOVE LOU

HARRIET PATTISON

8870 Towanda Drive
Chestnut Hill
Philadelphia Pa
U.S.A.

145

On way to Cairo

Dearest Harriet and Nathaniel,

Was greeted by Mazzariol and Scarpa with kisses on both cheeks and taken by motor boat to my Hotel very expensive old with a new Bauhaus front. I went out that night with a party for dinner, Scarpa presiding. It was one of those orgy-ious affairs which starts with little fish, shrimp, octopus, sea devil sardines, anchovies, mussels, dripping in oil and vinegar and spices, then pasta, wine of course at every mouthful and only then a fish course of "importante." Strawberries and coffee follow, topped off with liqueur. A gay, gay, full of praise and joy party. We walked and looked at the shop windows on our way back to the hotel.

The next morning I saw the site of the project. Wonderful but I can make it significant. I also visited the room in the Biennale where I am to exhibit. That night I had my own dinner, much more restrained yet somehow attractive. The next day Mazzariol took me on a tour of the city "by gondola." It was a rare break to be introduced to Venice by him. We ended up by visiting his Bureau in a palace, had lunch at his house on the Lido. A most pleasant and gracious afternoon. Then back to hotel and dinner, again with Scarpa, on the Rialto. This was another marathon gastronomique and to bed only after having stopped at the home of one of the architects where I had to show the slides I'd brought with me.

I needed to do this also because I had no idea up to then what I would show at the Biennale. After the talk and show which was an arduous thing because of the constant translations I got (what I wanted—a reaction) an idea of what they were expecting, which I found difficult to understand. This was a very late party and only this morning, accompanying Mazzariol to the airport, I got a satisfactory thought. I will finish later.

Love to you and Nathaniel

p.s. I noticed how little I observed the gondolas. They are superbly beautiful. The profession is handed down. Beautiful is the soul with strength of a tradition. Ugly is altering them except without change. I will make a study of the gondola. It adds enormous grace to Venice. They look like long wave strokes in the water.

Post card purchased in Rome. I had only a moment in airport. Now I will mail this one in Cairo. On way to Cairo. The view of this card is a village near Dhaka during the rains.

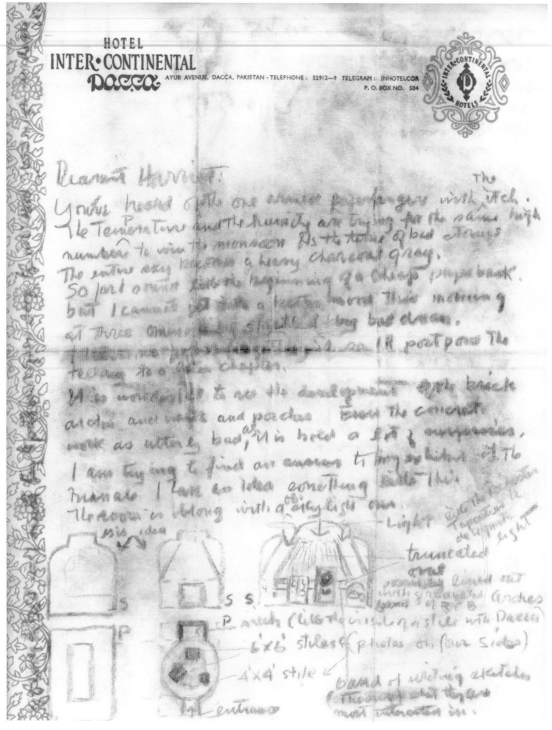

The room is oblong with a obl. skylight over. S[ection and] P[lan], as is. S[ection], idea. P[lan], niche (like the inside of a stile—with Dhaka arches). 6' × 6' stiles (photos on four sides). 4' × 4' stile (photos on four sides). Entrance. S[ection], light, truncated oval, possibly lined out with articulated bands of R[ed], Y[ellow], B[lue], like the Rochester tapestries to desegment light. Band of writing sketches (thought what they are most interested in).

Dearest Harriet:

You've heard of the one armed paperhanger with the itch. The temperature and the humidity are trying for the same high numbers to rival the monsoon. It's the titan of bad storms. The entire sky becomes a heavy charcoal gray.

So far it sounds like the beginning of a cheap paperback but I cannot get into a better mood. This morning at three, ominously startled by bad dream. Possesses no happy prognosability in it, so I'll postpone the telling to a later chapter.

It is wonderful to see the development of the brick arcades and walls and porches. Even the concrete work as utterly bad as it is holds a lot of surprises.

I am trying to find an answer to my exhibit at the Biennale. I have an idea something like this [drawings in letter].

Lou selected photographs like this one, of the members hostels at the capital complex in Dhaka, for the Biennale exhibit.

Dearest

See that stationary upstairs. That's what
I think I'm going to have to fight. I showed
the model or photo-drawings to Mr. Jacob
Solomon who is the one braid the funds for
the Hursa' Synagogue. He is a good man
but it took him some time to gather the meanings
and the scale.

Tomorrow I meet the planners of Israel —
the architects. Tied up with development —
Mayor Kollek (of Jerusalem.

I wasn't received like a conquering hero.
Kalmis came (young artist assigned to
assist me) I went to his house to give a little
present and then Solomon appeared.

I am very sorry about my stupid
Boston. I was so sure
that it wouldn't stop there on the way over
Fancy my frustration.
Darling don't worry baby about
your self evaluations. On ward, That
you constantly need confirmation of your
attitude and work is the same need that
crave for what ever item not ward
appearances may be. Let me always be
your confidence.
Will write you if everything is OK
or KO
Love to you and Nattaniel "my boy!"

Dearest,

See that stationery up there [arrow] that's what I think I'm going to have to fight. I showed the model and photo-drawings to Mr. Jakob Solomon who is the one to raise the funds for the "Hurva" Synagogue. He is a good man but it took him some time to gather the meanings and the scale.

Tomorrow I meet the planners of the area—the architects tied up with development—Mayor Kollek of Jerusalem.

I wasn't received like a conquering hero. [Ram] Karmi came (young architect assigned to assist me). I went to his house to give a little preview and then Solomon appeared.

I am <u>very sorry</u> about my stupid Boston. I was so sure that it would stop there on the way over. Fancy my frustration.

Darling don't worry baby about your self-evaluations downward. That you constantly need confirmation of your attitude and work is the same need others crave for whatever their outward appearances may be. Let me always have your confidence. Will write you if everything is OK or KO

Love to you and Nathaniel "my boy!"

Lou

At the urging of two young Israeli architects, brother and sister Ram and Ada Karmi, Lou had gone to Jerusalem the previous December to view the ruins of a synagogue known as the Hurva, which had been blown up during the Arab-Israeli War of 1948. The Karmis were advising philanthropist Yaacov Salomon (Jakob Solomon in Lou's letter), who wanted to build a replacement, and Lou now returned to present his plans to Salomon and city officials, including Jerusalem's mayor Teddy Kollek.

The dramatic presence within the old city of three religions' sacred monuments—the Muslim Dome of the Rock, the Christian Orthodox Church of the Holy Sepulchre, and the Jewish Western Wall—coupled with Israeli optimism following the Six-Day War in June, inspired Lou to put forth his ideas with speed and confidence for a new, democratic country that valued its architects as leaders.

For his Hurva Synagogue, Lou's inspiration reached beyond the Greek and Roman classics he revered to primal works of Egypt. He designed powerful pylons of golden Jerusalem stone, tapered inward while rising seventy feet in

The large Plasticine model Lou's office made of Jerusalem, showing, left to right, the proposed Hurva Synagogue, the Western Wall, and the Dome of the Rock. Lou wanted to preserve the ruins of the old Hurva as a temple garden, siting his building in the open square next to it.

eight pairs forming a square. The interior consisted of four massive hollow concrete columns, rising and flaring like geometric trees to almost meet in a canopy with slits to the sky. These brought silvery light to the sanctuary far below, which mixed with the golden light admitted through the gaps and corner entries between the pylons.

The cool, half-lit interior Lou conceived as sheltered from the climate and distractions of an outer world was bereft of objects other than the bema at the center, the encased ark and stepped seating for two hundred congregants with benches above for additional worshipers on high holy days. Surrounding this serene center were sixteen candlelit niches hollowed into the bases of the pylons.

It would be a singular structure and space, dedicated solely to prayer and belonging to an ancient world, in resonance with its name, Hurva, which translates from Hebrew as "Ruin." Lou was designing a modern temple for an ancient city, a great world synagogue to draw and unite Jews of all denominations through the power of an elemental architecture: all volume, surface, light, and texture, without doors, windows, furniture, offices, or art. It was a building that seemed to precede everything around it, reaching back to a primal feeling of spirituality, attempting to touch the essence of religion itself.

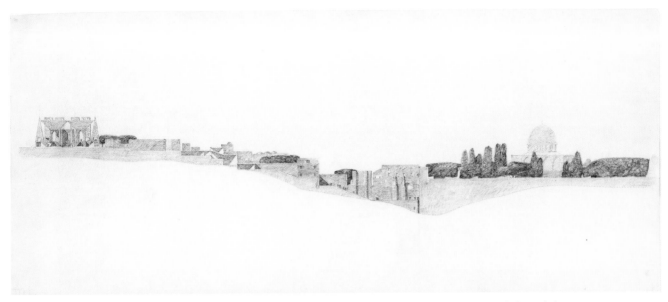

Lou's section drawing, showing the relationship between his Hurva Synagogue (left) and the Dome of the Rock (right). He was well aware that the mosque had been built over the ruins of the Second Temple of the Jews, and that his own building, while not intended as the third temple, would need to be worthy of its prominence in the ancient city.

An office model of the Hurva Synagogue, with Jerusalem stone pylons wrapped around a concrete interior.

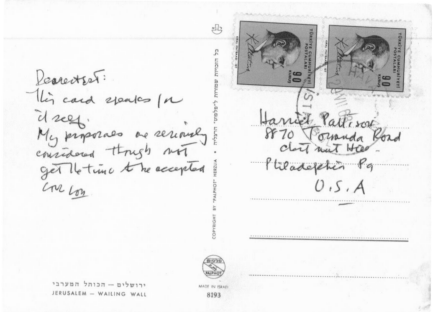

ISTANBUL TO TOWANDA ST., JULY 28, 1968

Dearest:

This card speaks for itself.

   My proposals are seriously considered though not yet the time to be accepted.

Love,
Lou

252

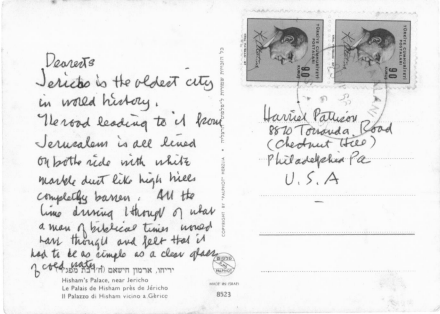

ISTANBUL TO TOWANDA ST., JULY 28, 1968

Dearests,

Jericho is the oldest city in world history. The road leading to it from Jerusalem is all lined on both sides with white marble dust like high hills completely barren. All the time driving I thought of what a man of biblical times would have thought and felt that it had to be as simple as a clear glass of cold water.

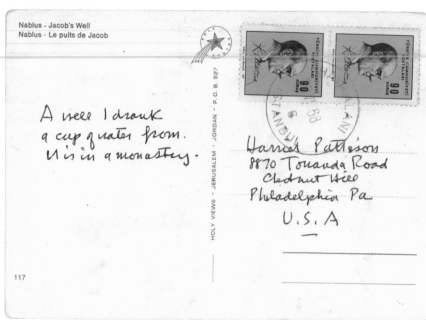

ISTANBUL TO TOWANDA ST., JULY 28, 1968

A well I drank a cup of water from. It is in a monastery.

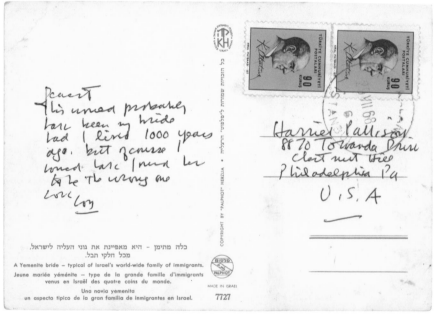

ISTANBUL TO TOWANDA ST., JULY 28, 1968

Dearest,
This would probably have been my bride had I lived 1000 years ago.
But of course I would have found her to be the wrong one.

                        Love,
                        Lou

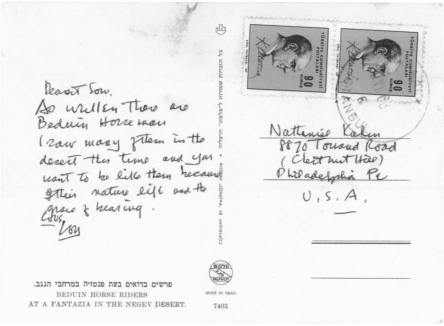

ISTANBUL TO TOWANDA ST., JULY 28, 1968

Dearest Son,

As written these are Bedouin Horsemen. I saw many of them in
the desert this time and you want to be like them because of their
native life and the grace of bearing.

Love,
Lou

Lou at the InterContinental Hotel, Jerusalem,
just after the trip to Mar Saba.

Lou loved his trip into the Judean desert to see the Greek Orthodox
monastery called Mar Saba. One of his traveling companions, the journalist
Dan Mirkin, wrote about how Lou had seemed like an old man on the journey,
tired and dozing in the jeep, but when they reached the monastery, he came
alive, running and jumping around the hills to get a better look at the stone
buttresses and wondering aloud what spaces they made possible within.

ISTANBUL TO TOWANDA ST., JULY 28, 1968

Dearests,
We took a dangerous hairpin narrow mountain road for several
hours to reach this secluded Monastery—Nothing else around—in
view of the Dead Sea in the heart of the Jordan Desert.

   Now it has only 14 monks. At one time there were 100 in the
same buildings.

MAR SABA CONVENT   מנזר מר סבא

Dearests.
We took a dangerous
hair pin narrow mountain
road for several hours to
reach this secluded Monastary –
Nothing else around – in view
of the Dead Sea in the heart
of the Jordan Desert.
Now it has only 14 monks
At one time there were 100 in the
same buildings

Harriet Pattison
8870 Towanda Road
Chestnut Hill
Philadelphia Pa
U.S.A

מנזר מר סבא בעמק נחל קדרון
MAR SABA CONVENT IN THE VALLEY
OF THE KIDRON
LE COUVENT DE MAR SABA DANS
LA VALLEE DU KIDRON
DAS MAR SABA KLOSTER IM KIDRONTAL

PALPHOT

MADE IN ISRAEL

8536

The National Assembly in Dhaka under construction during the monsoon.

Dearests,
I arrived in Dhaka and, for the first time, was not greeted by the entourage. My new secretary did not write ahead. I realize what a lonely polecat feels like without anyone else but another lonely polecat waiting for another polecat. "Die nudall dike fette Kumach hat deim Son boob so liek!"

The presentation in Jerusalem went well. Every one of the architects approved and especially Mayor Kollek—very imp. BUT I am not so sure of the religious groups in Israel. They are agin everything. But I was asked to proceed with the same basic thought. It so happened that one of the Israeli boys in my office (who worked on the project) also suddenly appeared in Israel and attended the meeting and presentation (a closed meeting but somehow there is always a little hole into which one can creep) which was strictly closed to only a few architects of Israel. SO—I put him to work digging up new info and it turns out to be a bit of luck that he is there—because those who are jealous of my work in Jerusalem would hold back what I need. He is equally ambitious—well anyway.

I am here in Dhaka now—and I already after the first day want to leave. I have already said that I must go soon. I hope sweeties that I can get away soon and be back soon—I love you so so much the two of you.

Lou

During Lou's weeklong stay in Dhaka, his clients in India had been trying to arrange a way for him to visit Ahmedabad on the way home. At this time tensions were rising between India and Pakistan (fueled in part by the fact that Pakistan was receiving financial aid from the United States while India was not), so Lou cooked up a scheme to visit India via the neutral Iran Air, quietly changing his ticket paid for by the Pakistanis. Over the next several letters Lou narrates the way the thin scheme unraveled, like a frayed piece of Indian cotton.

EN ROUTE DHAKA–KARACHI, WEST PAKISTAN, TO TOWANDA ST., AUGUST 3, 1968

Dearest ones:

I got away finally from Dhaka and on my way to Karachi where I expect to board an Iranian Airline flight to Bombay 5:30 a.m. It is now 10:30 p.m. Will arrive K. midnight. The airlines will put me up at the Midway Hotel near the airport.

Constant rain and violent storms. The winds are often horizontal, driving the rain thru any opening. No detail can stop it. I entered one of my buildings, the main one attached to the Hostels. The stairway landing at the bottom had four inches of water. It all came from some openings high up in the stair chamber intended to be closed with shutters. This detail was not issued. Sometimes I think I am doing the capital single handed.

You notice how sloppy my hand has become. It comes from the feeling that I am writing nothing of importance. I want so much to be always your most precious part.

The days spent here are like putting in time. Details are so neglected, space allocations on site so defiled, little concessions of land are given away without consolidating the land plan and our plot arrangement goes down the drain. It is a race against scheming arbitrariness and complete lack of feeling for what is intended.

Still! my sweet one life is good when I think of you two. Sweetness takes the place of rubbish fights of garbage collectors whose outlook is more garbage. Nobody means harm. It is all basically undue pressure placed by those who know not on those who know. My commissioner, Saddique, is a good man but those whom he works for turn everything to political expediency.

Love,
Lou

Sunday on my way to India (?)

Dearest Harriet,

I tried to outwit the Pakistani in using their ticket to help India pay the fare onward to Ahmedabad. I mentioned this to no one (except the office) that I intend to quietly arrive in Karachi and from there board the Arab Airline flight at 5:30 A.M. to Bombay.

When I arrived in Karachi at midnight, I was met by Mr. Kafiluddin and an army of his assistants. They knew that I missed the flight to London which left just at midnight and were there to help me to the Intercontinental Hotel in Karachi and prepare for a day's stay in Karachi talking over matters and leave the next day on the same flight. I was thoroughly trapped. Then I found out, while I was at the hotel, that there is a flight early, 7:30 A.M. to Tehran (Persia) where I could get a connecting flight to Bombay. Ahmedabad has wired a ticket for me in Karachi which I could not pick up because of the hour. I thought I could get this ticket transferred to Tehran. The connecting flight from Tehran being scheduled to fly at 22:30 hours and with my arrival in Tehran at 8:30 I figured I could see Persepolis, Darius' Palace, by way of spending the day in Persia beautifully.

I was off and arrived in Tehran all ready to have the enjoyment of still conquering the situation. Then I found out that I was really trapped even more conclusively. Sunday! No telegrams possible to Ahmedabad. All flights to Persepolis or Isfahan in the early morning only and also that it is a great distance from Tehran, resulting in flights being in the late evening—No go!

So here I am at the "MIAMI" hotel expensive dull frustrating no word no Persepolis. Time eating away at my plan to return early. I must go [on] to India.

I am so sorry sweetheart that as a schemer, I am but a child. But really I could not have told the Pakistani about India. They would have resented deeply my using their precious foreign exchange to help India.

I miss you very very much and I must say that I miss Nathaniel just as much.

Love,

Lou

Time weighs heavily here waiting all day for the next. The town is not very much. The people are not usual. They look handsome and historical. . . . I tried some shopping, did a little, met a young Persian in a coffee house. He helped me find some interesting bazars, but it was already late and decided there was too little time to choose well.

Tomorrow being Monday may bring some better luck [but] not good enough to work well for our plans to see each other before you leave for Maine. For a while I thought I could turn the whole thing in my favor by just going on to London and home, forgetting India, but I would regret this no end afterwards. So I've got to pay for my devious way which I had to resort to.

SHIRAZ, IRAN, TO FARAWAY, C. AUGUST 5, 1968

This is after a letter I have ready to mail but never found the moment. An American learns about time in Persia thru his sense of service as he knows it back home which leaves him dazed when at the airport he can't buy a stamp—only when [he] gets into town where, if the post office is open, he after standing in line for twenty minutes, has one and hopes that it is sufficient to cover the distance the letter has to go. So here [I] am with 4 hrs wait in Shiraz airport with an unmailed letter to you in my pocket and with time on my hands, but good because it makes me feel like writing, especially after I ordered a Turkish coffee which just appeared in front of me.

The "comedy of errors" I've been writing to you about—my cleverness about the Pakistani ticket and the way on to India is still with me. So far I haven't heard from India. If I had enough money with me I could have taken the flight on my own but as it is I must wait for India's ticket. I phoned Air India in Tehran from Shiraz at 10 this morning. They had as yet not heard. I am flying back at 8 P.M. from Shiraz to Tehran and maybe, MAYBE, I will find it waiting for me . . . .

I have never written a more uninteresting letter. I cannot enjoy my stay here though I found Persepolis (near Shiraz) wonderful but slightly less than I expected. This was never true of the Greek masterpieces. They only become more and more wonderful.

I am sending these two letters to Faraway because now I am sure that I will have to stay away longer than I expected—from my ever sweet heart. Nathaniel is by now fully a down Mainer but seeing you again must be the greater joy. With his grandmummy, uncles, aunts and cousins, and his special, special mummy, he has everything except his most beloved daddy. I know he loves me and that at this moment causes many tears to come. Good tears. Tears of hope and feeling of goodness.

Love,
Lou

Dearest,

I enclose a letter I failed to post. It was in my bag going thru it to prepare for my trip back to dear old U.S.A. This letter will reach you after I am back. It is all too too crazy. The letter enclosed now as I read it over was innocent of the frustrations I was to meet in Tehran. What a place for service. I might of just as well have been in the middle of the Sahara. Every place seems to close before it opens and when it does open it closes before you can get there. I have left innumerable messages advising how I might get a notion about my trip to India. No one understands and I am quite sure that without my further explanation you don't either.

. . . To get a stamp takes a taxi ride from my hotel MIAMI, which I was directed to by a well meaning Iranian, is in a quiet place alright. It is practically nowhere. I couldn't leave the place for fear that I might get thirsty on the road. They would find me completely dehydrated on my way to somewhere where it takes all day to get to.

But Persia has something, but it is all in the past! It is really the place where a drop of water commences a poem in praise. Desert. Desert. Desert. Water. A rose.

Now again, this letter enclosed didn't get mailed because I did not expect to be met at the airport in Karachi. I thought I would quietly fly to India. But as you already know, I was met by a crew, Pakistani, who were informed that I was flying off to U.S. I had to carry out their expectations and booked a flight to U.S. by way of Tehran and then came the Terror of Tehran, the no place.

Right now I am not in a laughing mood having decided to go back to Philly without having accomplished mission India. Now I am left with still having to serve India soon.

Please excuse my terrible griping.

Love,
Lou

Lou included this scrap of paper with his letter: "This is the note that the Hotel Manager gave me to present to the Taxi driver on my way to center Town." The note reads in Arabic, "Address: Takhte Jamshid Street—in front of Caspian Hotel."

One afternoon I stopped at Lou's office and joined several of the men standing about his desk, theorizing over the proportions and material for an emblem of the Alfred I. duPont–Columbia University Award for broadcast journalism that Lou had agreed to design. Should it be bronze or silver, or maybe gold? Should its form be a trophy, a medal, a baton, a scepter? How should it fit into the hands that gave and received it?

Before long Dave Wisdom, Lou's longest-term employee and self-appointed office manager, stalked out, angry that important projects were stalled by indecision over a trifle. As Lou's only contemporary among a staff of mostly young people, Dave was usually unflappable, rational, and sardonic. He was the loyal Quaker who came and left punctually every day and was essential for the office to function. It was he who often gathered up the pieces after Lou's cliff-hanging departures.

Still, Lou refused to be hurried, for the subject was about the communication of truth and how to form a gesture in an object that bestowed honor, like a knighthood, for a person's dedication to it.

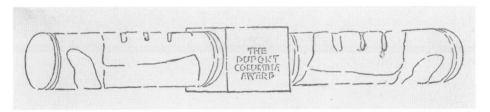

Lou's design for the Alfred I. duPont–Columbia University Award for broadcast journalism: a gold baton, first awarded in November 1969.

In the early fall George called me into his office, put a plan in front of me, and said, "It would be good for you to work on this." It was the latest version of the Kimbell Art Museum in Fort Worth, Texas, which Lou had asked George to help him with. I was thrilled but also scared; it was a big step up to serve as project landscape architect for a major building, and the challenges were daunting. It was a nine-acre site bordered by dusty streets on the outskirts of town, with Philip Johnson's Amon Carter Museum of American Art at one end and the Will Rogers Memorial Center, with its vast cattle barns and rodeo fairgrounds, adjacent. The land had a ten-foot slope, and a wide row of elms that had once lined an old road ran through the middle of it.

Already Lou's building had gone through many variations as he tried to work with the site. He had kept the museum to one story in deference to the view from Johnson's building, and with the wonderful idea of bringing in

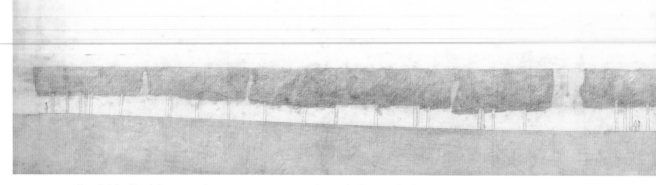

Lou's idealized fourteen-foot west-east section through the Kimbell Art Museum and its park site, expressing his desire to unify the building with the trees and the landscape. Sadly, the primacy of this relationship has been poorly understood in recent years, resulting in a loss of the balance between architecture and nature so eloquently expressed here.

a controlled slice of bright Texas light through roof slits in long modular galleries. At one point these modules took up the entire site, surrounded by an endless arcade, and at another he turned the modules at right angles, which was quite awkward. To deal with the slope, Lou had placed the building on a plinth, which made it sit too high at one end. From the start he had interrupted the modules with interior courtyards, but in the plan George showed me, he had split the building in half, allowing the trees from the old road to flow right through it. To me it seems that the moment Lou opened his building like this to nature, it was the beginning of a new order in his architecture.

I began by addressing the grading, suggesting that the building be taken off the plinth and dug more into the ground. This approach was helped

An office model of the scheme for the Kimbell Art Museum when I first began to work on the project, showing the vaulted modules broken into two wings to incorporate the existing trees.

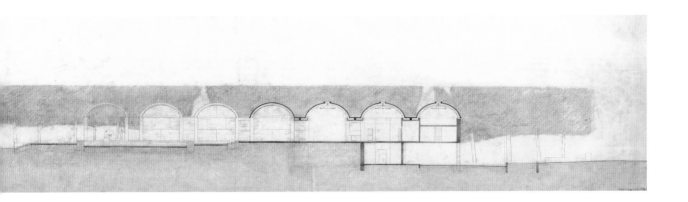

by a visit from the curator and director of the museum, Ric Brown, who interrupted his globe-trotting hunt for art treasures to stop by Philadelphia and let Lou know that the budget needed to be cut and the building made smaller. As a simplified tripartite arrangement of modules emerged, I encouraged Lou to move the building closer to the eastern edge of the site, opening it to the trees and the park, nestling it into the land, making it belong. At one point Lou tried removing the vaulted porches now facing the trees, but I objected. He sat with it for a day or so and then left them, saying, "You know the wonderful thing about porches? They're so unnecessary!" It would be two years before a true partnership between the Kimbell Art Museum building and its site was realized, and in that time, I was able to share in the creation of a great work and grow creatively as never before.

My early landscape plan for the Kimbell Art Museum, finished on October 29, 1968, the day I turned forty. Although I had helped resite the building, at this point I had yet to create a compelling setting for it.

"Mind is just Spirit in the rain." Lou in the Piazza San Marco, Venice, January 1969.

1969

Although Lou turned sixty-eight this year, he had the energy of a man half his age, often racing up the five floors of 1501 Walnut Street two steps at a time. It was a narrow, forlorn building of pale limestone and double-hung black-framed windows, barely twenty feet wide by a hundred feet long, but it was at the epicenter of the architectural world.

Working on Kimbell, I would excitedly climb those steps, where the contrast between George's tasteful carpeted "corporate" premises on the third floor and Lou's no-frills drafting rooms above always hit me with a bit of a shock. With bare floors, unfinished plasterboard walls, and woodshop furniture, Lou's office felt like a cross between an artist's atelier and a sweatshop. The un-air-conditioned fourth floor, with its smell of Plasticine and sawdust, was where Lou's magnificent models were built, while the fifth floor, the main drafting room and reception area, consisted of a couple of bentwood chairs, a coat stand, and a secretary at an IBM Selectric, the only piece of up-to-date technology in the place. To the right of reception was Lou's private office, and to the left, the open drafting room with its twin rows of drafting tables, each with a Luxo lamp, and drawings, books, models, and samples everywhere. The saving grace was superb natural light, which streamed in from windows facing the facade of the Drexel Bank, a monumental stone building modeled after a Florentine palazzo across Fifteenth Street.

During the day Lou would circulate from board to board and project to project, consulting with a single architect or a cluster of three or four, pausing to sketch ideas or revisions on his own roll of yellow tracing paper laid over the drawing being worked on, then escaping after questions with an exclamation or joke. He was a creator in perpetual motion, undeterred by the commotion of visitors, deliveries, ringing phones, and the throb of street traffic.

Sometimes I met directly with Lou and "his men," inspecting the latest Kimbell site model with Vincent Rivera, who rose from office boy to master model maker to architect, or with Marshall Meyers, the gifted project architect, whose poised oversight was to foil nearly all the skullduggery and attempted undercutting from Preston M. Geren, Associates, the by-the-book associated architectural firm in Texas. I was shy and kept my head down, but I began to know a few of the younger people in the office, including the lone draftswoman, Leslie Armitage, who was dating Argentine Carles Vallhonrat, and Edgar Engelskirche, a fun, dark-haired Bavarian who had fallen in love with Heidi Shleigel, who worked with me at George's downstairs.

Lou and I were able again to visit some of our Philadelphia haunts of a decade before, often meeting on the stairs to slip away to Zum Zum, where Lou might have a Rolling Rock and a corned beef sandwich, or down Walnut Street, past the newsstand, travel agency, and Taws art supply store, to the Colonnade, an old-fashioned cafeteria in the basement of an office building that served American fare—meatloaf or sliced turkey, mashed potatoes with gravy, and overcooked string beans—from a steam table.

My mother had died in November of the previous year, which was a deep loss, but I was comforted in knowing that she had lived long enough to see me, her youngest child, gainfully employed, and that I had had the chance to tell her I was engaged in work I believed in with all my heart: that I had found not just a profession but a calling. My world was a small one compared to Lou's, however, which continued to broaden every day as he grabbed his tiny valise with a couple of shirts and headed straight from the office to the airport.

Lou arrived in Venice in late January for the presentation of his plans for the Biennale convention complex. The office had made drawings and built a large model showing the three proposed buildings: a jewel-box entry off the lagoon, the Arts Exhibition Building, and the Palazzo dei Congressi, all nested among rare trees of the Giardini Pubblici.

Venice, with the wooded site between the lagoon and the Rio dei Giardini.

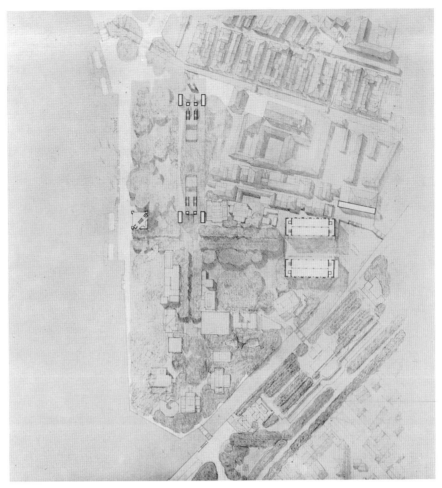

Lou's Biennale site plan, with footprints of the entry (left), the Palazzo dei Congressi (center), and the two wings of the Arts Exhibition Building (right).

The palazzo itself was amazing, a total original for a city that was also one of a kind. Uncharacteristically exuberant, this concrete-and-glass fantasy was to swoop across the gardens, touching down lightly on its piers like an object from outer space, barely disturbing the park's eight hundred trees. The building's emblematic presence, with its 2,500-seat auditorium sloping gently from both sides to a central stage, promised to be a destination of enhanced civic life, inviting people from all over the world to, as Lou put it, "Come here, meet others, and something good will happen to you!"

Deeper in the wooded site, Lou placed the Arts Exhibition Building, with two parallel three-story wings facing each other, containing fine art galleries and studios for artists. The eighty-by-two-hundred-foot piazza between the wings could be open to the sky in fine weather or shielded by massive bronze doors and a deployable glass and steel roof.

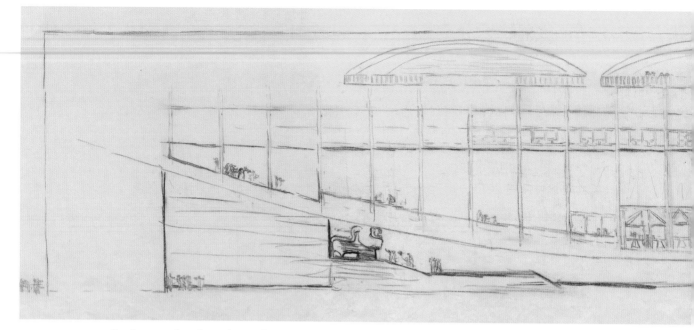

Lou's seven-foot-long charcoal presentation drawing of the Palazzo dei Congressi. Lou loved the gondolas of Venice, and the swooping form of the building was inspired partly by them, but it is also a channeling of the bowl-like space of the Piazza del Campo in Siena, which he admired.

The Arts Exhibition Building, with gallery spaces below and artist studios above. Half of the deployable roof is open to the sky in Lou's sketch.

Lou presenting the Biennale Festival of the Arts convention complex model at the Doge's Palace, Venice, February 1, 1969.

VENICE TO 8870 TOWANDA ST., PHILADELPHIA, FEBRUARY 2, 1969

Dearest Girl and Boy,
It went very well. Busy night and day to finish exhibit and then the press WOWEE! Leaving now for India. Will have a good chance to write.

Love,
Lou

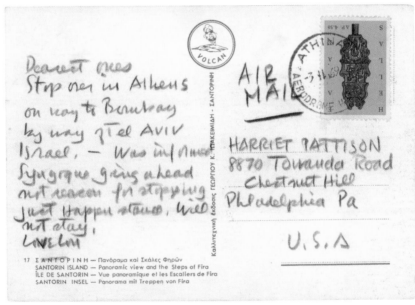

ATHENS TO TOWANDA ST., FEBRUARY 3, 1969

Dearest ones,
Stopover in Athens on way to Bombay by way of Tel Aviv Israel. —
Was informed synagogue going ahead. Not reason for stopping, just
happen stance. Will not stay.

Love,
Lou

AIR-INDIA

On board
the Magic Carpet

Dearest Harriet

I have had a constant streak of work
going while in India. The work is going well
but slow. They wait for my every decision
before proceeding. This time they waited for
nearly a year and a half. I have held them
back on my decisions coming almost to a
breaking point.

I have read nothing since my leaving. I wonder
about the reaction to the Venice presentation,
and I wonder most of all sweetheart how my
precious sweetheart and anothe precious sweetheart
are. So only in a few days sweetheart.

Love Coy

Dearest Harriet,

I have had a constant streak of work going while in India. The work is going well but slow. They wait for my every decision before proceeding this time they waited for nearly a year and a half. I have held them back on my decisions coming almost to a breaking point.

I have read nothing since my leaving. I wonder about the reaction to the Venice presentation, and I wonder most of all sweetheart how my precious sweetheart and another precious sweetheart are. So only in a few days sweetheart.

Love,
Lou

ZURICH TO TOWANDA ST., FEBRUARY 12, 1969

Beautiful Switzerland because all man made work is made small compared to the mountains.

Daddy

Lou in Zurich, February 12, 1969.

On the way back to Philadelphia from Venice and India, Lou gave a talk, "Silence and Light," at the Swiss Federal Institute of Technology (ETH) in Zurich. For Lou, Silence is the mystery one feels at the pyramids, and Light is the material world in all its forms and manifestations. He imagined that art arises from the threshold where the two meet each other, a coming-together of desire with what is possible. It seems to me that the roots of "Silence and Light" were already there in Ina, the concept Lou had written to me about in 1959, although he may not have recognized this. In the talk he said: "So I must put on the board something which I thought of only recently, what could be a key to my point of view in regard to all works of art including architecture. . . . And so, I put this on the board: Silence and Light."

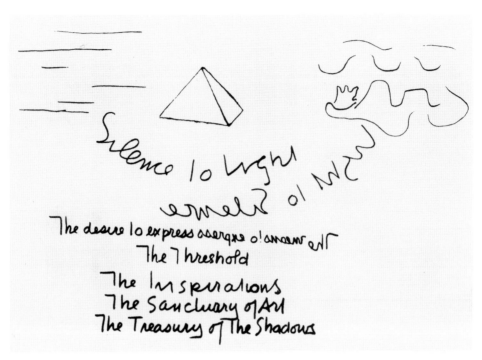

One of the many drawings Lou made around this time exploring his thoughts about "Silence and Light."

Silence to Light / Light to Silence
The desire to express / the means to express
The Threshold
The Inspirations
The Sanctuary of Art
The Treasury of the Shadows

For the occasion of the talk, ETH also mounted a comprehensive exhibition of Lou's work, organized by its architecture department and Ralph Baenziger, a young architect who had visited 1501 Walnut Street and had walked with Nathaniel, Lou, and me to Rittenhouse Square one weekend morning. Baenziger printed facsimiles of the panels from the exhibition, bound them with a transcription of the talk overnight, and handed several copies of the unwieldy volume to Lou as he left Switzerland for America. Lou liked the book very much and gave me a copy on his return. I treasure it to this day.

Teddy Kollek, Lou, and Buckminster Fuller in Jerusalem.

KING DAVID HOTEL, JERUSALEM, TO TOWANDA ST., MAY [29], 1969

Dearest Harriet and Nathaniel,
. . . I am in Jerusalem under the auspices of the Mayor [of]
Jerusalem. I have come from an artificial session on Religion with
all sects of religion present. Those silent are the only ones who said
something. It was a delight to meet Buckminster Fuller who when
he saw me kissed me on my lips . . .

Louis I Kahn

In June Lou traveled again to India by way of Jerusalem, where he presented a
revised set of plans for the Hurva Synagogue, as well as preliminary thoughts
for a new town in the barren hills overlooking the Old City. While there, he
spent time with Mayor Teddy Kollek, the architect Buckminster Fuller, and
the architect Moshe Safdie, who had worked in Lou's office from 1962 to 1964
and had recently launched his own career in spectacular fashion with Habitat,
the model community for Expo 67, the world's fair held in Montreal.

Dearest,

The city of Jerusalem is not like any other place. The outcropping of the hills and the houses are alike, stone and stone.

I saw the city, old and new, from a distant place which before the Six-Day War was the no man's land which neither Jew nor Arab ventured to cross. Those who tried to build were fired on. That sight from the distance was like a field of heather—lavender against the light of the setting sun. The stories of the Bible come to their setting to be continued.

I have been asked to build a small city on the no man's land. I wish I could have been a soldier in defense of it to feel the homeland devotion and not merely the architect. This field when studded with dwelling has still to feel this view of ancient Jerusalem. Like fine cuts of a hillside forest, gaps should be left where building cannot be.

In my absence the plans for the Hurva (synagogue and the environs) were badly interpreted. Tomorrow—Sunday—I must try to bring it back to its good meaning. Objections, completely ill-founded, have grown. What a constant bother to entrust thoughts to others.

Tomorrow, Sunday, I see the Mayor of Jerusalem, I see the head Deputy of Religious Affairs, I see the Prime Minister, the minister of Jerusalem Development, and other ministers. I fear the difficulty of leading people away from wrong notions. I may actually fail.

They are excavating deep into the ground discovering old ruins dating back to Biblical days. After tomorrow, I will write again. Monday, I leave for India.

Good night my sweethearts.

Love,
Lou

Lou in Ahmedabad, conferring with his friend, architect Balkrishna Doshi, and staff from the National Institute of Design.

I miss Nathaniel and you very much.

It was the day before the meeting of the ministers now headed by [Yigal] Allon in the absence of Golda Meir, Prime Minister, that I wrote you expressing my apprehensions. That day, I worked to sum up the reactions and adjust to them. The archaeological finding the uncovering of building under rubble caused by fighting now revealed points of departure I could not have anticipated; but it still remains surprising how much I did anticipate what would be found.

I [put] things together enough to make a presentation to the ministers after reviewing the modified arrangement with the Mayor of Jerusalem and the head of planning of Jerusalem. The ministers liked the scheme, praised it as inspirational. I left the meeting feeling a new confidence.

The same day the Mayor offered that I plan a large section of Jerusalem, the one I mentioned on free ground. This is a difficult decision for me to make—that is in regard to the—interest in building a little town and the time to do it. Associations become more and more intolerable—What to do?

Now I am arrived in the center of the Sun's touch. Still Jerusalem must claim priority. It was the period of the Hamsin, which means 50. Fifty days thru the year of heat and air stillness. White heat like the center of a furnace. Cars park only in the shade. The slightest touch of the sun on a car seat as you enter burns your skin off. Blankets must cover everywhere you sit or lean against in the car. I drank gallons of water so dehydrated is the body. But I know Ahmedabad can equal it.

I am told that my visits will have to be less frequent because foreign exchange is difficult and decisions must be made more on the site. This again is not easy for me because straying from my intentions are constant. Whom can I trust to make everyday decisions in my absence? I am now to meet Kasturbhai the head—to talk it over.

Love,
Lou

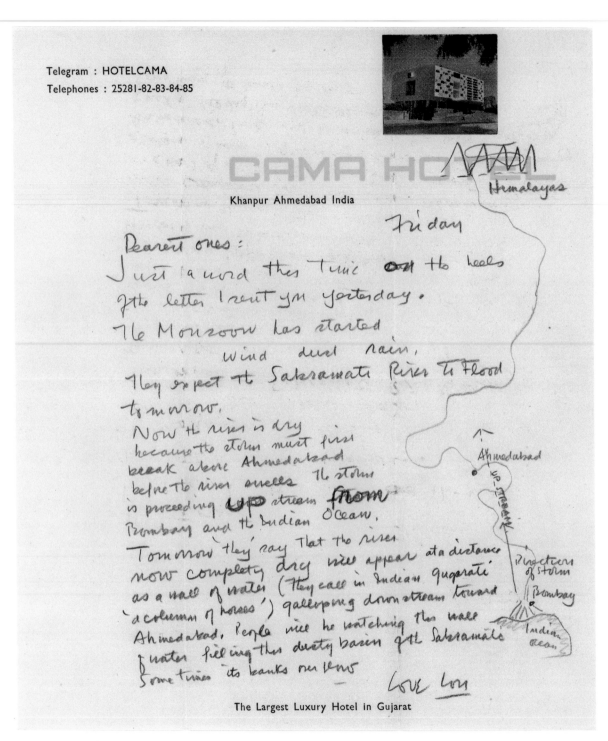

Telegram : HOTELCAMA
Telephones : 25281-82-83-84-85

Khanpur Ahmedabad India

Friday

Dearest ones:
Just a word this time on the heels
of the letter I sent you yesterday.
The Monsoon has started
                    wind   dust   rain.
They expect the Sabramati River to flood
tomorrow.
  Now the river is dry
because the storm must first
break above Ahmedabad
before the river swells. The storm
is proceeding UP stream from
Bombay and the Indian Ocean.
Tomorrow 'they' say that the river
now completely dry will appear at a distance
as a wall of water (They call in Indian gujarati
'a column of horses') galloping down stream toward
Ahmedabad. People will be watching the wall
of water filling the dusty basin of the Sabramati
Sometimes its banks overflow —
                         Love Lou

The Largest Luxury Hotel in Gujarat

Indian Ocean / Bombay / Direction of Storm / UP STREAM / Ahmedabad / Himalayas

282

Friday

Dearest ones:

Just a word this time on the heels of the letter I sent you yesterday.

The Monsoon has started

wind dust rain.

They expect the Sabarmati River to flood tomorrow.

Now the river is dry because the storm must first break above Ahmedabad before the river swells. The storm is proceeding up stream from Bombay and the Indian Ocean.

Tomorrow "they" say that the river now completely dry will appear at a distance as a wall of water (they call in Indian Gujarati "a column of horses") galloping downstream toward Ahmedabad. People will be watching the wall of water filling this dusty basin of the Sabarmati. Sometimes its banks over flow.

Love,

Lou

Saturday Night

Dearest,

That column of water down the river has yet not come. The river spread in front of my window is still a dry bed of sand. One of Corbusier's buildings is in my view on the opposite side. Brahmin cows, buffalo, camels, walk across all day. It has been raining and all low-lying lands are flooded. The rain is slurped up as it falls into the thirsty sand of the river bed. Flies of all description have come to life after only the second day of rain. Anywhere a light is they swarm to. I have had nothing but Indian food. I long for a lamb chop a la Harriet and a lusty hug from both my beautiful Nathaniel and Harriet.

Love,

Lou

A view from the northwest of the great plaza at IIM, with administration wing (left), library (center), and classroom wing (right).

Dearest,

Tonight I was invited to dinner to the Sarabhais'. They live out of town on the Sabarmati River in a house designed by Gira Sarabhai who composed it out of carved structural wood members taken from old houses which were torn down years ago. It is ingeniously done. They invited members of the family—all beautiful people.

We sat down to a dinner served squatting with attendants bending low to hand the dishes of food to you. There were easily 20 varieties of vegetables and fruit and chapati. After I unlocked my legs to stand, we took places to sit, I sharing a deep bed like sofa in which one sits cross legged. No sooner did I lean back when a rat flew out of the pillow in back ran thru my legs across the room and beyond. Gautam Sarabhai then told of a snake that came from the same place yesterday—a 7 foot poisonous one—they locked all the doors to contain him and trap him.

This is India. He explained that the rain fills the holes in the ground they live in and are forced out in the open. This is true of the rats too.

With all my love to Nathaniel and you.

Lou

Taken to great Mughal sites like Fatehpur Sikri and Mandu as well as to local
villages by Balkrishna Doshi, his architect associate and friend, Lou had absorbed
a feel not only for India's architecture but also for the ways in which it dealt
structurally with both searing heat and the torrential rains of the monsoon.
In his designs for the Indian Institute of Management (IIM), Lou used many
of these traditional solutions, including deep recesses to control glare, terraces
raised against monsoon flooding, and buildings oriented on the diagonal to take
advantage of cooling winds. But when it came to the lake that Lou had proposed
to control water and unify the campus, one of his patrons, Kasturbhai Lalbhai,
objected. As a devout Jain, Kasturbhai believed in the sacredness of all life and
did not want to be responsible for exterminating the mosquitoes that would
have bred in the water. The lake was therefore eliminated from the design,
although at the height of the monsoon it naturally occurs anyway, doubling
Lou's infinitely varied brick forms in watery reflection as he had imagined.

I marveled that Lou could change gears without delay. Returning to
Philadelphia, he spun back immediately into the Kimbell project, over which
I'd toiled for eight months. Groundbreaking was scheduled for July, but Lou
would again be in India, Dhaka, and Israel at that time.

TOP: An open-air hallway at IIM, overlooking the great plaza.

BOTTOM: The spaces between buildings at IIM become a rich variety of "outdoor rooms."

A procession of dormitories with cylindrical stair towers at IIM.

Mrs. Kimbell had requested a narrative about the landscape, so I gladly composed one. Lou and I edited it together, and Lou carefully copied it out by hand, giving it a personal touch that no typewriter could replicate. He asked me for a sketch, which I made on a page of notepaper to affirm the live reality of our design. Lou added his hand to my drawing with several labels, signed off with a few friendly words on its edge, folded it, and sent it with the letter overnight to Texas.

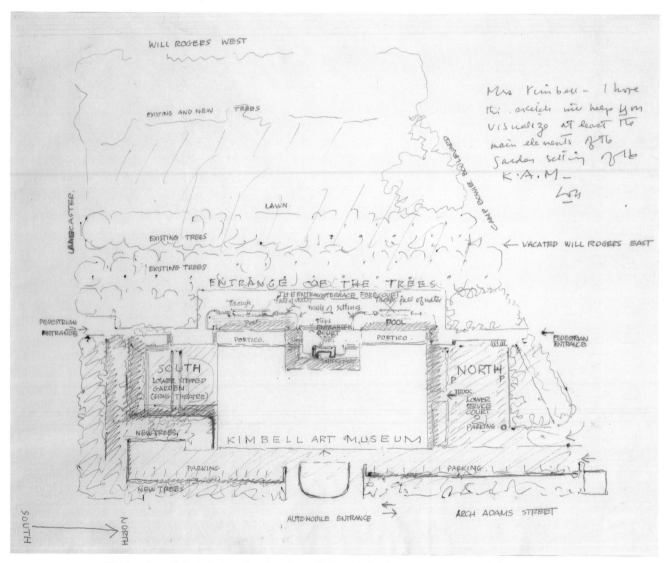

My drawing of the Kimbell site plan, June 1969, with Lou's note to Mrs. Kimbell: "Mrs Kimbell—I hope this sketch will help you visualize at least the main elements of the Garden setting of the K.A.M.—Lou."

Dear Mrs Kimbell:

I plan to come to see you soon to show and explain the Garden ideas I have surrounding the Kimbell Art Museum. I hope you will find my work beautiful and meaningful.

The entrance of the trees is the entrance by foot, which links Camp Bowie Boulevard and West Lancaster Ave. Two open porticos flank the entrance court of terrace. In front of each portico is a reflecting pool which drops its water in a continuous sheet about 70 feet long in a basin two feet below. The sound would be gentle. The stepped entrance court passes between the porticos and their pools with a fountain, around which one sits, on axis designed to be the source of the portico pools. The west lawn gives the building perspective.

The south garden is at a level 10 feet below the garden entrance approached by gradual stepped lawns shaped to be a place to sit to watch the performance of a play, music or dance the building with its arched silhouette acting as the back drop of a stage. When not in use it will seem only as a garden where sculpture acquired from time to time would be.

The North Garden though mostly utilitarian is designed with ample trees to shield and balance the south and north sides of the building.

The car entrance and parking is also at the lower level, running parallel to Arch Adams Street. This end too is lined with trees designed to overhang the cars as shelter. For this we must choose the right tree whose habits are respectful to the car tops.

When I see you I expect to bring a model, which should say more than my little words.

By now you know that I cannot be present at the ground breaking ceremony. Unfortunately I have emergency duties in India at the same time. In my absence I wish everything well.

I am confident that the work will progress well from now on. I believe everyone believes in the building and its good purposes.

I expect to return from India by the 13th of July. I will need a few weeks to firm up the material I hope to present to you for discussion.

Sincerely yours,
Louis I Kahn

TOP: The Canopus Pool at Hadrian's Villa in Tivoli, mirroring the imperial colonnade and sculptures, was a touchstone for the porticos and fountains at the Kimbell.

BOTTOM: The terrace of one hundred fountains at the Villa d'Este was pure Renaissance magic that inspired us in designing the water drama for the Kimbell.

290

The design for the landscape of the Kimbell Art Museum had developed along with the building until the two had merged into a single three-dimensional entity—a place. Lou had begun calling it "the Villa in the Garden," and indeed we had both drawn inspiration from the interweaving of landscape and architecture at Hadrian's Villa and in the Italian Renaissance gardens at Villa d'Este and Villa Lante, which Lou did not know well, but which I had loved since visiting them during my year in Italy.

The landscape for the Kimbell now included multiple levels, offering many ways to encounter the building, especially emphasizing the diagonal, oblique views and approaches. There were pathways, ramps, and steps, and a large sunken "Theater Garden" against the dramatic vaulted south wall that I imagined could be used for performances—plays, music, and dance—making the museum a destination after hours as well. I had pushed for this, and Lou embraced it instinctively, realizing that it made his building more relevant and challenging, rather than being only a repository for the visual arts. It was here, in a pool beneath crepe myrtles, that we had hoped to place the bronze Aristide Maillol sculpture of a floating female nude that was one of the first pieces acquired for the new museum; somehow the piece suggested the unity of all the arts that had once been in the ancient world, before commerce had pried painting and sculpture away from their brothers and sisters in the performing arts.

The use of water had also developed; gone was the dead reflecting pool between the porticos from earlier schemes, replaced now by fountains emerging from the entrance court and cascading into active pools before flowing around the building and falling into a grotto that I had designed for the Theater Garden. Lou called this "the odyssey of water," and we both wanted it to be realized in its entirety, as did George Patton in the office downstairs, where we set about detailing it.

Dearest,

I should not be entrusted to make a master plan by any one.
I managed it so to make life difficult to fly from Tel Aviv to
London—London to Karachi, Dhaka when I could have waited a
day and flown on to Karachi by way of Tehran (Persia) the next day
and not wear myself out by retracing my steps.

Just think of the Stupidity!!!!

I did terribly in Israel. One delegate of the International
Committee on Jerusalem condemned my synagogue as Pagan. Damn
it could be right but maybe Religion is only good when Pagan. The
one God—I don't know. I only know how I feel.—It all—this reaction
by—by an archeologist may be so. I suddenly saw my synagogue
hatefully, felt he was right but I defended it nastily—I did terribly.

I am writing in the plane. I have to bury my misery in drink. I
had a tall scotch. I felt angry about my travel nonsense and the way
things went. Right now I don't want to see Jerusalem ever any more.
I want to laugh about my own sense of religion. I am in a dream
world, which no one will share. Yet I know it is human and true.

So if I did not love you I would not have written. I may have to
go back to J. to save all avenues of expression, J. being one.

Love to Nathaniel and you,

Lou

Kent Larson's computer rendition of what the interior of the Hurva Synagogue
might have been like.

EN ROUTE JERUSALEM–DHAKA, EAST PAKISTAN, TO TOWANDA ST.,
JULY 4, 1969

Dearest Mommy:

I have left Jerusalem with heaviness of feeling. The synagogue is
being nibbled away at by the divided religious factions and little
critics doubting a bit here a bit there. They do not see I only
consider it an offering waiting for someone's eye and heart to meet
and to inspire me with new feelings for me to translate.

    But I may be unduly wary—

Love,
Lou

EN ROUTE JERUSALEM—DHAKA TO TOWANDA ST., JULY 4, 1969

Dearest Boy O' Mine:
The architecture would seem like ginger bakery to us.

To the people of the East it is an expression of delight to give delight.

I think of you always and with all my love.

Daddy

In the two postcards Lou sent from Dhaka on July 4, he did not note that the Pakistani stamps depict not only a historic mosque but also an image of his own National Assembly Building, which was, although still many years from completion, already iconic.

In August I went to a family meeting in Maine to settle our mother's estate with my brothers and sisters. As conflicts inevitably arose, I would telephone Lou. His advice was solid and measured, but suddenly I couldn't reach him. When I called his secretary, I was told he was having emergency surgery. I panicked, thinking I might never see him again. The next morning I heard that his gall bladder had been removed, and that he was out of danger, but I couldn't find out what hospital he was in, and I had no way to reach him.

Days later I received an envelope addressed in an unfamiliar hand. It enclosed a letter from Lou and a scrap of decorated script, meant to amuse me, but it made me sad. To this day I don't know whether he had disguised his handwriting to hide that he was writing to me from his hospital bed from his wife, Esther, or from my family, and especially my brothers, now in charge at Faraway. I remember wishing that the secrecy would end and that at last we could just be truthful with the world and be together.

 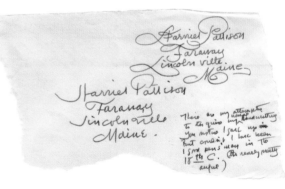

The envelope, perhaps addressed by Lou's secretary, and the scrap enclosed with the letter, reading, "These are my attempts to disguise my usual handwriting. You notice I gave up. But couldn't I have been 1 good pens'man in the 18th C. (It's really pretty awful.)"

Dearest ones:

Monday

I was correcting a paper I am writing and realized how meager is the superlative. When I say "It is good to see you," how warm are such words compared to "It is very good to see you," "I love you," and "I love you very much." The measure does not respond to the Psyche. The more the measure the more it becomes the language of science.

I promised a good while ago a foreword to a book on villages made without the architect. I see the world, this variegated play of green blue and rose, as a marble in space. —Alone, unique in its being in the full bloom of life giving. From out in space the work of the villager and the work of the architect resemble one another. Mars impressed me because its atmosphere is barely detectable which tells me that many millions of years from now it will have a richness of life giving ingredients shaped into being different from that on our earth and hopefully of such attitudes that their expressions have more reverence for the wonderful privilege to be alive.

2

As I looked thru my hospital window the drabness of man's work is more depressing than the deepest pain. I remember Aline Saarinen's relaying the words of Eero, who got up for a moment to look outside—"When I get well I am going to change this whole mess. Redesign everything." It seems so disgraceful the way we are crudding up the world with works motivated by moneychangers. How pure really are the villages made by craftsmen with great desires and eager fingers holding only the simplest of tools. How un-pure are the architects whose desire are beclouded by the knowhow of technology away from the hands akin to desire.

The office has been coming in to review projects. In my absence very little of value has come about. I am trying to work but the pain is still too great to allow concentration.

Do not allow yourself to be pressured. It is not as though you were buying from the market. I want to talk everything over with you. You need a happy solution. Use this time of vacation to gather all the angles. We'll go over them for good plans. I long so much to see you and Nathaniel and hear about the joys of Maine.

I have been reading a book on Edward Lear, landscape painter. A more luck-less story of struggle against the odds of undue modesty, not a full impulsive talent, little money, epilepsy, few friends, a fickle public, self-criticism. Constant is strain of these conditions. So hard for a man who wrote the nonsense rhymes of the "Owl and the Pussycat" etc., the only work from which he derived something of an income. It's a hard book to read with my own constant pain yet it has its good effects.

I will try to write often—With all my love,

Lou

In her will, my mother had left me something remarkable: Indian Island. Actually, no one else wanted it, and what was I to do with such a rustic place, which I could not afford? "Get practical, H'ie, sell it!" said my brothers, who regarded it as a nuisance rather than a marvelous gift. But I had different ideas, dreams really, remembering when Lou and I had gone there nine years before. Could this island in Penobscot Bay that was now unbelievably mine become a haven for the three of us? A place in the sun that Lou could come to, even for a few days, where we could be ourselves, far from intrigue or secrecy. A home by the sea.

Nathaniel and me on Indian Island.

Lou's drawing of the Temple of Karnak, Egypt, 1951.

PHILADELPHIA TO FARAWAY, AUGUST 1969

It is so frustrating not to be near you when you are so upset. I am tied to my pains and need for constant rest. I am not yet able to move about because of the internal pains but I do feel that I am getting better. I am really playing hooky from the hospital where I should have stayed a few more days.

Yesterday I had a beautiful dream. We were in Egypt in the life silent halls of columns. Nathaniel you and I.

Above all do not lose courage nor make anyone doubt your courage. Don't let your impetuousness rule decision. Ask for the time you need to make a workable decision about the island. Don't let Abbott pressure you or scare you with insurmountables. If you show your firmness to keep the Island and show your practical sense not to dive in, with planning though, fully and economically, then you will have the faith even of [your niece] Pam who certainly is so akin to you. I cannot write much now.

I love you.

Lou

Find a US Geodetic Survey of Indian Island

Dearest Harriet and Nathaniel,

I waited for you. Saturday all day. Sunday, I didn't get in because the elevator does not run. Climbing stairs as yet not advised. I was told by Edgar that you called those ten days.

I am trying very much to work. It is not easy—but I am getting along. Saw the surgeon who approves of my condition.

I read and reread your letter. With all the unexpected support of Margaret and furthermost the understanding of Pam you should feel a little less alone. . . . I am so happy you are happy. I know the precariousness of the whole situation but admire so much your response to natural inclination in you which said to hold onto the Island. But you must admit how close you came to surrendering to brain washing. . . .

Love,
Lou

Indian Island, Rockport, Maine, painted by Alexandra Tyng, Nathaniel's half sister.

My study sketch exploring planting options for the entrance court at the Kimbell Art Museum.

1970

Lou was a man of the city, but he had a strong connection to nature. He'd spent the first years of his life in a village by the sea in Estonia and had made summer trips to Canada and the Adirondacks with Esther and friends in the 1930s. On these journeys, as on the grand tour he'd taken to Europe in 1928, Lou drew landscapes as often as he drew buildings, lavishing great attention on trees, rocks, streams, and distant hills, sometimes with an idyllic hamlet nestled among them.

If there was no longer time for such excursions now, still Lou craved moments of escape to nature, and he loved to spend a few hours on the high back porch of our house on Towanda Street, amid layered shades of the Wissahickon forest with its towering tulip poplars, feathery hemlocks, sturdy oak and ash, and flowering dogwood that danced on the margins. Sometimes we would walk the Adlers' property together, admiring the copper beech, the horse chestnut, and the great Atlas cedar that spread its dark boughs over the lawn behind the main house. While Lou didn't know the names of these trees, he was exquisitely sensitive to their color, scale, and character.

From the start Lou's design for the Kimbell had been shaped by the line of elm trees that ran through the middle of the site. At first he had incorporated them directly into the building, allowing them to bisect it into two wings, but now that the building had a smaller footprint, they had become the main vista from the porticos and I added oaks to their number, extending and thickening the line.

For the fountains and the odyssey of water, I had to master new facts and techniques, and for the plantings I learned a new palette of North Texas plants, aided by a local landscape architect and an expert nurseryman. I specified a grove of crepe myrtles for the Theater Court and designed pathway layouts and shrub plantings to screen off streets and guide the visitor: pittosporum hedges, informal groupings of viburnums, rhaphiolepis, and cherry laurels beneath four varieties of oaks and London planes, with hollies and scattered redbuds—all to achieve harmonious sequences for each building face, while rising to the high drama of the entrance porticos.

A solution for the forecourt was vexing. I sketched many ideas, including a trellis with vines to evoke a villa grape arbor, but in the end a grove of low

trees in scale with the porticos felt right. It would be as if they had always
been there, and the building had been built to embrace them. I wanted to use
European hornbeams, as they had the desired character, but they would not
have survived in the hot Texas sun. The tree from the list that would achieve
a similar effect was the evergreen Yaupon holly. I detailed forty of them to be
planted on ten-foot centers. Walking beneath them, with the crunch of gravel
underfoot and the murmur of falling water on either side, one would leave the
busy world behind and enter the realm of art. Lou, meanwhile, was far away
in Dhaka.

INTERCONTINENTAL HOTEL, DHAKA, EAST PAKISTAN,
TO 8870 TOWANDA ST., PHILADELPHIA, JANUARY 17, 1970

'H'y,
. . . We have come mainly on account of the Ayub Hospital. Our
original concept was approved years back. The foundations were
installed and have been laying waiting for the super structure
for 2 years and more. The structure remains but the interior
has been changed a number of times and always for the worse.
Now they have attached two other hospital functions: Tropical
Medical School and Cancer Research Hospital. The nursing
wings (where the patient has his bed and services) have luckily
been made resourceful enough to take more anticipated beds. The
O.P.D. building (out patient department) is that archy building you
like. They think [the] building is more aesthetic than a building
has to be for its use. I TELL YOU THEY ARE WRONG
AS OUR AMERICANS ARE WRONG ABOUT PEOPLE
AND BUILDINGS.
   The doctors who are the only ones who know about the
functions in this country are completely suppressed by the
government people. They like my plans but I must wait for the
word of the politically installed director who is smart about figures
and stupid about lasting values. Everything is square foot and $.
   I have been here two days now and I have heard only complaints
mostly due to their out smarting themselves about the regularity of
payments to us. They hold back paying us. What can they expect
from us?—yet we have always more than served them and never
complained about the numerous changes made by a succession
of always new people in-charge critical of the preceding man in-
charge. We are in the middle and even thought to be inadequate

because we don't come with the commercial handle of "expert" in hospitals. You know the so called expert who is invariably the failure in his profession and must take up a specialty to be recognized. I explained at one point by the old adage, "an expert is a man away from home."

This [is] not a nice letter but [I] write it because I cannot sleep. It is 6 a.m. Maybe today will bring a more pleasant outlook.

Love,
Lou

As at Kimbell, Lou used porches for the "archy" outpatient building at the Ayub National Hospital in Dhaka. Here they not only offer shelter from the weather but also serve as a broad indoor/outdoor room where extended families gather, sometimes for days at a time.

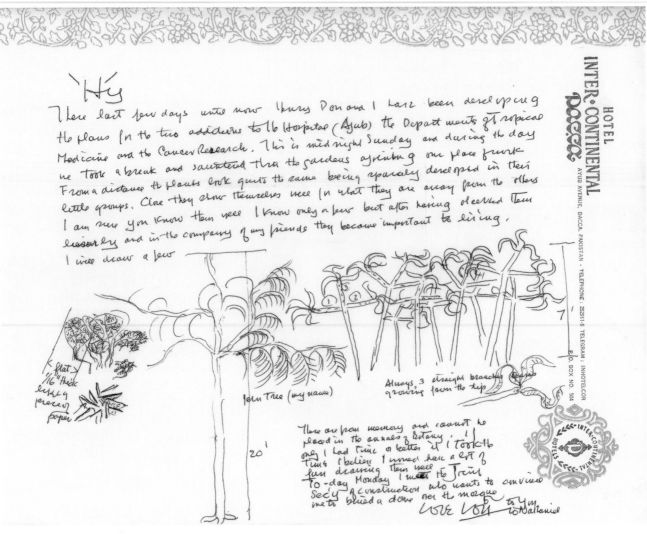

flat, ¹/₁₆" thick, like a piece of paper / fern tree (my name), 20' / Always 3 straight branches growing from the tip / leaves / 7'

'H'y,

These last few days until now Henry [Wilcots], Don [Barbaree]
and I have been developing the plans for the two additions to the
Hospital (Ayub): the Departments of Tropical Medicine and the
Cancer Research. This is midnight Sunday and during the day we
took a break and sauntered thru the gardens adjoining our place of
work. From a distance the plants look quite the same being sparsely
developed in their little groups. Close they show themselves well
for what they are away from the others. I am sure you know them
well. I know only a few, but after having observed them leisurely
and in the company of my friends they became important to living.
I will draw a few:

These are from memory and cannot be placed in the annals of
Botany. If only I had time, or better if I took the time, I believe I
would have a lot of fun drawing them well.

Today, Monday, I meet the Joint Secretary of Construction who
wants to convince me to build a dome over the mosque.

Love,

Lou

to you

to Nathaniel

In May Lou traveled to Rome to give a talk, managing to slip away to Tivoli
to see Hadrian's Villa again and also the Renaissance masterpiece the Villa
d'Este, perhaps for the first time. Then he was off to London to discuss his
latest commission—the Yale Center for British Art—with advisors to Paul
Mellon, the renowned patron of the arts and breeder of horses, who was
giving his collection of British art to his alma mater and paying for a new
museum in New Haven to house it. I didn't see it at the time, but the Spanish
Steps (shown in the following postcard) may have been an inspiration for the
elaborate stairway Lou would include in the first scheme for the Yale building.

Dear Harriet and Nathaniel,
I am writing with a pen I bought for you. My trip to London is postponed a day so will fly back on Thursday instead of Wednesday. I mailed the packages you gave me to London with a note explaining to each.
This stay is turning out to be a little holiday. Yesterday I visited Villa Adriana and Villa D'Este. Both are marvelous to see. The water works and gardens of V—D'Este are under...
Miss you both very much,
Love Lou

Harriet Pattison
8870 Towanda Street
(Chestnut Hill)
Philadelphia
Pennsylvania,
U. S. A.

ROME TO TOWANDA ST., MAY 25, 1970

Dear Harriet and Nathaniel,
I am writing with a pen I bought for you. My trip to London is postponed a day so will fly back on Thursday instead of Wednesday. I mailed the packages you gave me to London with a note explaining to each.

   This stay is turning out to be a little holiday. Yesterday I visited Villa Adriana and Villa d'Este. Both are marvelous to see. The water works and gardens of V— d'Este are wonderful. Miss you both very much.

Love,
Lou

On the evening of August 1, Lou saw Nathaniel and me off for Maine at the Greyhound bus terminal in Philadelphia. I called him from the pay phone by the wharf in Rockport the next morning, surrounded by boxes of groceries and a gallon of kerosene for the lights and gasoline for the pump. With no phone or electricity on Indian Island and with Lou on the way to Dhaka, we both knew it would be several weeks before we would talk again.

Tuesday afternoon
Dearest 'H' and Dearest 'N',
Am reboarding in transit from Geneva to Tehran (Persia) by way
of Beirut (Lebanon). I left Philadelphia with my half-finished
drawings and too little sleep. When I arrived in London, I was too
tired to write. I slept on the plane from London to Geneva and now
just starting out, I have the paper and the "go" to write. . . .

I see the both of you getting in that bus, the filthy platform, the
background to your beautiful faces. It reminded me of passages in
Dr. Zhivago of "misery and beauty." But your voice from Rockport
was like from a survivor of the Titanic. That dark bus beset with
self-concerned faces stunned by the heat and the low-ness of service
and ill regard for others all around. The bus attitude is intolerable.
Only those deeply in love and together can cut thru its degradation.
NO! Walk.

I look at it all from the all importance of self-expression. Just
how strong is this passion? Can it be so strong that one could
actually decide to walk from Philadelphia to Rockport!

My dearest ones, I will try to keep on my promise to write
every day.

With all my love,
Lou

Monday night—the night before Tuesday night, the night before
Wednesday night when I leave.
Hi 'H'-N,
Counting the days—what a bunch—did much work, all angles,
even landscape—kind of trees mostly—with Horticulturalist; very
nice man, knows a lot feels a lot about plants. Likes to give a tree
room to breathe. Will bring back some of his suggestions (studied in
Japan / is no composer). Will be fun to work out some of our details.

Negotiations on Hospital tomorrow, sad business, hoping to
come with sound idea, good only for them and m-ay-be even for me.

We are—the gang—discussing it tonight.

Lots of love,
Lou

Dearest 'H'e and Nathaniel,
Today I spent explaining the lighting of the site including the water
garden on the island. I have yet not seen Siddique who is away in
West Pakistan. After lunch I felt sickish went to my room. Took my
dysentery pills and took to bed. Got up at 9, felt well, went down
to dinner. The floods are the worse ever. Warnings everywhere
about water, Cholera, Typhoid. I am extremely cautious, yet a little
something might slip thru.

Word has gotten around that I am ready to negotiate on more
reasonable terms for the hospital. At this point, I do not know how
much good the Ambassador has done. Tomorrow, I meet some
authorities.

Love,
Lou

Incidentally, for dinner I had 2 bananas and 4 hardboiled eggs

Sunday
Dearest Angels,
I wrote you 4 letters from Pakistan. Mail is slow. Did you get
them? Since I have returned (Thursday night), I waited for a
call every morning figuring the logical time for your shopping.
I imagine now, since I got no call, that your shopping days are
numbered. I miss you both so so much. It must be great though on
the Island.

A day before leaving Pakistan, I was able to get some results on
the Hospital negotiation. Apparently the Ambassador—U.N.—
got through to the Governor of East Pakistan and other high
ranking officials. At one point the Department of Works sensed
that I had connections—because I was invited to see the Governor
without their initiative—usually the case. What did the Governor
have to say to you? What was the reason for the invitation? You
can imagine the same situation if I were visiting France and the
Governor of Provence were to invite me without the sponsorship
of the profession. I said it was personal and on their pressing me
farther, I said, "We discussed your conduct!"

I made a reasonable proposal all in all. Since they could not afford American engineers, I said I would propose using Pakistani professionals and pay them rupees and that I would strengthen my office in Dhaka, take a certain proportion of rupees for my profession to use in Dhaka. This seemed to have had effect and reopened negotiation. I could not have allowed my stay in Pakistan, for the express purpose of finishing the Capital Buildings, to have the atmosphere of competition. I feel I will be successful in having about $500,000 in dollars ($130,000 which they have paid me already in the past) for my use in the States, the rest in rupees in Pakistan.

Anyway Angels a word from you before too many days would do wonders for me. Don't you want to hear my voice too?

I am up to my neck and now on <u>Mellon</u>, which now needs undivided work to present the final preliminary drawings in September. Please pity me because I got back from abroad needing much rest. Only today do I feel up to the job. It was dangerous being in Pakistan this time. Cholera is everywhere because of the floods bringing water pipes in touch with sewer lines. I got 2 cholera shots there—my health cards were not up to date . . . I hope I am [not] harboring that damnable disease.

So long for now my angels with all my love

Lou

Lou believed that art should be seen in natural light. With lighting designer Richard Kelly and Marshall Meyers in his office, he'd devised a "natural lighting fixture" at the Kimbell to admit a slice of Texas sun through a long slit in each vault, filling the space with silvery light that shifts miraculously with the time of day and the passing clouds. At Yale too, Lou insisted on natural light, and Kelly was soon at work on an ingenious system of louvers and diffusing panels to bring in the softer New England sun through the roof—but the two museums are actually totally different.

The Kimbell grew out of the landscape, while the Yale Center for British Art is fundamentally an urban building, fronting on Chapel Street right across from his earlier Yale University Art Gallery. Lou incorporated shops into the ground-floor plan from the start. This would be a bustling place, a center of city and university life, not a hermetic fortress as so many museums are. In this sense the design owes something to Palladio of the Veneto, as Palladio's palaces, unlike his villas, were integrated with city life, often with interior streets or arcades running through them, and spaces of commercial activity on ground

Lou's drawing of his first proposal for the library court at the Yale Center for British Art, New Haven, Connecticut, with a thrilling open stair, worthy of Piranesi, leading to galleries above and shops below.

floors mingling public and private functions. Indeed, in one of Lou's elevations at this time he even playfully labeled Paul Mellon's building "Palazzo Melloni," in honor of the touch of Palladio it would bring to Chapel Street.

But above all, the building would serve the collection it was to house. Lou visited Mellon's homes in Virginia and Provincetown, Massachusetts, and was taken with the great George Stubbs paintings of horses and animals, the delicate watercolors of William Blake, and the luminous colors in the paintings of J.M.W. Turner. The interior of the Yale Center for British Art would be composed of rooms and galleries, intimate places as in a great warm English country house, with paintings hung densely, sometimes even floor to ceiling.

I loved everything about this building from the start, including that it was to be built on the site of the Waldorf Cafeteria, where I had first seen Lou Kahn on a snowy day in 1953, when I was a student at the Yale Drama School.

The library court with enclosed stair tower as it was built at the Yale Center for British Art.

PHILADELPHIA TO INDIAN ISLAND, AUGUST 24, 1970

H'ie and N,

Your call to New Haven from Rockport keeps recalling itself for your hurried sentences of desperate needs and my own feelings of inability to meet them straight on. Tomorrow, I will talk to Betty about it all with the hope that she will be able to give me about $450.00. What you are doing on the Island is right and important and I know how apprehensive you are asking Abbott to advance funds. I go along fully with your feelings of wanting to be independent, but I only wish I could make them shine more brightly with my more generous support. Now you know that you have not too long to wait before my participations (what an ill chosen word) will be befittingly unquestioned and free of questions (again should be full of love). I am broke now, so much so that I cannot, in spite of my "knightly" (natural) feelings, tap from a bottomless barrel.

The Baltimore thing [Inner Harbor] looks possible (I must write you about Perkins). The redevelopment in New York [Broadway United Church of Christ and Office Building] is getting close to something (the developer, a Mr. H., has agreed to me as architect) (I hate to use too optimistic phrases about them for after all their commercial overtones scare the hell out of me.)

Heidi and Edgar must be there now. How good those two are. I hope they are hopelessly in love and when they go back that they be honored by being given work to do. . . .

So, with very many loves,
Lou

Hi Nathaniel,

I miss you and Mummy very much. I guess I just love you both. The island must surely feel like your treasure, like a little piece of the wide wide world, made since the beginning, with every stone and every living thing a sign—for you to think about—of eternity.

Heidi Shleigel from George's office and Edgar Engelskirche from Lou's came to visit Indian Island at the end of August. We walked over the wild rocks, with Nathaniel leading the way, and talked late into the night by kerosene lamp about their plans. They had become engaged and were going to return to Germany and open a firm together, after taking a road trip to see America that fall. Edgar believed in Lou's mission of making the world better through architecture, and I think it was partly the faith of young people like him that kept Lou going through struggles like those coming up on a new project in Baltimore, and even at the Kimbell—where our plans for the landscape and the "odyssey of water" were about to be significantly curtailed by sudden budget cuts that seemed designed to punish the artist for dreaming.

Heidi and Edgar with George Patton, January 1970.

On envelope:

HARRIET PATTISON
INDIAN ISLAND
ROCK PORT
MAINE

BY AIRMAIL

PHILADELPHIA TO INDIAN ISLAND, AUGUST 24, 1970

Sunday—To snatch a piece of a working day that has in it the reward ever flowing.

H'ie and N,
Thought I'd send you an appendix to the letter of Sunday on Sunday.

Past Friday Perkins called. He is on the planning board of the Baltimore Redevelopment Authority. Said he, "Lou, are you enthusiastic about the project in Baltimore?" My first reaction was caution! Then I said, "The project offers the opportunity to design a structure of function, tying by means of a central concourse, all circulation to parking, shops, elevators, over streets—a structure distinctively itself in character, never really done before, but as I have always visualized as valid for large portions in a city. Why then should I not be enthusiastic and besides, I have no trouble with enthusiasm." "Aside from the hotel, apartment, office, shopping and recreation building," I continued, "Easy buildings to design in contrast, the idea of expressing a function, contrast of movement and living spaces, is truly what I have been waiting for to do since my first drawings of city architecture in 1950."

What did he mean by his question? Being in a position to influence the decision on who should design the project, I am sure he had someone else in mind other than me. This could also have been a friendly question, but had I shown any doubt by my apprehensions (which I have somewhat), I could have played into his hand.

Then I asked him, "Don't you think this project is exciting?" He said, "Of course it's a terrific project." Now tell me what could have prompted his question?

Had I not sealed the first letter, in which there is this little account promised, I could have included this one and saved 10 cents toward dire needs.

Again, my loves, keep well and don't worry your little heads.

Love,
Lou

PHILADELPHIA TO INDIAN ISLAND, SEPTEMBER 6, 1970

Sunday morning

What could have happened, so distressing, that cannot be brushed aside, only because we are both alive and in love. What problems of living, deserve to possess us, to blindness from beauty, the most venerable of all feelings. What else is there to worship.

Neil, Marshall, Shane, Edgar, Volker, Flanaghan and I are working to correct the mangled interpretations of our design in [Preston] Geren's working drawings. Dr. [Ric] Brown has ordered the parking court cleared of all bumpers, bollards, and trees. He considers the grotto a hazard and wants no part of the front court arbors. He demands a saving of $400,000, which he expects from these modifications. Geren has the confidence of the Board, he wants me to surrender the right to check shop drawings and proposes that I do not share in the division of fees. (This is just one of my problems.)

You know I am leaving for Persia Thursday night. School begins Thursday afternoon. Monday night, I leave for Fort Worth [and] will be in Fort Worth all Tuesday. Wednesday, I meet Dr. [Jules] Prown (Mellon, Yale), who will stay over until Thursday morning. I have no help on this most important meeting with Dr. Prown to prepare for the September showing of the project to Yale. He is nervous about the unconfirmed structure of the building. I am confident that it will be great.

Please don't be angry, think only of the beauty of our love. And now I will tell you that the Baltimore Project is approved. Soon we will be asked to begin it. I am sure it will mean, in a short time, the considerable easing of my financial position.

Lou

The Kimbell Art Museum during construction and tree planting.

I was shocked by Lou's letter about the drastic cutbacks at Kimbell and knew how they would reduce the power of the design we had all worked so hard to refine. Preston Geren's financial demands were especially galling. I sensed that Geren, as the "gentleman architect" of the associated Texas firm, had targeted Lou as an "impractical artist" from the start, and now he appeared poised to take over.

I mourned the demise of our plans for the Theater Garden grotto and blamed Ric Brown for not standing up for them. When I called Lou, I chided him for not doing something about it. He listened and was thoughtful of my feelings, even though he had so much more at stake—but he also had the experience and resilience to absorb undeserved failures and knew he would be able to make adjustments and restore most essentials. By the fall, Lou was winning the game again, and I conceded that Ric Brown actually shared his goals, although we never did get to complete the grotto with water cascading down into it, as we had dreamed. As with Jules Prown at Yale, Ric was a rarity among museum directors, championing architecture that challenged the sterile spaces and exhibit patterns that persist to this day. Ric and Jules both understood Lou's quip, "The first thing you want in most museums is a cup of coffee—you feel so tired right away."

In mid-September, as I worked to adjust the planting plans to accommodate the cutbacks at Kimbell, Lou left for Iran to address the First International Conference of Architects, in a place he'd always longed to see—Isfahan.

مهمانسرای شاه عباس

Monday –

Dearest Harriet and Nathaniel,

Sorry didn't keep my promise to write from London. The time was very short at change flights from T.W.A. and Iranian air lines and had to get up at 4 in the morning to catch the I. air to Isphahan. This morning was touring time to this marvelous place and in the after noon the queen (her imperial majesty) in augurated the session in a terrific Hall of 40 columns — a open air portico over looking ancient gardens.

At end of meeting I received those who were into views with the queen.

I spoke quite a bit with her. At one point when she questioned if it is helpful for the architect of her country worked in the various bureaus of the government or all work should be entrusted to the architect in practice. I advised her that there should be no questions in her mind. Only the independent architect can serve the country affectionably. I also said, which made her laugh, that "if the government departments have their own architectural office in their entire is the next thing they will want to dictate who should be female or who male. They are doing it up brown in a atmosphere quite imperialistic.

will write soon again
Louis Kahn

اصفهان ـ صندوق پستی شماره ۵۴ ـ تلفن ۶۰۱۱ تا ۶۰۱۷ ـ تلگرافی : شاه عباس

The queen / people assembled

Monday

Dearest Harriet and Nathaniel,

Sorry didn't keep my promise to write from London. The time
was very short. A change flight from T.W.A. and Iranian Airlines
and had to get up at 4 in the morning to catch the Iranian Air to
Isfahan. This morning was touring time to this marvelous place
and in the afternoon the queen (her imperial majesty) inaugurated
the session in a terrific Hall of 40 Columns—an open air portico
overlooking ancient gardens.

Immediately following there were interviews in small groups
with the queen.

I spoke quite a bit with her. At one point, when she questioned if
it is better for the architect of her country [to] work for its various
bureaus of the government or [if] all work should be entrusted
to the architect in practice. I advised her that there should be no
question in her mind. Only the independent architect can serve
the country effectively. I also said, which made her laugh, that if
the government departments have their own architectural office in
their control to dictate to, the next thing they will want to dictate
[is] who should be female and who male. They are doing it up
brown in an atmosphere quite imperialistic.

Will write soon again.

Much love,
Lou

Lou at a royal audience with Queen Farah of Iran, in Isfahan.

The Hall of Forty Columns, Isfahan, of later significance for the FDR Memorial.

HOTEL SHAH ABBAS, ISFAHAN, TO TOWANDA ST., SEPTEMBER 16, 1970

Dearest H'ie & N,

This is now Wednesday morning. The second session dealing with technology. The speakers will be Buckminster Fuller, Alexandr Ureyanoff, Oswald Ungers. The discussion yesterday on tradition was really quite excellent.

There is something in the air in Persia which is particular. The people are colorful. They look eagerly aggressive, men as well as women.

I walked around a great deal yesterday. Went to a place outside the hotel for dinner, open air court with trees and tables bedecked with fruit, colorful service, good dishes, and jovial company. Later, after dinner, back to the place near the hotel in a dungeon like room, serving drinks and dancing, that confrontation dance I can't do. You feel so lonely and dead when you love to dance but can't do the particular style. Went to bed late, got up early, had breakfast with Paul Rudolph. Now I must go to the conference.

Love,
Lou

By this time, Nathaniel was thriving in second grade at Germantown Friends School, but his first two years there hadn't been easy. He had begun at GFS

Lou carried this notebook on his trip to Iran, which he later left with me. These are likely the notes he used for his talk at the First International Conference of Architects in Isfahan.

under a cloud, which I shielded him from, but he was sensitive and surely picked up on the tension. In spite of the generally accepting attitude of the Quakers, some on the admissions committee apparently disapproved of my unmarried status and of his "illegitimacy," and one teacher had said she didn't want him in her class. But then Irene Wolf, who was the grandmother of one of Nathaniel's friends and a champion of mine, stepped in. When Irene, as the matriarch of a prominent Philadelphia family, said "My granddaughter is starting this year at Germantown Friends, and I am so happy to hear that Nathaniel Kahn will be in her class," it put an end to the debate, and Nathaniel was admitted to kindergarten.

Nathaniel made many friends at school, but he hit the first snag when the children were asked to draw pictures of their fathers. While one friend drew a picture that read "His name is Barry, he has a beard, he has a mustache," Nathaniel refused, saying it couldn't be done. He could not draw his father. He was sent to the school psychologist, who asked him probing questions that he reported to me. I told Lou, who responded by telling Nathaniel funny stories of his own struggles at school. Nathaniel told Lou all about the class, adding that there was even a family of guinea pigs and that he had been assigned to clean the cage. This alarmed Lou, and, thinking that his son, as a scholarship student, was being singled out for menial tasks, he insisted on a meeting with the kindergarten teacher. When he arrived, Lou announced to Mrs. Foulke, "My son is not here to clean the animal cages." But Mrs. Foulke, who had accepted Nathaniel in her class when the other teacher had demurred, explained calmly, "At a Friends school all children are equal and each one must take a turn caring for the animals and cleaning their cages." Lou was suddenly humbled and lingered at Mrs. Foulke's invitation to observe the little ones absorbed in their friendly tasks and games. Watching his boy building an edifice of giant wood blocks with other children, Lou was so beguiled that he ended by deciding it should be Nathaniel's turn to take the guinea pigs home to care for them over the weekend, cage and all.

Then, in first grade, Nathaniel was stricken with daily stomachaches and refused to go to school. Finally, in desperation I turned to Lou, who at first had no ideas. Then suddenly he said *he* would take Nathaniel. That did it; the next morning Nathaniel was ready to go. He took his father's hand and walked into first grade, with only a little complaint about his stomach hurting. "Mine too," said Lou, tenderly.

Lou stayed the morning in the classroom. I can still see him sitting in front of a circle of first-graders on a tiny chair in his dark suit and bow tie, telling the children about places in the world where things were done differently, like Venice, where everyone went around in boats instead of cars. The kids were enchanted, and Nathaniel was back on track.

After we left the school, Lou asked me to drive him not to the office but to the wooded northwestern edge of Philadelphia, not far from our house on Towanda Street. It was there, in a deserted luncheonette near an intersection, that I learned why Lou's stomach hurt. Marie Kuo, a talented Chinese architect who had worked for Lou in the 1950s and early '60s, had been killed there the day before, when her car skidded off the icy road. Her son was in the car as well—he was a few years younger than Nathaniel—and had survived the crash. Lou worried about the child and the husband Marie had left behind, but I could tell there was more to it than that. I did not know Marie or what she could have meant to Lou, but I was struck by his silent grief. I realized without words that he was telling me he had loved her. Later I learned that Marie and Lou had been lovers in the 1950s and that she had left architecture when she married. "What does it mean to love more than once?" Lou wrote me early on. I do not know the answer, as I myself have only truly loved once. Perhaps Lou was pondering the question again that day. I felt a pang knowing that Lou had loved others in his life, but I was grateful that he had let me into the deeper chambers of his heart, and I felt terrible for Marie and the family she had left behind.

In the following years, Lou began spending more time with Nathaniel. I think he knew his son needed him. To see the two of them playing on the floor or drawing together, or listening to Lou tell Nathaniel bedtime stories about his childhood, or the next installment of a tale he'd made up about a boy with a pet elephant, was one of the great joys of my life. Lou needed Nathaniel too—I could see how he turned to his son, putting his arm around him and pulling him close. Nathaniel also accepted things that I could not. When we would drive Lou downtown to the house he shared with Esther in the middle of the night, Nathaniel took it in stride, cheerfully bidding his father good night and making sure I answered Lou's quiet "See you soon" with an acknowledgment.

In the fall of 1970 Nathaniel had a marvelous second-grade teacher, Mrs. Cunningham, who encouraged his interests and wrote me about his talents at telling stories and as an actor. Nathaniel had become fascinated by King Arthur and the Knights of the Round Table, and Lou gave him treasured books on the story, with illustrations by Howard Pyle that they both pored over.

For Halloween, Nathaniel wanted to be a knight. Lou designed the costume, and together we all built it in the office. It was elaborate, made of many components cut from gray model-making cardboard held together with brass fasteners. Vincent Rivera made the sword and shield in the office shop, and Lou himself made a magnificent helmet, with a visor that went up and down. The armored shoes were a pair of Keds overlaid with articulated cardboard bucklings, and everything was spray-painted sparkling silver. It took some forty-five minutes for Nathaniel to get suited up, and that Halloween at Germantown Friends School, no one had a better costume.

Lou's sketch of a leopard for Nathaniel's shield.

Nathaniel in his knight's costume.

INDIA TO TOWANDA ST., NOVEMBER 23, 1970

Dear Nathaniel,
The Indians sure know how to draw elephants, horses, and people.
                              Best love to you and mommy.
                                        Daddy

The end of November found Lou traveling again, this time to Nepal and India after facing a fall filled with project deadlines: studios at Penn, Philadelphia Art Commission meetings, overseas talks, and intense work sessions in

Baltimore, New York, New Haven, and Fort Worth. It may have been on this trip that Lou had a startling experience at Balkrishna Doshi's house in Ahmedabad. A blind seer had been invited, and he singled out people in the room, telling them about their futures. When he came to Lou, he said, "You make things on the land that will be remembered as long as the sun will shine." He then asked Lou if he wished to know when and how he would die. "No," Lou said. Doshi or one of the guests mentioned something about Lou's wife and daughter, to which the seer had looked perplexed. "But you have three children," he said. When Lou told me the story, he said it was awkward in the room, as no one there knew about his personal life, but the fact that he told this to me was somehow very comforting. I sensed something was changing in him, as if perhaps he recognized the strain on everyone of living a life of secrets.

On October 26, 1970, on an Arizona highway, Heidi and Edgar's little Volkswagen blew a tire and veered into the path of a truck, and they were killed. Several weeks later a box arrived containing a note from them and a giant pine cone they'd picked up in Oregon on their journey across America. Half a century later, each Christmas I still unwrap that pine cone, remembering with tears those two beautiful young lovers and the dreams they had and would never fulfill.

The grief that struck both offices at 1501 Walnut Street affected the lives of all of us. George brought in two ambitious recent Penn graduates to handle incoming work, but the warmth we had shared when Heidi was there was gone. My friend John Moss left George's for a new landscape firm in town, led by Terry Schnadelbach, a talented young landscape architect, who then offered me a job as well. I talked it over with Lou and decided to take it. My work on Kimbell was done, and Terry's firm offered me a happier place to work.

The sketch Edgar made in the Indian Island guestbook, the morning he and Heidi left.

PART FOUR

The Garden and the Room

1971–1974

Lou and Nathaniel, Towanda Street.

1971

At sixteen, Alexandra Tyng, Lou's daughter with Anne Tyng, bravely reached out to me. She longed to know her little brother. When Alex found my telephone number and called me, I immediately supported her breakout from the conspiracy of silence, realizing that the two children would make better sense of the suppressed relationships than we adults had done.

I was struck by Alex's warmth and openness when she came to Towanda Street for dinner and an overnight stay. She was slim, with long red-brown hair, an easy laugh, and a carefree spirit, and Nathaniel took to her at once. Soon the two of them were talking on the phone regularly and hatching various projects, including an elaborate board game that took over most of the playroom on the third floor, with illustrations of a mythical land of soaring castles and dismal swamps. Alex drew and painted beautifully, and she wrote stories too, compiling them in richly illustrated scrapbooks. One revolved around a "dream family" in which many disparate members had been drawn together by their natural affinities.

Alex and Anne lived downtown, on ginkgo-lined Waverly Street, and Nathaniel began going there for visits. Anne welcomed him to her table and to her world of speculations about the geometric nature of history and the universe, which Nathaniel found mesmerizing. Unlike me, Anne was very confident in her ideas and presented them with authority. Her house itself seemed an extension of those ideas and an embodiment of her beliefs. It was spare and orderly, with geometric constructions hanging from the ceiling and a stair she had designed that rose to an ingenious angular addition at the top, containing only a large bed and a deck. The addition announced Anne's brilliance like a beacon, jutting out into space beyond the bland adjoining row houses and opening on all sides to views of rooftops and the sky.

Perhaps it is surprising that Anne and I became friends, but we did. In addition to the fact that we were both marginalized women, we shared a fascination for the ideas of Carl Jung, an abiding sense of idealism, and a desire to shape our own destinies, beyond what our "upstanding" families and our times expected for us. And of course there were our children—Lou's children. We enjoyed how they became close and were united in our belief that they should not be excluded from his public world, which indeed they were.

This came to a head in April, when Anne and I discovered that Lou had been tapped for the prestigious Philadelphia Award, and that neither of us had been invited to the ceremony. It was a double blow to my pride, as I had been a young friend of Mary Curtis Bok-Zimbalist, whose first husband, Edward Bok, had founded the award. Although Mrs. Bok-Zimbalist had died the year before, there would be many people I knew in attendance. I was so hurt and angry that I wouldn't speak to Lou for some time, but Alex, refusing to be left out, called his office and directly requested invitations. When they arrived, both Anne and I declined, but Alex and Nathaniel decided they would go together—on their own.

Distraught by my silence, Lou tried to make things up on the day of the event, having a package hand-delivered to Terry Schnadelbach's office on Delancey Street, where I was working. It contained two pairs of shoes and an ascot tie for Nathaniel, and the following note.

1501 WALNUT ST. TO 1924 DELANCEY ST., PHILADELPHIA,
APRIL 21, 1971

Dearest,
Tonight there will be no joy. Even if you were to be there, I am sure
I cannot feel it. Something has eroded. I know it from the little
enthusiasm I feel in my work.

I love you,
Lou

The tie situation—a salesman gave me the idea of using this red
handkerchief, folded like an ascot. If Nathaniel does not like one of
the pair of shoes the slip enclosed is negotiable.

That afternoon I went to Anne's house, and together we watched as our children marched off to the ceremony. Nathaniel wore the shoes but rejected the ascot, preferring no tie at all to "a scarf."

Alex and Nathaniel were laughing when they returned, regaling us with stories from the event until late: Nathaniel imitated an officious lady who was frantically rearranging chairs in the front row, explaining that there was no room for them, as the seats were for "important people," while Alex explained that the officious lady was actually someone they knew, the wife of one of Lou's men in the office. Afterward there had been a long receiving line, and Nathaniel was anxious about joining it, but Alex had convinced him it would be all right, and together they waited to greet their father. Esther Kahn stood next to him, and on seeing Alex, she clasped her hands behind her back and nodded, saying, "Hello, Miss Tyng," while she looked right over Nathaniel's head, taking the hand of the next in line.

But upon seeing his children, Lou had pulled them aside, hugging them both to himself and introducing them to the man next to him, who was Jonas Salk. Salk shook hands with both of them, and the kids were awestruck. Later they were introduced to Lou's sister Sarah, from California. The evening had been a breakthrough. Lou had acted from the heart, and an astonishing family portrait had been unveiled in front of Philadelphia society—although parts of the portrait remained hidden.

1501 WALNUT ST. TO 8870 TOWANDA ST., PHILADELPHIA, APRIL 24, 1971

Harriet,
For the fourth night, I haven't called. At times, and always on the phone when you are miserable, only that I have marred the beauty that you seek of life, overcomes me. I need the life the two of us could make. Yet, only the hope that it will come about is in my plan- less mind. The phone, my only nearness to you these days, promises no joy in reflection for the innermost love I dared to offer you. Our innocent little boy needs his daddy and I want so much to give him the love and guidance you express so well and know he needs.

Harriet, my dear sweet dear, in spite of the pain we cause each other, I love you and will always love you.

Lou

In spite of the children's enthusiasms, I stubbornly resisted Lou's efforts to resume communications, and only slowly let my anger die. Our rift would be healed, but to be treated with continued disregard, even as Lou expressed his enduring love for me and turned to me for assistance with his work, was increasingly hard to bear.

Eight-year-old Nathaniel could no longer remain outside our feud, but he would not take sides, and offered uncanny sympathy and compassion to both of us. While Nathaniel listened and comforted, Alex took on the paradoxes of Lou's private life with a persistent family activism that was beginning to have an effect. In June, Lou, Anne, Nathaniel, and I attended Alex's high school graduation, and later that summer Alex and Anne came to Indian Island, where Alex made the first of many paintings in a place she would visit often over the years.

Lou, Nathaniel, and Alex at Alex's graduation from the Friends
Select School, June 1971, photographed by Anne Tyng.

Nathaniel and Alex, Indian Island, Maine.

Anne, Nathaniel, me, and Alex's friend Linda Brookman,
Indian Island, Maine.

Waiting for your call after the one I missed. The letter I sent you to
Indian Island (sans Rockport) came back "no such address" "no such
person" I sent it on again . . .

At the last meeting of the Bicentennial I had a chance to
explain more fully some rudimentary ideas and also give them my
impression of some of their goals.

One goal is to give a historical in-look, out-look / as it was (past) /
as it is (present) / as it will be (future).

Everyone agreed when I pointed out that the future is not
predictable. That Beethoven did not write for the future, that
Einstein did not realize for the future, Edison did not invent for the
future. It was an act of today, that very day (not tomorrow)—the
only time of any creation. That the idea of projection into the future
is denying today which, besides being stupid, means trouble that the
have-not only feel more delayed, which really means denial because
tomorrow cannot be the day after the day before. This shallowness
would immediately be seen by Russia and all the unprivileged
nations where hopelessness is completely rejecting of promise.

Denise Scott Brown Venturi is also on this small committee. She
is insistent on small minded ideas. She wants to bring a classroom
in Sweden over to the Expo to demonstrate how a class is taught in
a foreign land. When I pointed out that the children would freeze
up and consider themselves in a zoo, she answered that they would
not [be] necessary to [show] because flashing lights of electronics
and signs and rockets and and and everything also that flash[es] and
burps would convey to the millions the message. I just stood there
amazed at the shallowness . . . but . . . she has the ears of people.

My dearest ones Nathaniel and Harriet please forgive the sudden
ending. Be good loving brave and above all Happy and even more
healthy and full of fun.

Lou

In 1976 the United States would mark its two hundredth anniversary,
and, as the city where the Liberty Bell had sounded and the Declaration
of Independence had been signed, Philadelphia seemed the obvious place
for a grand exposition. To pursue federal funding, the Philadelphia 1976
Bicentennial Corporation was formed, and Lou began developing schemes

to celebrate his beloved city. We spoke on the phone often about what he hoped to achieve: the creation of places that would provide lasting urban improvements, that would show how inspired institutions could better lives today, and that would lay the groundwork for greater cooperation between all peoples in the future. It was an idealistic vision, and it was soon overshadowed by the flashy proposals of Bob Venturi and Denise Scott Brown, whose brightly colored renderings featured mobile stages, covered wagons containing exhibits, "ethnic" food carts, playful historic structures, lighted signs, and searchlights crisscrossing the sky in a Pop art celebration of the American scene.

I understood Lou's desire to use the upcoming bicentennial to improve neglected areas of the city and to highlight "the institutions of man," but his initial proposal seemed out of scale and too much of a throwback to earlier times. I worried how useful his structures would be after the party was over. Then a new site was identified at Eastwick, and the project blossomed in a direction that was more connected to contemporary concerns and that included a role for landscape.

The new exposition site was near the airport, on the edge of Tinicum Marsh, where the Schuylkill River joins the Delaware. It was an industrial wasteland bordered by refineries and fuel tanks, beneath two highway overpasses—a tabula rasa of scarred earth, requiring a solution beyond what architecture alone could provide. Aided by my experience with Ian McHarg's ecological analytics, I was able to help Lou develop a plan that grew organically from the land itself.

At one end of the site Lou placed structures he called "The Courts of the Physical Resources," and at the other, "The Courts of the Expressions." These would be dedicated, respectively, to science and art, and the space between them—the "Forum of the Availabilities"—was an energized place of inspiration that would give rise to new solutions, new alliances, new ways of living on the earth.

I encouraged Lou to integrate the site not with pathways but with a canal crossed by bridges, which he did. We then located pavilions for the participating nations on either side of the canal and threaded them together with a garden matrix of green walls. Later I suggested adding tree-grove parklands at both ends, in the hope that the site would remain a landscape organism after the festival, to germinate a verdant city neighborhood. We imagined cars and planes passing overhead and noticing, in the midst of the postindustrial wasteland, a vision of a new kind of city, alive with green vegetation and flowing waterways.

The Courts
of The
Physical Resources
The source of all presences

The Forum of the Availabilities
(The street.)
The meetings of Human & Physical Resources

The Thresholds
Where the urges to express
Meet the possible

The Courts
of The
Expressions

The Houses of The Nations

Lou's master plan for the Bicentennial Exposition at the Eastwick site, which strikes me now as an embodiment of his concept of "Silence and Light."

Lou's plans for the bicentennial were never realized, federal funds were deployed elsewhere, and the celebration that eventually took place in Philadelphia was muted and disappointing. Lou would not live to see 1976, but one of his creations ended up as part of Operation Sail, the remarkable regatta that brought ships from around the world to New York Harbor on July 4 of that year. Commissioned by the conductor and captain Robert Austin Boudreau, the fanciful steel music boat that Lou had designed opened, like a glittering clamshell, into a full-scale concert stage. *Point Counterpoint II* survives to this day, pulling up to towns along coasts, rivers, and lakes and offering free concerts to local audiences in the best of America's showboat tradition.

Lou's ship, *Point Counterpoint II*, underway.

1501 WALNUT ST. TO INDIAN ISLAND, AUGUST 14, 1971

Hi To (HE) Hi To (NK),
So now it is the story of the boat that slithered away and then caught in the act and came home. This should teach it a lesson—a boat needs a sailor.

This is Saturday, the last day for me to finish the revision of the talk I gave in Detroit. I have it all to do—well nearly. Tomorrow is typing day. Jeannette, after loafing all week, could not accommodate me for that day. She had plans. I will get an old secretary.

I got the extra $100.00 but too late to deposit, so will Monday—O yes—first thing before I get up "even"—deposit.

And now instead of the best, that is me, but the <u>very</u> best, that is you, how is your vacation and the distance from your most beloved, that is me, not complete I hope because I need you to love me and distance makes the heart more fondly. . . .

I found a book for Nathaniel's library. Did you hear that Nathaniel? It's called *The Wonder Clock: or, Four and Twenty Marvelous Tales, Being One for Each Hour of the Day* written and Illustrated by Howard Pyle.

I will gather together some drawings of the [Korman and Honickman] houses for you to study. Please—they are far from right—be kind. I must get started on my writing.

Love,
Lou

334

Lou in Detroit with architects Edward Larrabee Barnes and Minoru Yamasaki, designer of the World Trade Center, then under construction.

In June Lou had been awarded the gold medal from the American Institute of Architects at the annual convention in Detroit. "The Room, the Street, and Human Agreement" was the title he gave his acceptance talk, which he was now editing for publication. In the talk Lou imagines a dialogue with Wallace Stevens, inspired by a poem I had read to him from Stevens's *The Auroras of Autumn*. The line "the sun is secretly shining on a wall," from "The Bouquet," particularly resonated with Lou, and he paraphrased (or misremembered) it in his own way—finding through it a way to articulate his feelings about the mystical nature of architecture.

> The great American poet, Wallace Stevens, prodded the architect, "What slice of the sun does your building have?" To paraphrase: what slice of the sun enters your room? What a range of mood does the light offer from morning to night from day to day from season to season and all through the years. Gratifying and unpredictable are the permissions the architect has given to the chosen opening on which patches of sunlight play on the jamb and sill that enter, move, and disappear. Stevens seemed to tell us that the sun was not aware of its wonder until it struck the side of a building.

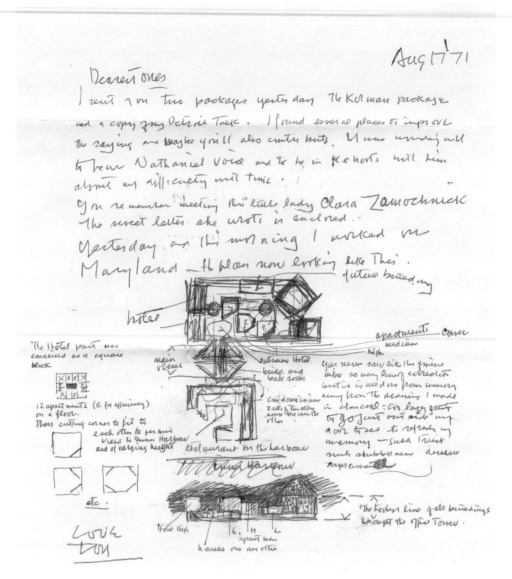

[TOP: site plan] *hotel / entrance hotel / bridge and ball room / main street / condominium, 2 sets of two story, house one over the other / restaurant on the harbor / Inner Harbor / future building / apartments / corner / medium / high.*

[BOTTOM: elevation] *Hotel high / houses one over other / apartments h, m, l [high, medium, low] / the highest line of all buildings except the office tower.*

[LEFT: plan diagrams] *The hotel part was conceived as a square block / 12 apartments (E for efficiency) on a floor / then cutting corner to fit to each other to permit view to Inner Harbor and of varying height / etc.*

Dearest ones,

I sent you two packages yesterday. The Korman package and a copy of my Detroit talk. I found several places to improve the saying and maybe you'll also contribute.

It was wonderful to hear Nathaniel's voice and to be in kehoots with him about my difficulty with time.

You remember meeting this little lady Clara Zamochnick. The sweet letter she wrote is enclosed.

Yesterday and this morning I worked on Maryland—the plan now looking like this.

You never saw [a drawing] like this of mine before, so many lines of correction, but it is all done from memory away from the drawing I made in charcoal: too lazy to go just outside my door to see to refresh my memory—such [trust], such stubbornness deserves reprimand.

Love,
Lou

Although I was working for Terry Schnadelbach, I was now also moonlighting for Lou on several jobs, including an estate for the Korman and Honickman families, the Wolfson Center in Israel, and Baltimore's Inner Harbor development project. Spreading out plans on the kitchen table on Indian Island, I would make sketches, often by kerosene lamp, to send back to Philadelphia, then call Lou from the pay phone at the five-and-dime when we went ashore to discuss ideas. It may have been an inefficient way to work, but the surroundings of sea and sky inspired ideas I wouldn't have had in the midst of the city.

The Inner Harbor development was the kind of large-scale urban design Lou had always wanted to do, but he had trouble settling on solutions for this prosthetic slice of Baltimore, split by a thruway. While he bridged the bisected areas with a city ballroom and met the developers' high-occupancy requirements, he had greater interest in the interstitial spaces than in the "easy" buildings he drew. Those buildings disappointed me, though I laid out public gardens and water features for them. Ultimately, it was the developers' profit-driven crowding that sapped Lou's desire to design "a city place like no other," and within a year he would let go of the project without reluctance, although he could ill afford to lose it financially.

Presenting the scheme in Baltimore.

Lou's perspective of a central concourse for the Baltimore Inner Harbor project, reflecting his concern with the spaces between buildings and how they communicate with each other.

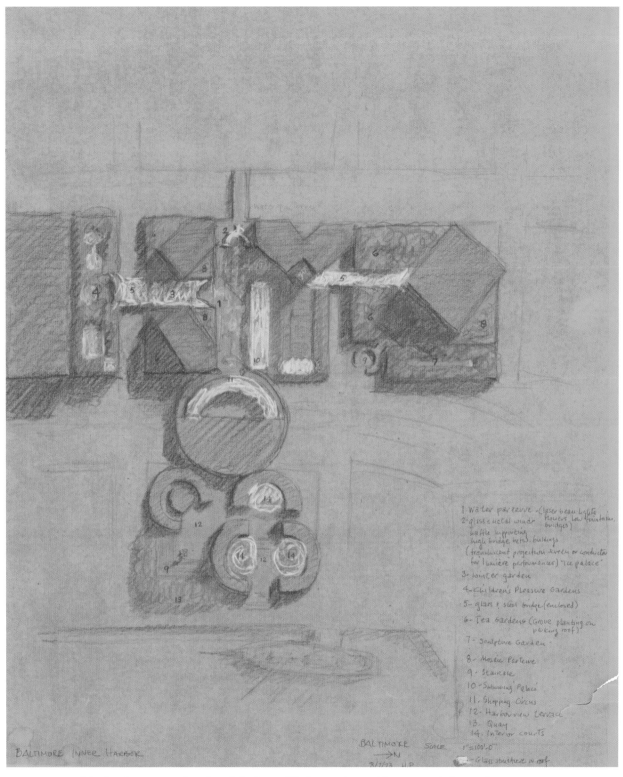

My sketch over a sepia print of the Inner Harbor project, with suggested plant and water features to enhance views, movement, and activity within the central area.

Dearest

I am now at the Kennedy airport on my way to Delhi. with stay over in London. London is closed on Sunday will visit for first time the British Museum — maybe can get some interesting post cards for our collection. The ride from Philly was 4 hrs — bridges clogged roads stuffed it is a hell — as they say traffic near New York is one continuous garage.

I will try to come back sooner and may be able if they have mercy after seeing the few drawings I made of the first issue of the plan. I started the plan with the aid of Henry's analysis by recognizing the orientation problems of sun and wind. So gave a series of narrow courts to catch the breeze and shield the sun — its just a start — If they see something in the start they will I am sure be merciful.

Be a good girl and guard the enormous strength of your sweetheart by not racing him hither and thon

I feel a bit late we going in one direction to get to the Abs — although I have done so much to get things going the time Tel Aviv, Baltimore Kansas City, Normans all are rather late enough until I get back.

I think I am going to just relax now and take Katmandu as a vacation too. Will you be at least merciful. But after all I do want so much much to see you on the Island Lets hope YES

Love Lou

Dearest,

I am now at the Kennedy Airport on my way to Delhi, with stay-over in London. London is closed on Sunday, will visit for first time the British Museum—maybe can get some interesting post cards for our collection. The ride from Philly was 4 hours—bridges clogged, roads stuffed, it is a hell—as they say, traffic near New York is one continuous garage.

I will try to come back sooner and may be able if they have mercy after seeing the few drawings I made of the first issue of the plan. I started the plan, with the aid of Henry's analysis, by recognizing the orientation problems of sun and wind. It gave a series of narrow courts to catch the breeze and shield the sun—it's just a start—if they see something in the start—they will, I am sure, be merciful.

Be a good girl and guard the enormous strength of your sweetheart by not racing him hither and thon.

I feel a bit like one going in one direction to get to the other—although I have done so much to get things going this time, Tel Aviv, Baltimore, Kansas City [Office Building], Kormans, all are satisfied enough until I get back.

I think I am going to just relax now and take Kathmandu as a vacation too. Will you be at least merciful? But after all I do want so much much to see you and the Island. Let's hope yes.

Love,
Lou

Spent a lonely day in London. The place is shut down on Sunday. The Cumberland Hotel is a dismal imitation of a 1st Class Hotel (so noted by Indian Air Lines). But I was exhausted from the long line of days and days of no sleep in Philadelphia and finally a night on a 747 Air India. Those big things do fly easily and are roomy, first class you know. Oh for sleep and that's what I did most in the Cumberland. I did walk a stretch in the Westminster area. It is really very very much like [an] elegant home. Urbanity at its modest, yet slightly very secure, very sedate, but above all, home-like scale. I don't know, brick is pretty great, and the way it is handled by the British, damned bloody all right . . .

Been reading Dickens *Oliver Twist* by chance of having picked up an early 20th century book of [George] Cruikshank's watercolor illustrations. . . . It is a very eye appealing book. You and Nathaniel should enjoy.

Love,
Lou

KATHMANDU, NEPAL, TO TOWANDA ST., SEPTEMBER 3, 1971

Friday

Dearest Harriet and Nathaniel,

I may have told you that I am designing the Family Planning Building in Kathmandu. I brought with me some plans Henry and I got up the day before I left. When I saw the plot I realized that no building can go on it before the entire area has plan direction so I got to work. This was not easy because I had a severe backache, I had to lie down frequently not being able to stand or sit without nauseating pain. Only today I got up feeling relieved of its severity. The second day I got the idea for the site which is below the level of the streets.

To use the lower level as a car entrance communicable with plaza above. All plots will face the plaza and have lower level auto entrance.

The entire site is about 75 acres. The central idea is to place buildings for people's services, ordinarily people do not know where to go for their needs. This place cuts the lost motion:

1) For their family and personal development
2) For people who will get information on farm and city enterprise
3) Banks for loans for worthy projects
4) Surveys of all sorts
5) Information leading to scholarships to further studies
6) Health instruction, etc.

The Land Planning office likes the idea and have called in all the commitment to those promised land on the site. That 2nd day I made a drawing of the site plan—got a few hints on presentation to certain officials. The 3rd day I gave a public-official presentation in the auditorium of the Bureau of Mines and today, after spent all day on the plans of the building itself, completely changing what I brought with me and presented early this evening the plans.

I am so sorry sweetheart that I had to send the telegram about getting back early. I could not budge the rupee business! But next time, I will insist that they pay the ticket in Indian rupees which has negotiable means. Sorry, also, for the dry business of the plans.

Love,
Lou

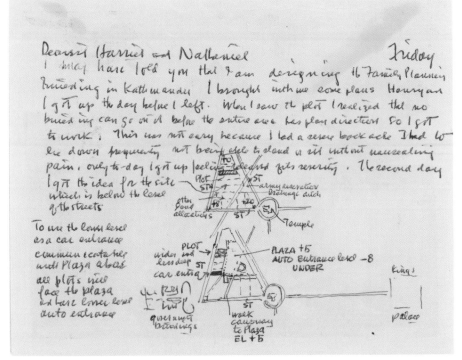

[TOP: existing site] *PLOT / ST [street] / ST [street] / army reservation / drainage ditch / temple / +20 / ST [street] / +8 / other land allocations.*

[BOTTOM: Lou's proposal] *PLOT wider and less deep / ST [street] PLAZA +5 / Auto entrance level -8 under / King's palace / ST [street] / walk causeway to Plaza EL [elevation] + 5 / government buildings / car entrance.*

343

Lou's many ideas about Nepal's government services complex in central Kathmandu crystal-
ized into a singular vision soon after he saw the site. The freehand scheme he drew in the
three days he was there resulted in this site model, made upon his return to Philadelphia.

The Family Care Center, Kathmandu, Nepal (1970–75), the rightmost building on the
triangular site in the model above, would be the only part of Lou's plan to be built.

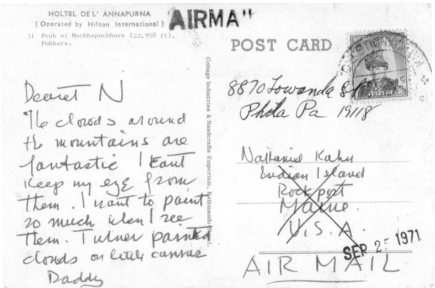

ANNAPURNA, NEPAL, TO TOWANDA ST., SEPTEMBER 5, 1971

Dearest N,
The clouds around the mountains are fantastic. I can't keep my
eye from them. I want to paint so much when I see them. Turner
painted clouds on little canvas.

Daddy

Exterior of the Class of 1945 Library at Phillips Exeter Academy, Exeter, New Hampshire (1967–72).

Lou circled November 9 on his office calendar; it was Nathaniel's birthday, and Lou showed up to join the group of nine-year-olds as they played darts and bobbed for apples on our porch on Towanda Street. This was also the day that a great line of high school students at Phillips Exeter Academy in Exeter, New Hampshire, carried all the books from the old library into the new one Lou had built, along with a dining hall, at the center of Exeter's neo-Georgian campus.

What had those schoolboys thought of the pair of unadorned brick buildings, set at a dynamic angle to each other, rising in the midst of their picture-postcard New England town? They were neither overtly modern nor neatly traditional. To this day they stand in challenging contrast to Exeter's patrician environment, resembling the old mill and factory buildings along the nearby Merrimack River and demanding a reaction from anyone who approaches.

In my last semester as a student at Penn in 1967, Lou had brought me in briefly to help with planting ideas for Exeter. I worked on pathway layouts to connect the two buildings as well as suggesting the idea of a planted space beside the library with benches, where students could meet, talk, and study in the sun. Lou was very thoughtful about how young people learn in different ways and need varied spaces for studying, and we even developed a plan for a rooftop library garden, which would have been a magical space to retreat with a book. These ideas were never further developed for budgetary reasons, but perhaps they will be reexamined someday.

If the exteriors of Lou's library and dining hall gesture toward New England mill works and the hard-toiling laborers on whose backs the wealth of the Exeter region had been built, the interior of the library suggests an

Lou's drawing of the roof garden we imagined, with places to read beneath espaliered trees in large earthen pots.

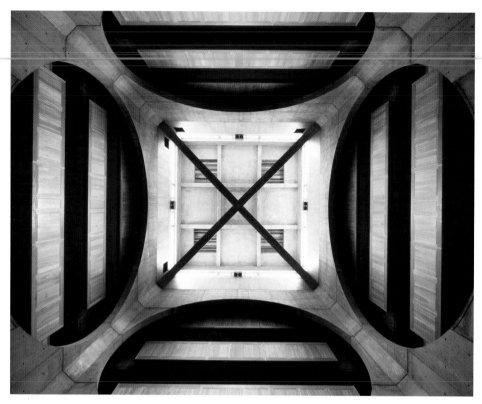

Looking upward in the Phillips Exeter library's central court.

entirely different inspiration—the works of the French utopians Claude-Nicolas Ledoux and Étienne-Louis Boullée, whom Lou had celebrated in the book *Visionary Architects*.

Entering the library through the low brick arcades, those students carrying books must have been shocked by the wonderous interior they encountered. Then as now, one ascends a majestic curving stair on treads of travertine to the sudden revelation of a soaring central hall, reaching up past layered shelves encircled by huge concrete structural frames to massive crossed beams far above, reflecting sunlight as if from heaven. The dramatic height and grandeur of this space with its heraldry of books hearkens back to the interiors of great castles, and it also suggests the awe-inspiring spaces one might have encountered in Lou's religious sanctuaries in Philadelphia and Jerusalem that were never built.

OPPOSITE: "A library is a place where you bring a book from the darkness into the light." Looking across the central court at Exeter.

348

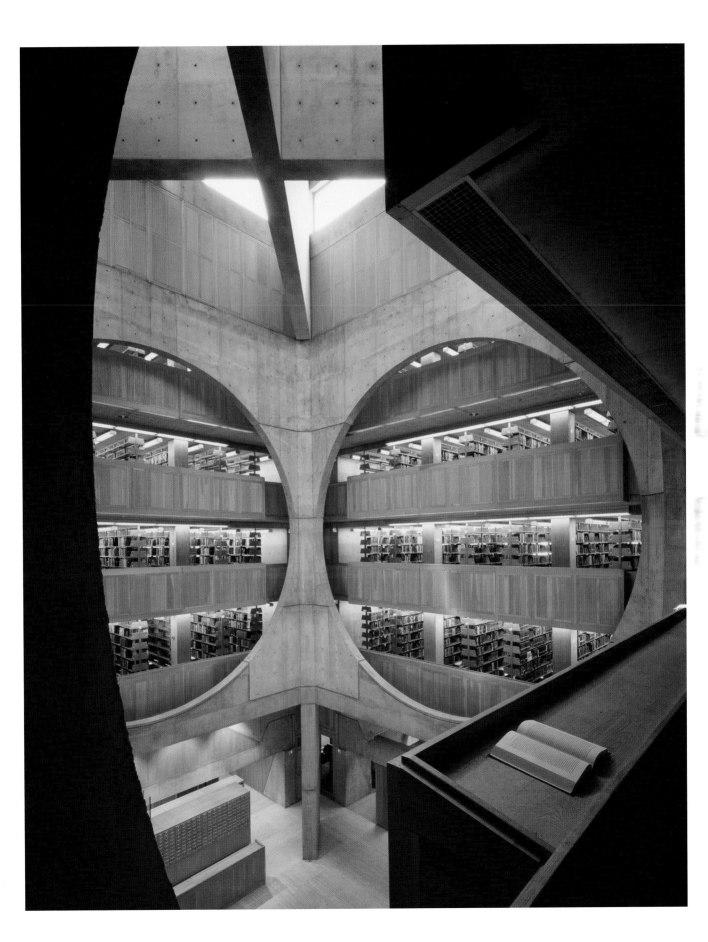

Lou in the auditorium of the Kimbell Art Museum during the final inspection, 1972.

1972

When Lou spoke of our lives being shaped by accidents and circumstances, I couldn't agree, believing that fate plays a role in them as well. But I must admit that I might not have gone to work full-time for Lou were it not for the faulty wiring that caused a fire in Terry Schnadelbach's office in the summer of 1971. Luckily the fire broke out over the weekend, so no one was around, but the Delancey Street office was totally destroyed. The outcome was life-altering for all of us, beginning with Terry, who was sufficiently insured to rebuild his practice.

Terry set up shop in a renovated warehouse across town, acquired a partner, and sought out regional planning commissions that redirected the firm toward more entrepreneurial goals. This weakened the role of design people like me, but we rallied around the boss, and there was a strong camaraderie on the day we helped movers assemble a battery of furniture and equipment in the new space. Suddenly the iron-cage elevator door opened and out stepped Lou, unannounced. He strode up to Terry, seized his arm—as he had once playfully immobilized Philadelphia mayor Frank Rizzo's—and exclaimed over the wonderful space, brickwork, and natural light in what had to me seemed a dreary place. Then, like lightning, Lou was down on his hands and knees, helping put things together, and everyone was laughing and enjoying themselves.

If the energy of this white-haired luminary inspired Terry and his young crew, the incongruity of Lou's presence in that environment told me that I didn't belong, and the light went out when he left. I had begun work on a park plan that didn't suit Terry's agenda, and it was clear to me, before it was to him, that I needed to move on. But where was I to go? I hadn't a clue about marketing myself, did not wish to return to George Patton's office, and had no license yet to practice on my own.

I spoke to Lou about my situation one night over supper, and he listened intently. Then, after a silence, he said simply, "Come work for me." Of course, this was what I'd hoped he might say, but I think Lou had also realized that my sensibilities and skills were being wasted, and that he wanted them for his own projects. I expect my work on the Kimbell landscape, seen in recent progress photographs, also helped Lou justify my presence and face the

Lou in his corner office at 1501 Walnut Street, Philadelphia.

personal risks of giving me a place in his office. And so, whether by accident or fate, I moved back to 1501 Walnut Street in early 1972.

When I joined the office, Lou had little money for another person on his payroll and no extra space amid architects in his drafting room, where my presence might cause a stir, so he uncovered a fourth-floor hideaway adjoining the storage area as a place for his in-house landscape consultant on a retainer. My drafting table faced a wall of windows, and I kept the door with its frosted-glass panel locked to avoid confrontations when Esther Kahn paid a visit. She arrived every month, checking Lou's calendar and finances, or showed up as his vizier when he was away, and would be drawn to the fourth floor to rattle my door and complain to anyone in the workshop about its being locked. Though this may have amused the staff, I dreaded those occasions, and Nathaniel commented that I acted "like you're living in somebody else's house." But I was confident that I belonged, and I knew that Lou needed me.

I was to learn about 1501's fourth and fifth floors from the inside now, and how Lou comported himself there. He was still the wrestler of his youth, taking on the forces of mediocrity and defending architecture with all his mental and physical strength. He needed teammates but not followers in this arena; "The man who serves me best is the man who serves himself," he said. He chose able "clerks of the works" for far-flung assignments, yet he was attentive to every detail, overseeing the creation of all the models and hardline drawings from his charcoal explorations and making notes that were to be followed and defended at all costs.

I saw Lou for the first time among his people: a dynamo operating between concepts and materializations, ignited like the sparks in his eyes, with uncanny insights—ideas that made their way onto rolls of drawings that he carried tucked under his arm, like battle plans, to the diverse places he was constantly traveling to, far from home.

What saved Lou from burnout was drawing alone, late at night. On breaks, he would circulate in the silent office, leaving notes and corrections on the drafting boards to be addressed the next day. He would rarely draw directly on your work; instead, he made his own drawing on yellow trace laid over yours. It was efficient but also respectful, even tender.

And there was the weekly ritual of teaching. At past jury sessions, I'd seen how Lou's mind worked in the studio, critiquing a student's presentation while testing his own ideas and teaching himself. But now I saw that students were also essential to the operation at 1501. They came from Tokyo, Istanbul, Ahmedabad, Tel Aviv, Buenos Aires, grassroots America, and the Ivy League. Some of them, spotting a charette in 1501's lighted windows at midnight, volunteered for piecework, hoping to be hired, as many were. They provided a tireless outlay of energy to meet office production from a welter of forms at the highest level of creativity, and many of them settled in Philadelphia and stayed on for years.

Several members of Lou's staff, like Dave Wisdom, Henry Wilcots, Marshall Meyers, and Vincent Rivera, I knew already, but now there were new people I was coming to know. Hema Patel, Reyhan Larimer, John Lucas, Gary Moye, Winton Scott, Tony Pellecchia, Keith Donald, and Karl Krumholz were among them.

A few had short-term visas, like Shane de Blacam, from Dublin, whose delicate sketches Lou admired, and Jacques Fredet, a fiery-haired Frenchman who cared as fiercely about architecture as he did about revolution. And there was Gabor Szalontay, a mysterious Hungarian who was never formally employed in the office, but who slipped in for late-night talks, comparing, as Lou said, "on equal terms, a piece of sculpture by Phidias and a word." Tall, handsome, with a conspiratorial accent, Gabor wore but one suit, but he wore it with the air of a boulevardier, and he was rumored to have bicycled to freedom during the 1956 revolution. Gabor and Lou would sit late at night at a drafting board, mostly in silence, waiting for just the right word to appear— as if it might unlock a hidden power from which a new kingdom would arise.

Still, the Walnut Street office was no Taliesin. There were no amenities, just the work. Lou's corner room, bright with daylight from windows on two sides, held a door mounted on sawhorses for a desk, a brass telescope, a large

Piranesi plan of ancient Rome pinned on the wall above a wooden bench piled high with books, and a scrap of orange textile from the tapestry of the First Unitarian Church that he rolled out to nap on. The Bicentennial model was mounted above a single shelf of books treasured for their illustrations by George Cruikshank, Gustave Doré, Eugène Viollet-le-Duc, and Leonardo da Vinci, as well as a dog-eared copy of German classicist Werner Jaeger's *Paideia*—Lou's bible for ancient Greek customs and philosophy. The windowsill facing Walnut Street held tchotchkes, including archaic clay sculptures and a tiny Buddha head I had given him, while the window behind his desk faced the Drexel Bank across Fifteenth Street. Lou pointed to how the sun brought out rainbow hues in its stone walls, often sitting at his desk until all the light had faded from the sky before switching on an electric light.

Lou mapped his thoughts in red Winsor & Newton notebooks that he bought at the Taws art supply store around the corner. What he wanted most of all was to write the new fairy tale—because, as he said, from the fairy tale came locomotives and airplanes and all the wondrous institutions that spring from the imagination of man.

What would Lou have made of computers? He didn't drive a car (he had landed a Ford in a ditch the one time he tried, back in the 1930s), nor was he mechanically minded, but he was no Luddite. He had great respect for engineering, pushing his engineers August Komendant (a fellow Estonian) and the wonderful Nick Gianopulos to the limits of what was possible and beyond. I think Lou would have respected the ability of computers to model possibilities quickly, but he would have rejected them as a generator of design, even as he would toss out a drawing without hesitation if he felt it was merely pretty or seductive and not of real substance. For Lou, drawing was a way to reach toward what was true, and this had to be felt, not calculated.

A glance at one of Lou's office calendars shows every hour of his day filled by meetings, talks, and classes, with frequent travel to seven countries overseas as well as American work sites. He had a total of eighteen projects simultaneously underway the year I joined the office. The only time he had to collect himself was in the middle of the night, after his office went home, or when he escaped to an afternoon movie or a baseball game with architect Ricky Wurman, whose company he enjoyed, or when taking a fast walk (never a stroll) through the city, sidestepping cars like a matador intent on dispatching them. One bus took revenge, however, and ran over his foot. And Lou never passed a beggar—a fellow, he'd say, "just temporarily down on his luck"—without emptying his pockets.

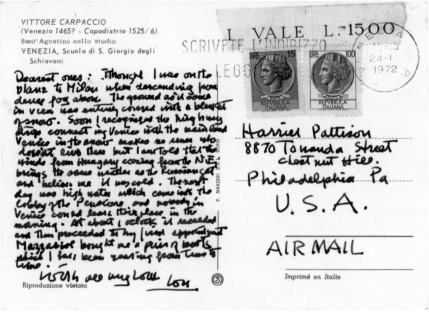

VENICE TO 8870 TOWANDA ST., PHILADELPHIA, JANUARY 24, 1972

Dearest ones:

I thought I was on the plane to Milan when descending from dense fog above the ground as it came in view was entirely covered with a blanket of snow. Soon I recognized the highway strip connecting Venice with the mainland. Venice in the snow makes no sense [to] who doesn't live there but I am told that the winds from Hungary

Lou on a tour of Venice's Jewish ghetto.

Lou crossing the Giudecca Canal in a boat, looking toward the future as always.

coming from the N.E. bring the same weather as the Russians get and believe me it was cold. The next day was high water which came into the lobby of the Pensione and nobody in Venice could leave their place in the morning. At about 1 o'clock it receded and then [I] proceeded to my first appointment. Mazzariol bought me a pair of boots which I have been wearing from time to time.

With all my love,
Lou

One project that took on an accelerated pace, now that I was a full-time employee in Lou's office, was a small city garden for Martin and Margy Meyerson, just across the Schuylkill River from the University of Pennsylvania, where Martin was the new president. The Meyersons had lived in the Darwin Martin House (designed by Frank Lloyd Wright) in Buffalo, saving it from demolition, and as city planners they were eager to exchange Penn's suburban mansion for one in town with a Kahn interior.

It was wonderful to engage with such buoyant and enlightened people as the Meyersons, but I recall standing in our coats in their chilly living room and viewing the narrow, walled backyard through a bay window with a sense of unease. Lou had already borrowed space from the yard for a sunroom, making it even smaller. How could I make this garden worthy, despite its minimal size? Coming from Chicago, where city gardens were a rarity, I had only one memorable precedent: if I made my design half as good as the

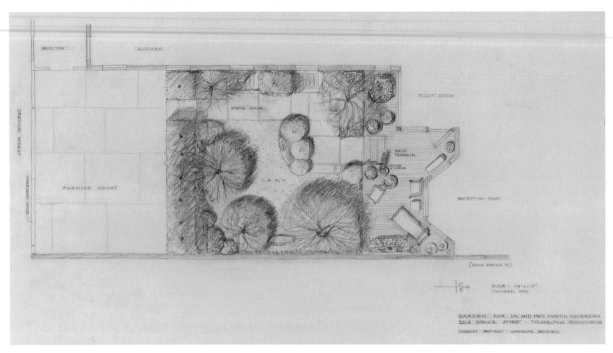

My plan for the Meyerson Garden, Spruce Street, Philadelphia.

exquisite Art Deco garden by my mother's friend Gertrude Deimel Kuh, doyenne of Chicago landscape architects in the 1930s, I would be all right, I told myself.

I centered the design on a carpet-sized lawn for small receptions, secured all around by evergreens. There was ivy for the brick walls, boxwood, laurel, and holly hedges, and a lacebark pine at the far end, creating the illusion of distance. For historic reference I added a rare franklinia, descendant of John Bartram's original specimen, named for the university's founder, Benjamin Franklin. And I unearthed pots and classical bronzes from Penn's arboretum storage to be loaned for a terrace that extended the footprint of Lou's sunroom to the outside. The Meyersons welcomed my ideas, as well as choices of interior artworks and tropical plants for the sunroom to dispel the winter's gloom for shut-ins like George, the family's giant housecat.

On March 22, after Jerusalem's mayor, Teddy Kollek, met with Lou to review progress on the Hurva Synagogue and the Jerusalem Hills project, Steven Korman, a partner in his family's Philadelphia real estate firm, stopped by the office. He had the money to build one of the two houses that he and his sister, Lynne Honickman, had persuaded Lou to design for a seventy-acre tract in suburban Fort Washington. Lou found his eager and attractive young votaries hard to resist, although public and international

The Meyerson Garden terrace, Spruce Street, Philadelphia.

commissions left him no time for such residential work other than weekends when he was in town.

"Like an African savannah!" Lou had exclaimed as we walked through the tall grass of the site with Steve Korman and his wife, Toby, as well as Lynne and Harold Honickman the summer before. It was a hot day, and Lou had thrown his jacket over his shoulder as we joked about lions up ahead and circled about for bearings—the least landmark to tell where to place a house—then struggled up a hill through scrubby trees to a barren overlook. Lou had everyone laughing over our safari as we bivouacked in the grass, and it was lovely to be with young people my age—although it was bittersweet contemplating houses for couples when I so wanted a home with Lou.

In the end only the Korman house would be built. It was a tender mission, imagining life for young parents with protected areas for their sons' play, while mooring the house in that grass sea with its horizon of low hedgerow. I was to imagine mowing parts of "the savannah," mounding and paving bits of it, and planting trees to merge house and land, while Lou would tussle over details with builder Steve, with whom he found a real connection, even sharing feelings of inadequacy compared with his craftsman father, Leopold, one night over a bottle of vodka. "My father never respected me," Lou apparently said, "because I never did anything with my hands."

Toby and Steven Korman with their boys, Mark, Brad, and Larry, at the building site, Fort Washington, Pennsylvania.

I have often wondered why Lou took this modest commission while he was so inundated with the large-scale work he had sought all his life. I think building a modern house for one young family, something he couldn't do for his own children or for his immigrant parents, who moved from one Philadelphia tenement to the next before escaping to California, gave him something he needed. It allowed him perspective on the sweep of his life and to engage in the future in a very personal way—projecting his hopes for a dawning era of openness and acceptance that transcended his own time.

We had planned to site the Honickman house atop the hill and the Kormans' in the grasslands, both accessed by a private road with gravel courts, which I laid out along with terraces, gardens, and outdoor recreation spaces. I tucked each house behind driveway curves and suggested orienting them to their longest view, offsetting the orthogonal footprints with curving forms to initiate flow between the two dwellings. I regraded the land in three dimensions to energize the common acreage with added vistas and destinations. There was to be an orchard and a pond for the Honickmans and, for the Kormans, a tennis court, pool (with a protective ditch or "ha-ha"), and woodlands. My desire was to unify and characterize a "family seat," distinct from splintering land into suburban lots—a now ubiquitous practice that was just then beginning to destroy the natural topography of many great tracts of open land in the Philadelphia region.

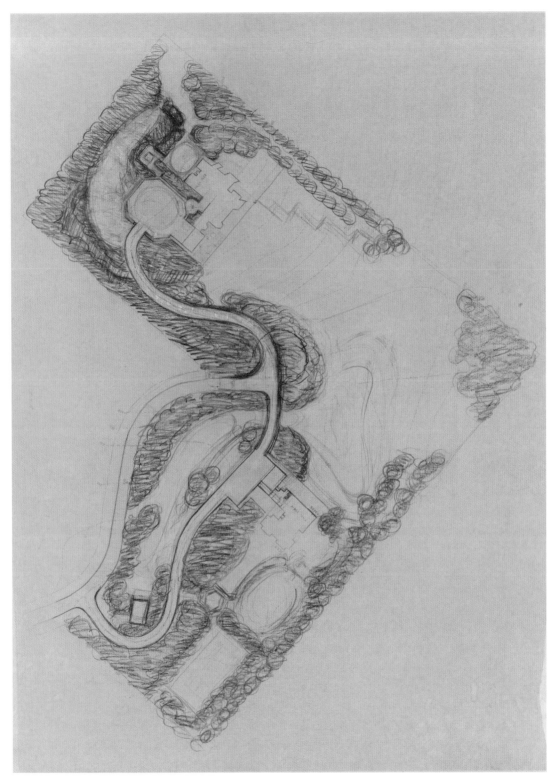

My initial master-plan sketch for the Honickman House (above) and the Korman House (below), with layout of roads and plantings as well as "outdoor rooms" extending the houses into the landscape.

The Korman House under construction, held in composition by tall brick chimneys.

Of course there was ample local precedent for the American "country house" landscape I was pursuing, beginning with John Penn's eighteenth-century "The Solitude" on the Schuylkill River, moving through the works of Frank Furness and the estates of architects like Mellor, Meigs & Howe (George Howe had been a friend and partner of Lou's in the 1940s). But this new generation was pursuing a different lifestyle, more informal, accepting, and unpretentious. I liked the Korman and Honickman families exceedingly and enjoyed modernizing design sensibilities in my own mind to serve the new, streamlined chic of this fun-loving crowd, while encouraging them to steer clear of the clichés of suburbia.

With the Honickman house on hold, the Korman house went ahead without delay. Materials had changed from stone to cheaper wood, but what Lou made of the cypress was wonderful. I had everything to do to make over this lonely place into something worthy, fast and on a budget. I took Nathaniel and a school friend with me one day and used their play on the construction site as guides for what the three Korman boys might do. I had to establish a heritage for the house, which looked small to hold down a big, bare slice of land. I exaggerated minor dips and rises in regrading this farm acreage, deepening swales and raising mounds to create movement, and I extended the house in a series of "outdoor rooms" for the pool and

The Korman House seen through the mature pine forest. The cypress walls are weathering to a rich gray, as Lou intended.

tennis court. But the rest would have to be accomplished in time, with bold plantings of trees and detailing with shrubs and ground covers.

Once the drive and parking courts were determined, my planting plan followed, to build the impression that the landscape had invited a country house to nest within it "as if it had always been there." Wanting to select native trees in a zone so richly endowed, I chose colorful tupelos, sycamores, and American arborvitae for wet areas, and oaks, tulip poplars, and maples for dry land. I interspersed them with pines, hollies, and occasional spruce as evergreen backbones to screen off vistas for privacy and to sequence discoveries along the drive. Finally I added a few specimens that would be knockouts at maturity: a Kentucky yellowwood, an ornamental beech, and a (non-native) katsura, supplemented by understory dogwood and redbuds. My boldest move, amassing white pines for a dense, quick "forest," was soon to provide an end-of-the-road sense of arrival in "Korman country."

Approaching along the curving drive and through parting trees, visitors today find the Korman house nestled in a mature landscape, but the long vista

The tall living room in the Korman House, looking out on a fresh snow, with the piano Lou played one night shortly before his final trip to India.

is intentionally withheld until one enters the living room and encounters it as a surprise—an iconic exchange between an artful inner serenity and the drama of the natural outer world. In the far distance, sycamores still line an old county road, beckoning the next generation to further sculpt this land and the adjacent hilltop, perhaps informed by what Lou and I once imagined for "the savannah."

Lou took time out from work at the office to advise me about a job that I was now grappling with on weekends in my home studio on the top floor of our Towanda Street house. It was a master plan for a three-hundred-acre estate on North Haven Island, Maine, for Thomas Watson Jr. and his wife, Olive, whose son was married to my niece. Tom had flown Nathaniel and me in his plane over the property the summer before, and as Lou sat at the drafting board he'd given me, tucked beneath the dormer eaves, I presented my ideas for the master plan. It was daunting, with an airstrip and family compound to contend with, as well as houses for many children, a horse barn, a fish farm, and roads

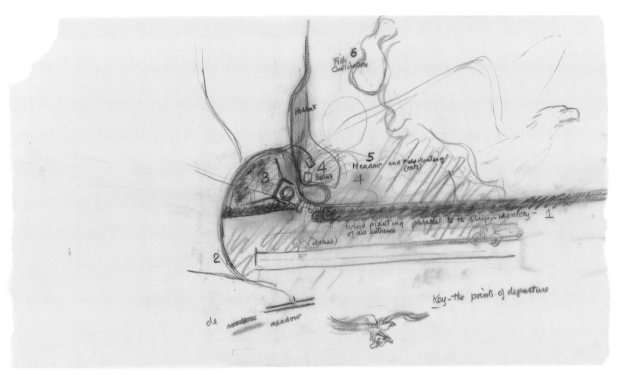

Lou's sketch of one area of the Watson estate, with Nathaniel's eagle taking flight from the airstrip.

and pathways that needed to be threaded through a dramatic landscape of woods, meadows, beaches, and overlooks.

What followed was a peerless Beaux-Arts lesson in proceeding between the large-scale and the particular, treating all the individual units with proportionate consistency. I was not to be intimidated by the scale of the project and the varied possibilities, but instead trust my instincts from the beginning, seeking a governing form. The plan should be clear and readable, as seen from the eye of the bald eagle Nathaniel told Lou he'd seen soaring over the airstrip.

The view from above was critical to Lou. He had a book of Leonardo drawings that he pored over, and it was not the inventions or anatomical and plant studies that captivated him but rather the topographic sketches of dramatic landscapes and terrains drawn from the air. Lou's sense of landscape was broad and from above—a perspective I felt a natural affinity for and, with his help, began to develop. Sometimes we would leaf through my landscape books together, admiring Frederick Law Olmsted's parklands and those of his eighteenth-century English predecessors, or comparing garden fantasists Fletcher Steele, Beatrix Farrand, and Roberto Burle Marx to Italian Renaissance masters, or seeing how modernists like Dan Kiley and Sweden's Gunnar Asplund reimagined the sweeps of André Le Nôtre's landscapes for Louis XIV.

An office model of Government House Hill Development, Jerusalem.

TEL AVIV TO TOWANDA ST., MARCH 15, 1972

My lovely dears H'ie & N,
If only time could—would be stilled.

If happenings could be cut away, that what is, is what was.

The clutter of need snuffs out desire. What a mess of imitation of imitation.

The artistic is taken for Art.

Hotels are Pop art the way they have become: leering.

I am designing a hotel—can I make so lonely a place?

BARCELONA TO TOWANDA ST., JUNE 10, 1972

Dearest Harriet and Nathaniel,
Have been in Barcelona now for 3 days without a change of shirt or suit.

My bag is lost in transit and cannot be traced.

I saw a good bit of Gaudi. It is wonderful in spirit. I am raring to tell you all.

Love,
Lou

Conceived in 1883, Antoni Gaudí's Sagrada Família was under construction at the architect's death in 1926 and remains unfinished to this day. That an art requiring the greatest effort to produce is the longest to last is perhaps a comfort to the creator; nevertheless, the realization that one might never see one's work finished was a simple fact ahead of each day's labors for someone like Lou.

Upon seeing Gaudí's masterpiece, how could he not have thought of his own great work in Dhaka? When he wrote this postcard, Lou had heard nothing about his building for a full year. In 1971 relations between East and West Pakistan had disintegrated into a brutal war in which Dhaka had been bombed and devastating numbers of East Pakistan's Bengalis had been murdered by the Pakistani army in an act of genocide. During this time, Lou had no idea what the fate of his building would be, but still he continued to work on it, saying, "There will be a time after the war when they will need this building." And so it was. In July the office was contacted by government officials, and in August Lou returned to Dhaka with Henry Wilcots, the gifted and trusted project architect on several of his commissions, including the capital complex. Lou and Henry had no idea what they would find upon their arrival—a building, or a smoking ruin.

The capital complex as Lou would have seen it, flying into Dhaka after the war, 1972. The National Assembly was still ten years away from completion, but it had survived the war unscathed.

Lou and Henry Wilcots in Kathmandu, after their return to Dhaka.

Dearest Harriet and Nathaniel,
Arrived in New Delhi last and lost all connections to Dhaka. The
Indian Air lines have given us a hotel room—we have a long wait
for a flight from Delhi–Calcutta–Dhaka.

The drawings lost in the destruction of war had to be reprinted
which we did and brought the new set of drawings with us. We had
to pay $300.00 over weight. Luckily Henry had a credit card. Did
you receive my hurried note to you (the note which instructs to put
$600.00 in your account. I asked you to send your bank number to
Kathy) just moments before we had to leave the office for the Air
India flight from New York?

The meeting with the Governor went swell; had a lot of people
with him. The agent of the General State Authority told us that we
are entitled to draw from a fund established, set at ½ of 1 percent
of the fee on what we estimated to be 30,000,000 as the cost of
the project. This makes it possible to continue studies even before
formal arrangements are made. This is <u>good</u>.

The usual trouble of communications and services have hit us.
Typical of these parts. I just hope we can be on our way. Nothing so
far is confirmed, and this is <u>bad</u>.

Here is joy, happiness, health to both of you and to that part of
the family who understand and love us.

With Love,
Lou

Dearest pussycats,
Tomorrow we leave for Kathmandu. Our dealings here [in Dhaka]
seem to be normal. The buildings look very well very like the
unexpected. They don't hate us. They are trying to be reasonably
unreasonable, merchants who know a bargain and know how to
exact it from the helpless seller. It's human in its most idealess pose.
I was struck down by dysentery. In bed all day the second day on
and off the - - - and nausea when I rose from bed. I took those pills,
6 at a time, big ones, 6 × a day. What a mouthful, but it did the trick
and the next day fit, but not quite like a fiddle.

Love,
Lou

Dearest Harriet and Nathaniel

Have left Kathmandu for Delhi
Much confusion on travel since
conformation of flights on Indian Airlines
not possible in States. Air India is ok,
but Indian Airlines are local. Tourist
jambo adds to the difficulties.

Kanya and I are now on our way to Ahmedabad.
I have decided not to go to Israel yet since
I had to leave the project undone to the office. I thought
when I left for the East that the idea was sound and
could trust Frede and Keith to interpret. I am
now that is not possible. How embarrassing
I return to _ I received photos of the _
to take to Maya Kollek only to make apologizes.
I have now the plan to come back earlier with
Henry and get to work on it directly. I will
have to fly back the 2nd or 3rd week in September
with something worthy. Maya Kollek _ that
I teckon _ waiting for me London Tel Aviv and back
I will have to pay my own way to London and back.
So it is going.
To day I tried to confirm a flight back to
New York on the 2nd of September. It may
prove to be impossible. I have a confirmed
Indian back London New York 14th Sept

Sept — the time I was to return from Tel Aviv. I
may be obliged to stay in London 3 days just
because I cannot fly any other way than by
Air India. What a mess that would be when
I so very much need the time. Flying back with
Henry would make it different also because of
our plans you and me.
I have asked to be helped in all directions I may yet
find a way I am so lonely for the two of you

In Dacca I proposed a new scheme for the site

[TOP: site plan] *court / new secretariat buildings as high as the assembly building /
crescent lake / park*

As you can see it is very different from the scheme I have always
had. the secretariats in my previous scheme had reason not to be
3,000,000 sq ft. Or need a new at all. I placed it opposite the
assembly

[BOTTOM: section] *assembly / park / secretariats*

I promised to make a model of this idea. I must win
over the new ministers with the vastly superior idea

Pray for me sweethearts. The world becomes more
and more exciting with every _ you earlier time
for us.

With all my love _

I got some old Victorian coins (silver and copper) minted
in India. and 2 Mogul coins of the 14th century for Nathaniel.

Dearest Harriet and Nathaniel,

Have left Kathmandu for Delhi. Much confusion on travel since confirmation of flights on Indian Airlines not possible in States. Air India is OK, but Indian Airlines are locals. Tourist jam adds to the difficulties. Henry and I are now on our way to Ahmedabad. I have decided not to go to Israel yet since I had to leave the final model to the office. I thought when I left for the East that the idea was sound and could trust [Jacques] Fredet and Keith [Donald] to interpret. I am sure this is not possible. How embarrassing it would be if I received photos of the model to take to Mayor Kollek only to make apologies. I have now the plan to come back earlier with Henry and get to work on it directly. I will have to fly back the 2nd or 3rd week in September with something worthy. Mayor Kollek wired that I. [Israel] ticket is waiting for me, London to Tel Aviv and back. I will have to pay my own way to London and back. So it is going.

Today I tried to confirm a flight back to New York on the 2nd of September. It may prove to be impossible. I have a confirmed ticket back to London and New York for the 5th of September—the time I was to return from Tel Aviv. I may be obliged to stay in London 3 days just because I cannot fly any other way thru my Air India. What a mess that would be when I so very much need the time. Flying back with Henry would make it difficult also because of our plans, you and me. I have asked to be helped in all directions. I may yet find a way. I am so lonely for the two of you.

In Dhaka I proposed a new scheme for the site.

As you see it is very different from the scheme I have always had. The secretariat in my previous scheme had 300,000 not as in 3,000,000 sq ft. [I] need a new place. I placed it opposite the assembly.

I promised to make a model of the idea. I must win over the new minister on the vastly superior idea. Pray for me sweethearts. The world becomes more and more exciting with many promises of an easier time for us.

With all my love,
Lou

I got some old Victorian coins (gilded and copper) minted in India and 2 Mogul coins of the 14th century for Nathaniel.

Sunday

Dearest Harriet and Nathaniel,

I had to cancel trip to Jerusalem. Received telegram of trouble
in office—rent, telephone, pay. Tried to cable you—no service
except thru Bangor, came to-day and before looking into
trouble—nobody in office—I write to you in hope that you get
this right away. Nobody apparently, has come thru with our needs.
Terribly frustrated not being able to stop on Indian Island, so
looked forward to, no word from you—Did you receive my mail?
Went back with Henry [from Dhaka] on circuitous route—many
changes—long lines of security checks terrible crowding of the
planes—went 2nd class because of Henry—dog tired but raring to
straighten out things must not lose heart even if I must let people
go—so hard for me to do.

When I wrote you last, I felt worried about not finishing the
work on Jerusalem and having to take with me to Jerusalem work
that I did not see completed. Now with the turn of events, I find
it better all except for having to return without seeing you on the
Island. I thought of several ways . . . [but] rescheduling flights with
Labor Day and the hordes of returning tourists, nothing was in the
remotest way possible.

I bought you about 5 yards of home spun silk—off white—for a
dress . . . [For] Nathaniel, as I wrote, some silver coins issued during
the reign of England in India. . . . Also for Nathaniel, I bought a
Tibetan hood made of suede lined with fox and for real cold days.

Come home soon! Call please to let me know when!

With all my love,

Lou

Lou had planned to visit Indian Island. Nathaniel was counting on it and had
straightened up his workshop in the barn in preparation, wanting to show
his father the boat models he was building. But when he heard what Lou was
going through, having just returned from Dhaka to find the office falling
apart, he shook it off and hid his disappointment with a smile and a caper.
Such was Nathaniel; nothing would come between him and his daddy. I too
saw the bigger picture. Lou's building was all right. It had survived in a kind of
miracle. Years later I heard a story that may be apocryphal, but I embrace it all

Nathaniel at the barn door, Indian Island.

the same: that the enemy pilot hadn't bombed the National Assembly Building because it looked like a Mughal ruin. Lou would have chuckled at that, but deep down it would have made him terribly proud.

Back in 1963, Lou had written to me in the woods of Vermont from Dhaka: "I am sad my sweet dears, because I see the image of the Assembly Building as though it were a reality and I feel the helplessness of my financial situation. I could give in and take a gander. The building may turn out well and hopefully break even. I could refuse the terms and never see the work of a dream. What should I do?"

Lou had taken that gander, and although he was falling deeper into debt, the work of a dream was turning out magnificently. The capital complex had survived a war. What was once the artificially created "second capital" of Pakistan had emerged as the only capital of a wholly new and sovereign country—Bangladesh.

The Kimbell Art Museum opened to the public on October 2, 1972. I wasn't there for the event, as I was not invited. Lou took Esther. Project architect Marshall Meyers and his wife, Anne, attended, as did George Patton and his wife, Sydney. Lou didn't have to tell me that the building and its landscape had turned out well; I knew that already, although it would take more than a decade before I experienced the project for myself.

With the Kimbell Art Museum, Lou felt he had reached a level he had never touched before: "When I saw it finished it seemed that I had nothing to do with it at all and that another hand had done it," he remarked later that fall. As a young man Lou had set out to be an artist and then turned to architecture as a profession that would fulfill him and give him a higher purpose—but a voice of his own in his chosen field had been hard-won. The mastery and control that came naturally to him in drawing took several decades to achieve in architecture. With the Kimbell he had fully found himself, and somehow also come back around to his own beginnings, creating a "sanctuary of art" that was also a work of art in itself.

Lou revered art as the highest human endeavor, and with the Kimbell, he touched the art of architecture as never before. Filled with light and movement, changing with every day and passing cloud, united with water, trees, and the sky, the place was alive as only a work of art can be.

From this time on, an energy flowed from Lou, like a star burning brightest even as it reaches its end.

PAGES 376–77, ABOVE, AND OPPOSITE: Kimbell Art Museum, Fort Worth, Texas.

Nathaniel's photo of Lou and me at Towanda Street.

1973

February 20 was Lou's seventy-second birthday, but that was the last thing on his mind when he came to my room in the office with a parcel. He deftly unwrapped it on my desk, saying with a flourish that it was from New York. The parcel contained site information from the state's Urban Development Commission (UDC) for a stunning new project—a memorial to Franklin Delano Roosevelt.

It had been twenty-seven years since the president's death, but in that time, four major architectural design proposals for a national memorial to join those of Washington, Jefferson, and Lincoln in Washington, DC, had been rejected. These successive defeats rallied a group of FDR relatives and supporters, including kingmaker William Walton and architect Philip Johnson, to seek an end-run alternative. Partnering with New York officials, they proposed a state memorial for its world-renowned resident and onetime governor on a prominent site, to be designed, in a unanimous choice, by architect Louis I. Kahn.

There was no one better prepared in heart and mind for this commission, which Lou regarded as the greatest honor of his career. Roosevelt was Lou's lifelong political hero: for his bold defending of immigrants; for his New Deal programs, which had given Lou work, designing housing during the Great Depression; even for his championing of public works and aspects of civic well-being, which had greatly inspired Lou's ultimate artistic focus on building "the institutions of man."

Lou was ready for this long-overdue call to create a unique American memorial. He unfolded the topographic drawings and spread out a pack of photographs like a winning hand at cards, eager to share with me what he knew of the site, on the southern tip of New York's Welfare Island in the East River, midway between the crowded shorelines of Manhattan and Queens. The site was a bare peninsula of rocky spoil, excavated from the digging of the subway tunnel beneath the river, and offered a prime opportunity for cooperation between architecture and landscape. Lou made it clear that we would do this one together from the beginning.

Suddenly I realized the gravity of the challenge: that I would participate in a historic moment, engaging not only my professional abilities but also my memories and feelings for the public figure who had informed my life more than any other. I heard in my head the sonorous, enunciated phrases broadcast in FDR's fireside chats, and my mind filled with a flood of memories of those years. Of "the War": its beginnings in fearful accounts of Hitler's advance through Europe and fleeing refugees, the shock of Pearl Harbor and the eerie drawdown of all the "boys." And of my brothers, in perilous, distant battles in the Pacific, and of the explosive bursts of news heard on the radio and splashed on movie screens, and of the high drama between doubt and hope disrupting minutes of "normal" lives, awakening all America to the universe of humanity. I flashed too on the day of Roosevelt's death at Warm Springs, Georgia, and how my young life had dissolved in tears. How to distill those feelings and seek a true authenticity in design? Then I recalled the thrill I'd felt, as a child aboard a sailboat in Penobscot Bay, when the president's yacht steamed past and we glimpsed him seated on the fantail. That was golden and real. FDR embodied my love for my country, and his personal courage gave me courage. I would give this project everything I had to give.

We were going to be hard-pressed to come up with results in time for a planned mid-March presentation, and Lou must have spent an hour that day at my desk, looking at the photos and sketching the walk he'd made over the four-acre site on yellow trace laid atop an engineer's survey. The empty land had but a single feature at the north end, the castle-like neo-Gothic ruin of the smallpox hospital designed by James Renwick in 1846. I could see it was a beauty that resisted dying in that forsaken spot, a quarantined area of this island that had once held the city's sick, poor, and delinquent, but was now being redeveloped into a residential community of mid-height apartment blocks and services. Whatever was to be built at this open end, reserved for the memorial, would have a permanent panorama of the river and the Manhattan skyline, with the United Nations structures in full view—it was guaranteed to become a landmark.

The moment he saw the site, Lou said, he knew where to start: he would consolidate the island tip as a triangle, with seawall and riprap protection against the river's six-foot tides, and square off the apex for a memorial structure. With these thoughts, he opened it to me to explore ideas for the rest of the site. Before he left, he said, "Remember the Catlin books I gave Nathaniel? Take a look."

What was I to make of the long, narrowing strip of land but a processional? A journey, then, a symbolic American one, summoning the spirit of the great, wide, wild continent George Catlin had portrayed in his

An engraving from George Catlin's *North American Indians*. Lou admired the way Catlin captured the magnificence of the North American landscape.

books on Native Americans and a journey made through those lands, giving way at the southern end to the architect's built order in the midst of the river.

My first move was to raise the ground, adding soil at the broad end of the long site and feathering it to the tip to give a third dimension and dramatic sloping profile, boldly signaling to the opposite shores that there were things happening here. I heightened the edges further with lines of trees and began to experiment by cutting through the land with a central path and a succession of landscape spaces along the route of the journey. I gradually simplified these natural "rooms" until they were eliminated altogether, creating one great green room, sloping, narrowing, and bordered by allées of trees. The shaded allée pathways would converge before the memorial structure Lou was exploring in a series of drawings.

Several days later, Lou began to draw—as always from the bottom up, as one builds—but he went off the top of the yellow trace. It was the beginning of his colossal sixty-foot-high cylinder-within-a-cube memorial scheme. It was shaped like an old stone bastion one might encounter at the mouth of a harbor, only its surface was of stainless steel, the material he was using at the Yale Center for British Art. But here Lou was bending the material into a scintillated composition of inner balconies, niches, and rooms, creating a kind of vertical theater of spaces—a radical experiment in expressionism, fusing high art and high tech.

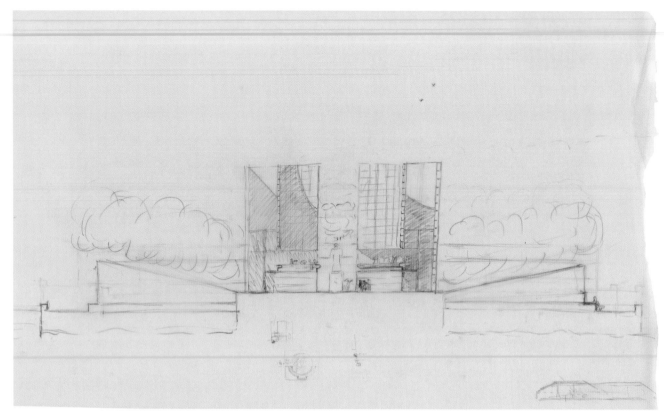

Lou's section drawing of his stainless steel "bastion" scheme for the FDR Memorial.

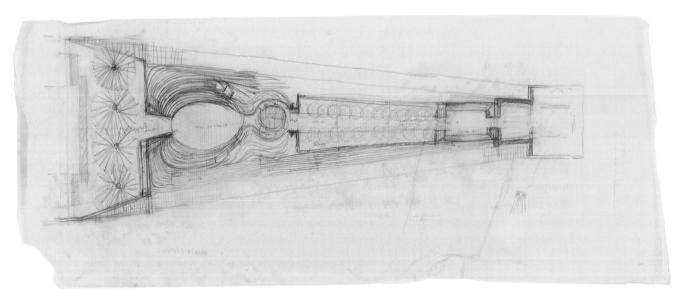

My first "kitchen sink" plan for the FDR Memorial, incorporating a little bit of everything, with cedars of Lebanon marking the entrance and an amphitheater with grass slopes.

I loved this monument as much as Lou did and tried to match it, suggesting pollarded linden trees for the allées, like the Tuileries in Paris or Berlin's Unter den Linden, but it was a move Lou dismissed immediately as "Kaiser Louis" and "not American!" After considering American beech, I had to recognize that the site was too small for avenues of large trees, and I needed to rethink the scale and find other ways of expressing the desired monumentality. But all this was rendered moot when the cost estimate for the bastion scheme came in at three times the $2.5 million budget. There was no way to save Lou's steel dream, and with just three weeks left before a planned April 24 presentation, he had to reform the entire concept.

"I like to believe that the room is the beginning of architecture," said Lou, and he channeled that idea into a new concept, creating a roofless space, eighty-four-feet square, at land's end. Its two parallel L-shaped walls framed a central pier that faced the trees and rising ground to the north, and created a dramatic "window" to the south, opening onto the East River, the United Nations, and the horizon.

Lou called this primal structure "the Room," and it evolved quickly. It harbored niche spaces, different levels, and stainless steel "baldacchinos" arcing from the walls. Mindful that the metal might still prove too costly, Lou developed an alternative version with cantilevered concrete as well. These canopies—be they gracefully sprung metal or cantilevered concrete— along with a pair of granite slabs for benches and a lowered slot to create a sharp edge and continuity with the river, defined the austere space that Lou populated in drawings with a fiddler, a child, and dancers as a place for "human agreement and inspired use."

Responding to the raised mount I had proposed for the north end of the site, Lou conceived "the House," locating it under the mount to contain the social, interpretive, and service spaces that would have been included within the steel bastion of the original scheme. I integrated a rose-garden terrace into the House, and we thought of the place as a tribute to Eleanor Roosevelt and her legendary Hyde Park hospitality. It mattered to Lou to provide this gracious clublike atmosphere, in observance of the Roosevelts' goals of providing dignity and well-being for all. Inspired partly by the forty columns at Isfahan, we defined the entrance to the memorial precinct with a grove of forty trees, at a larger scale than the trees defining the allées, to create a sense of mystery and discovery at the outset.

Between the tenth and the twenty-fourth of April two large pastel drawings for the Roosevelt Memorial and two models of the Room were produced in the office, in an extended charette of multiple all-nighters. Once,

Lou's ten-foot pastel presentation drawing of the FDR Memorial—a section through the entire project, from "the Room" through "the Garden," "the House," and "the Grove."

Lou's pastel presentation plan of the FDR Memorial, with our landscape composed of an entrance grove and a tapering green, flanked by allées of low trees. The Room, as shown here, is the simplified concrete cantilever version of the design.

A detail from the section drawing, showing the House with exhibit rooms, meeting spaces, and rose garden.

during a break in this work, Lou compared our partnering to the legendary architect / landscape architect team of Edwin Lutyens and Gertrude Jekyll, which filled me with pride. He suggested we call the project "The Garden and the Room." He repeated the words, liking the sound of them. I liked the sound of them too.

HOTEL AMIGO, BRUSSELS, TO 8870 TOWANDA ST., PHILADELPHIA, MAY 7, 1973

Dearest ones,

The Travel life is like serving a term. When the term will be over seems to be the possessor of the being. It must be like the condemned, who can think of nothing but the time of release. I say this because I gave no one a thought while on my way and even when I arrived in Israel and at the hotel my thoughts were away from all but the objective of coming back. I confess that I did not write to you, my dear ones, only because life seemed rather empty, pointless.

I had dreams, some amusingly ridiculous. I forgot them but I will conjure up substitutes, or even remember them. I had intended to jot them down but I tell you so far nearly everything was a drudgery, in spite of the smoothly going meetings and prospect of interesting work.

I was well greeted everywhere. I was driven to Haifa Caesarea (Roman town on the Mediterranean) and Acre (the site of a famous battle between Richard Coeur de Lion and the Saracens during the Crusades). There I found (bought) a Greek coin (I hope it is authentic, looks so) for Nathaniel . . .

My bag did not arrive the same time in Belgium as I did. I hear now, the next day, that it is on its way to the hotel. It feels strange to live in the same shirt for the 3rd day. Saw Yves Lepère et al last night; ate at a wonderful restaurant, simple yet very particular, so characteristic, of restaurants in Europe. Up late, went to a bar. Saw this morning that fine man and former student Willy Sernelles with his fisherman's beard and wearing the same goodness I remembered him by 6 years ago.

I lecture this evening at 5. I have lunch this afternoon at 1 with the U.S. Ambassador. We drive to Louvain-la-Neuve for the 5 o'clock lecture—it is the place where I am to build the new library. Well so long for now, must run along.

Love,
Lou

Nathaniel and Lou atop a jungle gym in front of our Towanda Street house.

In late May, Lou found time to help Nathaniel build a Plasticine model of the Acropolis at the office and also to attend the "Olympics" at Germantown Friends School, where we watched fourth-graders compete and celebrate their year of studying ancient Greece. It felt wonderful standing with Lou among the other parents of Nathaniel's classmates as our boy won the long jump and the twenty-five-yard dash. In June, en route to Tel Aviv, Lou stopped to see the Bishop Field Estate in Lenox, Massachusetts, where he agreed to advise on a residential development by a young entrepreneur, James Hatch. A pair of architects who had left Lou's office were working on the project, and he asked me to design a sample house plot for them. In working up a scheme, I visited the site, which turned out to be an original Beatrix Farrand design. This led me to investigate Farrand's career as a pioneering female landscape architect and to write about it in my chapter of *Maine Forms of American Architecture* (1976), edited by Deborah Thompson.

When Lou resumed work on the memorial in July, I joined him in revising plans for a review at the end of the month. Dissatisfied with concrete, the UDC's representative on the project, Ed Logue, had requested a new version of the Room in stone. As Lou contemplated the challenges of this, I delved into refining the Garden's landscape, further exploring the scale and layout of the trees. It was around this time that Lou made a sketch for me of an obelisk, labeling it five hundred and fifty-five feet in height. Next, he sketched the memorial, which was the equivalent dimension, only horizontal. "This," he

My Dearest ones:

It was such a good thing to receive your little letter with our selves at the Olympics with our little hero

The little little little looms so full of Joy in the depressing state of big trying to be bigger bigger all bigger emptiness and un happyness – bladderague

I know you are having fun and above all the good feeling that a part of the world is your domain.

I am working on Mellon – did a big job of straightening the confusion of the drawings.

Have made a scheme for the monument in all stone

I have included a copy of the reports from the USIS over seas of my tour of Belgium Germany and France

Love Lou

[TOP: plan, left to right] *statue / sloped stone bank / flat lower path to water / earth bank, green / rising paths flanked by trees either side / green lawn / house under*

[BOTTOM: perspective, left to right] *stone roof / high pillar for the gate (like the ones making the 2 porticos at the side)*

The open space of the rising lawn and trees with no wall to the side has the feeling of a gap with the monument the last accent on the island!

said, tapping the memorial, "has to be as good as that." He tapped the obelisk. I realized later that the obelisk was the Washington Monument. Such was Lou's ambition for the work.

My Dearest ones:

It was such a good thing to receive your little letter with ourselves at the Olympics with our little hero.

The little little little looms so full of joy in the depressing state of big trying to be bigger bigger all bigger, emptiness and unhappiness-bladderesque.

I know you are having fun and above all the good feeling that a part of the world is your domain.

I am working on Mellon—did a big job of straightening the confusion of the drawings.

Have made a scheme for the monument in all stone.

I have included a copy of the reports from the USIS overseas of my tours of Belgium, Germany and France.

Love,
Lou

Lou wrote this letter to us in Maine the day before presenting a version of the memorial to the UDC "all in stone." I was charmed by the columns and was glad to see that the House had survived cost cuts, and also that the banks of the landscape had been left as grass, which I had suggested, fearing that there would be too much stone in the new scheme. Based on the letter, I made a large layout drawing of the site before returning to Philadelphia in early September.

The changes, however, did not satisfy the UDC's Ed Logue, and he registered disapproval by letter, splicing in complaints from his staff on August 29: "The columns fall into the domain of stage setting (and) subdivide the Memorial compounding the axiality. If the Statue of Liberty were located down river . . . However, the view will be ordinary." On September 10, in receipt of Logue's letter, Lou penciled to Jim Campbell, his draftsman, "I still don't have a design . . . We'll have to gird our loins."

When I delivered my memorial rendering to the office on the thirteenth of September, it was unusable. Everyone was nervous—no one knew what Lou's next move might be. What could he show the VIPs for the planned ceremony on the twenty-fourth, when Welfare Island was to be officially rechristened Roosevelt Island? Lou had to await orders at a meeting in New York on the nineteenth, and when they came, they were savage and humiliating. He would be permitted to exhibit his earlier drawings but was to label them "studies." With cost estimates coming in at $3 million, the House was to be eliminated. Likewise, the stone-roofed colonnade had to go. It was a mess.

Lou returned from the New York inquest, tore into his old plan, and ignored orders. What he drew for me the next day on a slip of paper was, I thought, horrific. The Garden was gone, replaced by two earthen tumuli that sacrificed the lawn and the allées and pocketed a straight path to the Room, which was cut back to a minimum—no colonnade, no canopies. Its austerity, at least, sat well with Lou, though he initially kept four pillars as token steles for inscriptions. But our rich landscape ideas for a memorial were reduced to a single gesture. For me, it all looked funerary, a path to a mausoleum. I was sick at heart.

I dived into the new scheme, making a soft lead study of the site, while John Haaf, a young architect assigned to the project, drafted contours for a new site model to be fashioned in wood layers, for which a belt sander was purchased at the last minute, the sound of it grinding away at the Garden reminding me of what had been lost. As many hands were cutting out, sanding down, and gluing together Lou's peculiar design, against the midnight hour, against desires, against Logue's orders, I tried to think of it abstractly as tomb architecture from Egypt, but I didn't believe in it, and asked Lou to put me on another job.

Lou assigned me to a commission he had accepted the year before from John and Dominique de Menil, to design an arts community for a bungalow neighborhood of Houston, next to the University of St. Thomas. He had high hopes for this one, on discovering that its émigré patrons were discerning collectors and generous philanthropists who had already built the beautiful Rothko Chapel for the university. The project was to be located in a working-class neighborhood, which the de Menils hoped to engage with a low-profile campus to present their experimental ideas and collection. They wanted to provide not only a place to display and store the art but also studios, auditoriums, and living quarters for a society of artists and students, all interwoven into the surrounding neighborhood. What an inspiring project to work on; gardens in Texas, again!

Lou began this campus with a grove of royal palms next to the Rothko Chapel, in symbolic expression of his belief that "the school began with people sitting beneath a tree," and from which he unfolded low, small-scale

Lou's sketch of "the Storage" on the de Menil campus. The gallery modules remind me of the room Lou drew for his Biennale exhibition in his April 28, 1968, letter.

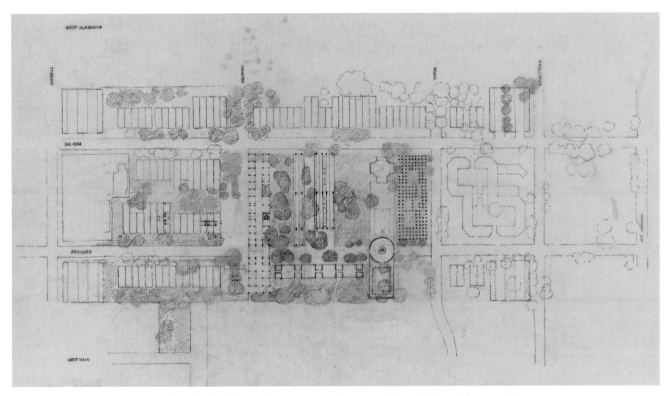

One of my plans for the de Menil arts campus, Houston. From left to right: hotel site, studios, "the Storage," Rothko Chapel, grove, University of St. Thomas.

buildings connected by arcades along the bordering streets to encourage a spontaneous flow between study, work, and living. Dominating the central green at cross axis would be "the Storage," for exhibiting art in open racks amid gardens and connecting porches built like stables in this settlement, which included a small hotel. In an eerie echo of the villages Lou had known, he attached fanciful domes and towers to the hotel, which somehow brought the distant lands of Africa, India, and the Middle East to the new West.

The de Menils' radical and anti-elitist ideas for a locus of inspired environments and availabilities resonated deeply with Lou's teaching and works, and he favored the project, turning to it intermittently during this year, though John de Menil's death cast doubt on its future.

Preoccupied as he was for much of the year by the FDR Memorial, Lou took on another major overseas project, teaming up with Kenzo Tange of Japan on a master plan for Abbas Abad, a satellite city for Tehran. The program set aside the northern half of a fourteen-hundred-acre site pleated with ridges off Iran's Elburz Range, for residential development, while the plateau, connected to the capital, was for a new urban complex of commercial, cultural, and government use. Under the spell of his recent visit to Isfahan and the semblance of royal patronage, Lou took on the work, and in preparing to visit the site early in November, he asked me to provide him with facts about "Persia."

Soon I was describing how the qanats (subterranean canals), badgirs (wind towers), and double-skin structures (which Lou had already employed in several projects) provided natural solutions for Tehran's dry desert heat; how deep porches behind grand portals led to shallow, dark interiors enhanced by mirrors and gold leaf, and inner courts and fountains; how people slept on their flat roofs but also used them, linked with multistoried aqueducts and bridges, as pathways for travel and socializing; and how city dwellers, with rug or tent, escaped to foothill streams, forests, or gardens in nature worship, free of rituals.

While others were building a Plasticine site model for the Abbas Abad development, I sketched ideas for melding natural valleys into parklands, laid out lake sites, and clustered housing on ridges in various landscape studies.

On his return from Tehran, Lou stopped in my room to report that the FDR Memorial scheme he had submitted back in September to the UDC had elicited a blistering reply from William Walton. Walton, who had piloted the project from the beginning, had rejected all but revisions to the Room, and ordered a return to the April scheme, in which "the park and memorial areas would be bound together," but with a lowered mount and reworked "peripheral walks." I was surprised, then quietly thrilled on December 3 when Lou, whose own choices had failed him, surrendered to Walton's terms and agreed to present final schematics, in a cliff-hanging nine days. I quickly retrieved the work where we left off before September, and joined the memorial charette with little more than a week to rescue our foundling project.

Adding to the drama in the office, national politics had been building to a pitch of discord over the Watergate scandal. The unseating of Vice President

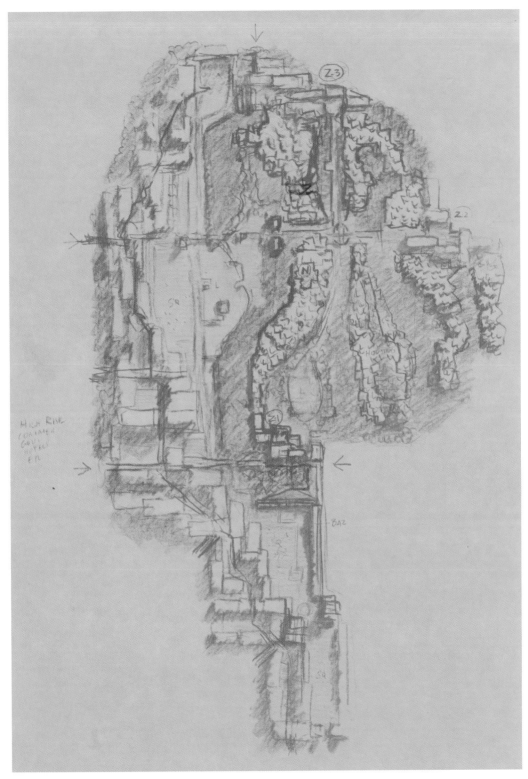

My site study for Abbas Abad, with valley-park areas, a thread of mountain-fed water courses, residential areas on higher ground, and civic centers at lower elevations near lakes and crossroads.

One of my sketches for the revised Garden at the FDR Memorial, December 1973.

André Le Nôtre's Hundred Steps at Versailles.

Lou's sketch of the final version of the FDR Memorial, from the staircase to the head of FDR at the entrance to the Room. He wanted the trees to be low and orchardlike, spaced closely together, with their unclipped branches fully enclosing the green space within.

Spiro Agnew and the Saturday Night Massacre in October would presage President Nixon's resignation in six months, and a sense of impending disaster was unnerving everyone, including Lou, making him fire up all efforts to overwhelm the obstructions, take back his mistakes, and reclaim his vision of the hope that the country so badly needed. The atmosphere seemed to make our last pitch for the memorial a do-or-die pact and an act of belief and patriotism.

While Lou, with help from John Haaf and others, focused on detailing the Room, I turned to the Garden, to rework it without the House and to recover the drama of the journey through the landscape by multiple pathways. I specified grass steps with stone risers for the lowered mount, funneled the ascent through trees to break at the summit onto a lawn with forced perspective, and detailed simplified tree allées on either side to walk beneath. I broke the allées at a forecourt before the Room, where crowds might gather. To control access, I explored creating a canal across the site between the ruin and the steps, with boat landings—an idea that Lou liked, but was afraid to explore for budgetary reasons. I regraded the peripheral walks while Lou, insisting on a full return of the Garden mount, designed a set of stone stairs. Feeling that Lou's first thoughts weren't strong enough, I showed him the Hundred Steps staircase at Versailles in my book on the gardens of André Le Nôtre. This clicked, and the one-hundred-foot-wide staircase Lou detailed next was marvelous, performing a powerful architectural introduction, anchoring the site and bookending the Garden with the Room. We liked the idea too that this great stair would create an expectation of grandeur that would then be subverted surprisingly when, upon reaching the top, the visitor would encounter not an imperial statue but rather a garden.

We saw it as a village green, an idyllic scene sheltered by enclosing trees with people in random pursuits, pastoral or sporting, with a sculpture in the distance, at the entrance to the Room.

Lou had originally wanted to include an allegorical piece by the sculptor Giacomo Manzù, but Walton proposed an FDR portrait sculpted by Jo Davidson, which Lou embraced as an idea he himself had explored in early schemes. It would be of a powerful head, alone, free of frailty; Lou enlarged the visage many times over, and framed it within the entrance pier for a one-on-one personal meeting with the man who had used his power for the good of all humanity. That resolute but open visage is the way we encounter Roosevelt still on our coins, or as my generation recognized him, disembodied but vital in radio broadcasts of his "fireside chats."

All of this fitted with Lou's existential and unifying minimalism—using the simplest means to achieve the broadest effect, but ingeniously played, with contrasting scales, placements, and pace; so open to the environment that a single flag or memento might compromise the project's symbolic and free spirit. What might emerge now with utter clarity would be thrilling: architecture and landscape, working together in harmonious agreement to create an American memorial.

In his desire for perfectly proportioned simplicity, Lou reduced the Room to seventy-two feet square, defining its walls with granite blocks six feet on a side and twelve feet high, leaving a one-inch gap between them. Originally he had wanted to cut two slits in the walls at angles that would allow a ray of sun to enter the Room on Roosevelt's birth and death dates, but even this he stripped away.

In the rush to finish the design, we were unable to resolve the space between the ruin and the great stair. The geometry had changed, making it too tight to accommodate the grove we had envisioned, and as a placeholder I

The final presentation model of the FDR Memorial from the south, showing the Room in granite.

suggested bringing back the large trees from my first "kitchen-sink" scheme to create an entry sequence. Hoping for the kind of suspense and awe that I felt in the theater at the rise of a great footlighted curtain, I visualized a shimmering stand of copper beech and felt that Andrew Jackson Downing's admiration for a fifty-foot specimen at nearby Throggs Neck in 1859 somehow ratified my choice. And so we detailed five big trees, resolving the presentation visually but fully intending to revisit this area and, if possible, restore the Grove, as the memorial went to working drawings later.

In just nine December days of a third charette, like those of April and September, only more intense, Lou had reversed direction, reclaimed original ideas, and presented a final scheme for UDC approval. He promised a "realistic" model for a January meeting with the president's son, Franklin Roosevelt Jr., that would include details and a confirmed budget—now $4.1 million.

"Lou, I think you've done it!" would be FDR Jr.'s resounding acceptance at the January 8, 1974, meeting. He confirmed this with "I congratulate you!" following agreements over document delivery dates and construction schedules, with groundbreaking set for May.

The memorial seemed to be on the fast track toward construction, which meant there could be no delay in detailing the lighting, selecting materials

The final presentation model of the FDR Memorial from the east.

for walls, riprap, and paths, and specifying the tree blocs. I would follow through on getting recommendations for delicate tree lights as opposed to floods, which Lou disliked, and I chose a dense, medium-size European hornbeam for the allées. This matched Lou's January 8 tree description, specifying that the trees should be "of the low overhanging type, requiring little or no clipping." The hornbeams would remain at the right scale as they grew, and could form the green tunnels representing the wild beauty of the American continent, in dialogue with the designed order of the forecourt and the Room.

The key for us was to maintain the true balance between landscape and architecture, and to offer the experience of an American memorial, unprecedented in its freedom and hospitality, without excess of symbols, signs, or barriers. We hoped to locate the amenities planned for the House in the hospital ruin, which had to be negotiated in the future, and also for the full installation of the entry grove, but the die was cast. The Garden and the Room would be built, with desired refinements to be realized later, thus securing Louis Kahn's "horizontal" masterstroke and commemorating a great president at a time when the country needed it, on the southern tip of New York's Roosevelt Island.

As Christmas approached, a sense of relief settled over the office. We had come through a crisis, and Lou and I were very close as the days grew shorter. One afternoon he came to Towanda Street, bringing carving tools

and two blocks of linoleum. He had drawn a picture of angels with their hair entwined, surrounded by abstract holly leaves, and with Nathaniel he set about transferring the drawing to a block and carving it for a Christmas card, as they had done the year before. Nathaniel was quite adept with the tools now, and as he worked, Lou wrote something on the smaller square block, and then Nathaniel carved it. We rolled out silver ink on a piece of glass and printed a first card. The angels danced brightly on the cover, and inside was one word: "Joy." Lou had spoken a great deal about joy lately, and how it was all that mattered in the end. Together, as the darkness of night gathered around our house in the woods and I lit the candles for a supper for the three of us, there was no other word to describe what I felt.

Dearest

If we were alltogether together
your feelings of the weight
of responsibilities would disappear
When you are depressed it means
I don't inspire you when I am
depressed it means you don't
inspire joy in me.

Yet I know there is Joy in us
more than we can enjoy
in a lifetime. and a Joy we
yet don't know.

Coy

1974

Lou's note left on my desk:

> Dearest,
> If we were altogether together your feelings of the weight of
> responsibilities would disappear. When you are depressed it means
> I don't inspire you. When I am depressed it means you don't inspire
> joy in me.
>
>   Yet I know there is joy in us more than we can conjure in a life
> time and a joy we yet don't know.
>
> Lou

I have no more letters, only this note Lou left on my desk and a few of my
own to spark memories of the winter days leading up to the fateful evening of
March 17. After the resolution of the Roosevelt Memorial crisis, somehow I
thought Lou would be able to ease up for a bit, but there was never any slack
at 1501. Projects overseas needed decisions, and within a week of the new year
Lou was off to Dhaka. Soon it would be Tehran and Tel Aviv, with a trip to
India planned for March.

One afternoon, as we walked through Rittenhouse Square to the New
School of Music, where Nathaniel was to play violin in a recital, Lou suddenly
stopped and had to sit down. We sent Nathaniel ahead, and I joined Lou on
a bench. I was frightened and wanted him to go to a doctor immediately, but
he shook it off, saying he felt better, and we went on to the concert, where
Nathaniel played Mendelsohn's "On Wings of Song." But this had been the
second such incident. The first had happened during the fall, when on the way
to visit an ailing Francis Adler at the University of Pennsylvania Hospital,
Lou had been short of breath and looked pale.

After the incident in Rittenhouse Square, I insisted Lou see a heart
specialist, which he did, and apparently the physician pronounced him "fine."
But I had a foreboding that I couldn't shake, and one day as we lingered over
lunch at the Colonnade after the noon crowd had dispersed, I spoke about
my fears. After a long, reflective silence, Lou said, very gently, but spoken
deeply as a vow, words I will never forget: "I will wait for you." Taking off his

glasses to wipe them, he let me into the mystery of what he could fathom of a continuum, and for a moment he, who reveled in life, had stepped beyond it.

Saturday morning, the second of March, Lou, Nathaniel, and I took the train to New York, and while Lou met over lunch with Mrs. de Menil, Nathaniel and I went to the Metropolitan Museum of Art to see a medieval tapestry exhibit with Nathaniel's friends Malcolm and Diana Wright, whose parents were close friends of mine. Having hurried through the exhibit alone, Lou caught up with all of us on the Met's front steps, and together we window-shopped and had hot chocolate on Madison Avenue before Lou detoured on another errand ahead of joining Nathaniel and me in Penn Station to catch the 7:05 train to Philadelphia, which Nathaniel remembers being short of seats. Nathaniel has also never forgotten how, when we arrived that morning, Lou took him to the men's room underground in Penn Station and suddenly remarked, "This would be a terrible place for a man like me to be in trouble." In two weeks and a day, Lou's premonition, if that's what it was, would play itself out in that very place.

After a day of such closeness in New York, it was terribly painful to part ways at Philadelphia's Thirtieth Street Station as we returned to Chestnut Hill and Lou went across town to the house on Clinton Street. On Monday, Lou and I exchanged cross words in the office stairwell and on the street as he hailed a taxi. He stepped into the front passenger seat without a backward glance, and sped off to Penn. I had been working all morning on the Tehran project with Egyptian architect Farrokh Sabouri and was frustrated that Lou had no time to talk to me.

I recall another incident from around this time: Nathaniel was in the office with me, and Lou had promised to come to our house for dinner. But when we descended the stairs to the lobby, he stopped and said he really couldn't make it, there was too much work to do before going to India. "Come on," I said to Nathaniel angrily, and went out the door onto Walnut Street. But Nathaniel didn't follow me. As he told me later, he went up the five flights of stairs and found Lou sitting on the top step with his head in his hands. He put his arm around his father and said it would be OK, and Lou looked at his son with tears in his eyes.

Early on Thursday morning, the seventh of March, Lou and I met at 1501 to "make up" over our quarrel and pledged to take a long lunch, in spite of Lou's rush to cover all bases before his departure to India. Of what followed, I have an account in my red notebook. We chose the Hoffmann House this time—a quaint German restaurant with dark walnut walls that Lou admired. Bullet-eyed windows let in light beams from the narrow street. There were tiny lamps at each white-clothed table, with gleaming silver and glassware

Lou and Nathaniel at Towanda Street, winter 1974.

and black-vested waiters like hovering clergy. We had not been there since the early days, and we sat by a wall, far from the vacated bar. The atmosphere was dim, hushed, confessional. Neither of us bothered with the food we ordered.

I pleaded with Lou, and he listened: I did not want to be just his lover, we were far more connected than that. We had weathered so much, and our love had only deepened over time. I was willing to do anything to help him with his work, but there was a whole realm of family life that I wanted to give him too. A home. Truly a home. It was so clear how much he loved being with us; why did he not commit to it? It was intolerable to keep living in the shadows. It was disrespectful and cruel. I understood that Esther took care of many things for him, but how could he continue so long in a double life? When I pressed him before, Lou had said he had wanted a divorce, but that Esther had prevented him. I questioned this now, saying that maybe he was using Esther as an excuse. If he wanted to leave, he could—it was up to him. I spoke about the island, too; I wouldn't invite him anymore because it was too hard to be disappointed so many times, when he promised to come and then didn't. I couldn't go on like this.

Sweetest Lou! He heard my pleas, my hopes, my anguish, saying, "I believe you! All except what you say about using Esther as an excuse, but you couldn't know that—and you have told it to me with love. I accept it."

I remember feeling sorry that I had put my grief on him when I saw the hurt in Lou's eyes, but I had challenged him to choose. "I will try to come live with you," he said. "But don't let that man who is too interested in watching us see you cry. Let's go somewhere else." And then, very softly: "I will try, for you two are my loves." Lou's tenderness was overwhelming. I felt he had understood what it was like for me, and that he truly wanted to honor our love. Wandering back, arm in arm, we stopped at Sessler's Bookshop, where I admired an early print of Stonehenge. "Don't just like things because they're old," he teased me, and in the elevator he joked with Ernie, the elevator operator, about the creaky cage never arriving even with the floors.

The second Friday in March, I attended Lou's talk at Bob Engman's sculpture class in the basement of Penn's Fine Arts Building. Lou described the glories of color to the students, speaking about the magic of light and the tapestries on show at the Met. The space was suffused in stone dust, and the dank fragrance of clay evoked my longings for a life in the arts when I visited my brother's studio at the age of these students now. Lou then spoke about a vision he had of the debut of Shakespeare's *Much Ado About Nothing* at the Globe Theatre—how the past happened once and could never be re-created, and that in his vision, all the players fell to dust as they performed, but that became "a golden dust of tradition," descending as inspiration for us.

Afterward we went for a quick lunch off campus before Lou returned to the university for his two o'clock class. The next day Nathaniel and I briefly stopped at the office, which was in turmoil before Lou's departure. It was late when we left. We hugged each other on the fifth-floor landing, and then Nathaniel and I walked down the stairs. We paused at the bottom and looked up at Lou, who was peering over the banister, waiting to catch a last glimpse before we disappeared. He waved down to us, and we waved back. He would only be gone for a week . . .

In the next few days, there were signs at the office that suggested otherwise. One morning I peered into Lou's private room and was shocked to glimpse Esther sitting in Lou's chair at his desk. The image triggered a disturbing vision, and I quickly escaped to my room. Another incident on Saturday, March 16, frightened me. I had stopped at the office with Nathaniel after a theater matinee in town. While chatting about Abbas Abad with Farrokh, who seemed to be the lone Saturday worker, I had a spontaneous hemorrhage that left spots of blood on the floor. It was alarming and unexpected, and I quickly broke off to drive home.

Sunday was St. Patrick's Day, and Nathaniel and I waited at home all day for Lou, certain of the day, March 17, but not the hour of his return. A little after seven we left the house and drove to a convenience store for some food.

I was distressed, as we heard nothing that night or the next morning, but I reminded Nathaniel that his father sometimes missed or delayed his flights.

On Monday I took Nathaniel to spend the first day of his school vacation at a friend's house, then drove downtown to work. The fifth floor at 1501 was a hive of baffled, leaderless workers. Where was Lou? Rumors abounded from surmises, reports of rescheduling, and multiple incoming phone calls and outgoing inquiries: What was his itinerary? What airline? Was there a passenger manifest? What time was it in Ahmedabad? In London? Lou must be in transit, because he hadn't called in, but where was he? Esther came and left several times, as did others through that day and the next. From Lou's phone, I called my brother Willy in California to see if he could help.

Tuesday began the same way as Monday, but people who showed up at the office were demoralized, and hopes were diminishing. There were no more leads, and senior people in the office began to focus on New York, local police, and the missing persons bureau. A surprising calm came over me. I knew Lou was dead. I left at two o'clock and picked up Nathaniel. On the way home, I stopped at the church of St. Martin-in-the-Fields in Chestnut Hill where we had a few moments of utter silence in the dim light of the stained-glass chapel. How else to prepare Nathaniel?

It was four o'clock on Tuesday when the office secretary, Kathy Condé, telephoned me. Nathaniel recalls hearing my question—"Is he dead?"—and then my hanging up. After her call, the phone rang again. I picked it up, and there was silence on the other end. But I held on, wishing to hear again Lou's "Hah–riet," with that at once astonished and slightly admonishing "Hah!" But I waited in vain for that voice.

We walked over to the brow of the hill by the Adlers' house and watched the sun go down behind the distant, barren ridges, still blackened from brush fires in the fall. Nathaniel asked me if we would ever be happy again, and I could not answer him.

Later, I wrote: "My dearest Lou, you are here with us tonight. Your eleven-year-old son, so eloquent, speaks of you: that you knew you could not live forever, you sensed your time was come. 'So, don't ever be sad. He worked so hard the last ten years—if he hadn't, he would only be an honored architect, but he became a loved architect. His room, so spare, without even a light. He was the light.' " Already halfway through my life, I then had but a fraction of our boy's wisdom to weather my sorrow. But I knew I had to be strong and keep it together somehow.

On Wednesday morning I drove to the Chestnut Hill station newsstand, where Lou often waited for me to pick him up. I bought the papers and read the front-page stories of the peculiar circumstances of Lou's death. He had collapsed in the men's room at Penn Station around eight o'clock on the night of March 17. He had been found faceup, and oxygen had been applied, but to no avail. Apparently the police had initially been unable to identify him, and when they did, they called the office, thinking that was his residence. Finding no one there, they had treated Lou as a missing person, and he had lain unclaimed for two days in the city morgue.

We heard later that Lou had not listed his home address on his passport. Those of us who were close to him have always attached symbolic meaning to this, despite latter-day efforts to explain his two-day disappearance as a simple bureaucratic mix-up. What was home to Lou? For years I've kept the belief that he truly wanted to make a home with Nathaniel and me, but perhaps "home" could never be a specific place for a boy whose family had moved so many times, and whose nature was to explore. Lou's life was a journey that led into the light, commencing in childhood, when he reached for glowing coals in the fire. His death in Penn Station—a public place of transit—seems fitting for a man who could not be pinned down but was always on the move, trying to engage with the world and make it better through his art.

There is another story surrounding Lou's death in Penn Station that continues to haunt me: a respected art dealer from Philadelphia crossed paths with him there that night. She spoke to him briefly, and then she watched as he went to a phone booth. Some time later, she saw him go in the direction of the men's room, but did not see him on the Philadelphia train afterward. Who had Lou tried to call? One can only assume that the call did not go through, as no one, not Esther nor anyone else, heard from him that night. It happened at precisely the time when Nathaniel and I had left the house to go to the store. I have always imagined our phone in the kitchen ringing, with no one home to answer it, and Lou on the other end of the line, standing in a phone booth in Penn Station. I shall never know if that is what happened.

Shortly before Lou's funeral on Friday, March 22, the wife of one of Lou's men telephoned Anne Tyng, informing her that, as Esther Kahn's spokeswoman, she was in charge of arrangements. She wanted Anne and me to know that we needn't come to the service; indeed it would displease Lou's widow if we did, she said, and then hung up. I did not know that woman, although Anne knew her well. It was deeply upsetting to be met with such insensitivity, but neither Anne nor I surrendered to it, and we made arrangements to attend Lou's public service with our children.

The city turned out for Lou. Chestnut Street was closed off Friday morning outside the Oliver H. Bair Funeral Home. It was packed by a citizen crowd that only parted for the official motorcade and closed ranks in the chill air for the duration, as there was no room for their legion inside. I think that tribute alone would have mattered most to Lou.

Tom Watson, my niece's husband from Boston, accompanied Nathaniel and me that morning, and my brother Willy flew in from Los Angeles as well. On the way in from the airport, Willy's taxi driver told stories about Philadelphia's admired "wizard" before leaving him off blocks away because of the closed streets. Willy waited for us on the landing above the funeral-home lobby: tall, soberly dressed, with a Silver Star Medal pin in his lapel. Nathaniel, in a suit and tie, remarked later that he thought his uncle looked very distinguished.

Stepping into the crowded main room where the casket lay, we were greeted by ushers who directed us quickly to a side room away from "the family." Anne Tyng, too, was sequestered, but Alex boldly broke loose and walked to the front of the main room to sit with her half sister, Lou's daughter Sue Ann. She saw Nathaniel, and asked if he wanted to join her, but Nathaniel chose to stay with Tom, Willy and me.

It was stifling as a rabbi began a dirge over the assembled mourners. A eulogy filled with platitudes followed, and seemed—as it was piped to us in the side room over a loudspeaker—to be about a man that bore little or no resemblance to Lou. Willy dozed as the Kaddish was recited. Then there was an awful rushing sound as hundreds rose and the simple casket was hoisted onto the shoulders of several of Lou's friends and men from the office. They carried the casket along the aisle and down the grand staircase. As the double doors opened, a great clamor arose from the street. I gripped Nathaniel's hand as we began to beat our way out through the crowd. Although I was aware of arms extended to greet or support us and caught sight of a few friends and two boys from Nathaniel's school with a father, we were for the most part unrecognized amid a multitude of strangers.

We watched as the casket was loaded into the hearse, but did not join the funeral procession or the burial at Montefiore Cemetery. I could not bear to see Lou lowered into the ground. Tom flew us off that afternoon to Boston in his own plane, lofting us out from the grief and tumult of the world. I sketched the pilots from my seat in a red notebook Lou had given me, unwilling to reflect on the shattering of dreams.

I heard later that, before Lou's body was closed in the casket, someone had laid a branch of holly on his breast. I thank the unknown person who placed it there, if they did, with our love.

Aerial view of Four Freedoms Park, Roosevelt Island, New York, 2012.

EPILOGUE

It is a beautiful fall morning in October 2012. I have emerged out of Manhattan's traffic and skyscrapers inside a crowded cable car that lifts off and carries me in a noiseless flight over the East River to Roosevelt Island. The other passengers are young workers and island residents, as well as some, like me, who will be guests at the opening ceremony for the recently completed Franklin Delano Roosevelt Memorial, now named Four Freedoms Park, designed by Lou with my help.

The island comes into view. At its tip, I see the gleaming memorial for the first time. I am dazzled by it and wonder what it will be like, after thirty-five years of waiting for it to become a reality. Lou and I worked together over a period of thirteen months on the project, and had not quite completed the schematics before Lou's sudden death, but his optimism about the merit of this design, "demanding presence" in the world, allowed me to hope that this last of his great works would be built in my lifetime. Suspended above the river, I am a time traveler, my mind rippling through the years between March 1974 and this moment.

Lou's work was his life, and his Philadelphia office was like an artist's atelier. When he died, it simply shut down; many of us were let go within days. Most of the projects in the office—de Menil, Abbas Abad, and the Hurva Synagogue among them—evaporated or were assigned to other architects, while the buildings under construction were quickly divided between two small firms formed by people in the office to complete the work. Marshall Meyers and Tony Pellecchia took on the Yale Center for British Art; David Wisdom, Henry Wilcots, and a few others took on Dhaka, with Henry dedicating a full ten years of his life to seeing that vast project through. Dave and Henry also inherited the Roosevelt Memorial, bringing in Mitchell/Giurgola's New York office for the necessary state license. I suppose it was deemed "awkward" to include me, as Esther was in charge of Lou's estate. Unfortunately my exclusion meant that the one person who could speak for the memorial's landscape and accurately communicate what Lou intended for it was rendered mute. Working drawings were developed through 1975, with the intention of breaking ground soon, but New York City's escalating

Nathaniel and me, fall 1974.

financial woes resulted in the project being mothballed, with the plans shipped off to Albany, where it seemed they would languish forever.

As for me, I wondered what I would do in that collapse after Lou's death. With no work and next to no money, I felt cast, along with Nathaniel, into deep shadow. I withdrew, like a Chekhov character banished to the provinces of Chestnut Hill. I began to build a life around that community, serving on local land-use and library boards and attending Nathaniel's school events, and with these connections I received some modest commissions for local gardens and landscapes. In Maine I was also fortunate to be able to consult on a number of estates and private homes, which allowed me to express my love for that dramatic landscape.

It was difficult to get up the courage to return to the world of downtown Philadelphia, but I did, seeking jobs from architects who were willing to hire me after my success designing a garden for Joe Jordan's AIA award–winning Philadelphia Center for Older People. Over the years, I was fortunate to work with a number of talented architects and designers, among them Joe Jordan, Aldo Giurgola, Peter Bohlin, Ed Jakmauh, Ehrman Mitchell, Otto Reichert, David Polk, Robert Couch, John Caulk, Richard Glaser, Peter Saylor, Susan Maxman, Alice Farley, Marguerite Rodgers, Judy Chang, Bernard Cywinski, and Rafael Villamil, producing plans and landscapes for college campuses, corporate headquarters, hospitals, parks, roof gardens, and private residences.

I teamed up with my mentor George Patton on several projects, too, including the Pennsylvania Avenue project in Washington, DC, for which

Lou in Ahmedabad, India, March 15, 1974.

we developed a design that I believe would have been a welcome addition to that city. Unfortunately, Bob Venturi and his firm, who had been awarded the architectural portion of the project, unceremoniously took over the entire site and edged us out. It was then that I was keenly reminded of all the struggles I'd seen Lou go through, and remembered his words to me: "Be stern because you resist your own destruction, smile because you know it doesn't matter."

In those years directly following Lou's death, I dreamed of him often and was overcome with waves of grief, but I had to make a living, and a home for Nathaniel, so I kept moving. I was blessed with the same wonderful friends who had been there all along for me, as well as members of my family—especially Eddie, who visited frequently and helped me get by. The parents of Nathaniel's friends gathered around us, too, treating Nathaniel as one of their own, and our landlord, Dr. Francis Adler, took on the role of beloved "grandfather." It was he who taught Nathaniel how to tie a necktie.

Although we lived far from the limelight of Lou's world and were actively excluded from it, there were some who sought us out, including Gabor Szalontay, Carl Linn, Carles Vallhonrat, and Balkrishna Doshi, who came all the way from India. On the evening he and his daughter visited Towanda Street, Doshi told us of Lou's last days in Ahmedabad and of how he had spoken about "doing one's own work without expectations" and how one must "love one's beliefs and attempt the incredible . . . thus life becomes art." Doshi felt his friend's presence "in the silences," and as the candles flickered and the wind rose in the trees outside our house, I felt him there too. Doshi gave

In the portico at the Kimbell Art Museum, Fort Worth, Texas, 1985.

me two photographs that were taken on March 15 in his Ahmedabad office, shortly before Lou left for the airport. They are the last images of Lou alive, and they have remained close by me ever since.

The summer Nathaniel graduated from college, in 1985, my dear friend Mariette Russell took us both to see the Kimbell Art Museum. Lou's "Villa in the Garden" was even more marvelous than I had imagined—the silvery light inside was a revelation, changing with the passing clouds and endowing the art, from Egyptian sculpture to Matisse, with freshness and life.

Walking in the porticos, looking across the shimmering water of the fountains through the trees to the mysterious beyond of the park, I was filled with gratitude for having been a part of creating this place, so different from any other museum in the world. Though the essential relationship between the building and nature has now been compromised by a poorly placed addition, the idea of a new kind of museum—that of a great house within a garden landscape—remains.

The following year, Mariette took me with her on the most remarkable trip of my life, to India, Bangladesh, and Nepal, where, amid the glories of the designs realized after Lou's death, we met the people Lou had served and written to me about. The Indian Institute of Management was like a city of

The National Assembly, Dhaka, Bangladesh, completed in 1984, ten years after Lou's death.

dreams, part of the past, part of the future, with students meeting and talking and playing cricket in the varied spaces between buildings, and ducking the sun in cool brick porticos—reminded always of the wide world beyond by the great circular openings letting in the sky. When Doshi and his wife and family welcomed us in their beautiful house and garden, I felt Lou near again and understood why he loved this place so far from home. The Indian people understood him. He was not "idealistic" or "impractical." He was an artist and a teacher in search of the truth, as best as he could find it.

Dhaka was a shock. Nothing can prepare you for the buildings Lou created there. That they exist at all is a kind of miracle that gives one faith in humanity. To see the National Assembly reflecting itself in the lake under the brilliant sun or in the rain is to encounter Architecture itself, as Lou spoke of it, with a capital *A*. With its monumental forms rising out of the water, pierced by great geometric shapes, it might have been built a thousand years ago or yesterday. And as much as it is a creation of a "Western" man, it does not impose any ideology; it simply inspires awe and a sense of belonging exactly where it is. Walking through the interior streets Lou created, with their layered spaces and mysterious light rippling down the walls, or shining in shafts through the dust in the air, I was reminded of Lou's paraphrase of

Interior of the National Assembly, Dhaka, Bangladesh.

With Balkrishna Doshi, Ahmedabad, India, 1986.

the Wallace Stevens poem I had given him: "What slice of the sun does your building have?" The assembly chamber at the center of the structure, with its sunlit concrete canopy far above, feels like a place where it would indeed be possible to reach beyond differences to the "human agreement" that Lou so greatly valued.

At the time I visited Dhaka with Mariette, in the mid-1980s, Lou's work on the Indian subcontinent was still relatively unknown to the world, represented only as it was by a few photographs that barely scratched the surface. This began to change in the early 1990s, with *Louis I. Kahn: In the Realm of Architecture*, an exhibition organized by the Museum of Contemporary Art in Los Angeles, which brought the true breadth and depth of Lou's work—both built and unbuilt—to broader attention. But as comprehensive as the show was, the man himself somehow receded into the shadows. Lou was presented as nearly a mythical figure, whose personal life didn't much matter and was best left unexplored.

All this changed with Nathaniel's film *My Architect*, about his search to know his father beyond the limited vision he'd had of him as a child. Released in 2003, the film captured the public imagination both in America and abroad and was nominated for an Academy Award. In it, the man who was Louis Kahn walked the earth again, with all his warmth and struggle. I marveled

417

The Room,
Four Freedoms
Park, Roosevelt
Island, New
York, completed
in 2012.

that the film was so filled with love, with no hint of bitterness, and at how Nathaniel himself had become an artist in his own right.

My Architect also helped rekindle interest in building the Roosevelt Memorial. Thanks to the efforts of US ambassador William J. vanden Heuvel, the Roosevelt family, and a few visionary donors, $54 million was raised, and with the guidance of Gina Pollara, a young architect with a passion for the project, construction began in 2010—which brings me again to this day in 2012.

The cable car lands softly, and I disembark, heading with the crowd to the southern tip of Roosevelt Island. I pass the nineteenth-century ruin of the smallpox hospital, which we had hoped to repurpose to provide services for visitors, and enter the precinct of the memorial itself. There are the beech trees that we had added as placeholders, hoping eventually to reinstate the entry grove, and there are the great granite stairs, one hundred feet wide, rising before me. I climb them with great anticipation, and although I know what to expect, I am surprised all the same by the green that opens before me, flanked by allées of low trees. The green is filled now with people celebrating this remarkable achievement, and the ceremony that unfolds is beautifully orchestrated, with speeches and clapping. I am thrilled and surprised to be acknowledged before that crowd, as Lou's landscape architect on the project. My great longing was to live a life in art, and with Lou's help I had found a way to do it. The work allowed me to transcend myself and be part of something bigger and more lasting.

Later, as the crowd disperses, I make my way down the slope, stepping from the Garden into the Room, with its vista across to the United Nations and downriver to infinity. I am overwhelmed by what has been achieved. While there are elements that I wish had remained truer to Lou's and my original intent, the Room is marvelous. Its scale is both intimate and grand. It is peaceful, yet demands engagement. It stands with timeless solidity, rendering all the rooms in the skyscrapers of Manhattan across the river somehow insignificant. With its great granite blocks vibrating next to each other, one inch apart, it is a physical embodiment of Lou's mythic moment "when the walls parted and the column became." Lou spoke of beginnings, and how he loved them above all else. The room, he said, was the beginning of architecture. And so it was. I had come not to the end of something, but to the beginning.

I still have a key to the post office box in Rockport, Maine, where every summer for years I received my mail, including so many letters from Lou. I cannot forget how those letters gave substance and flow to the richest fifteen years of my life, and I am not surprised that my heart still leaps when I open the box with that same excitement of long ago, when there waiting for me would be an envelope in Lou's inimitable hand. Perhaps I imagine that a letter might still arrive, having been misplaced or incompletely addressed, as Lou's letters sometimes were. It is not so fantastical, the missing address, for the place Lou wrote to did not really exist. It was a place we created together in our minds.

The shadows lengthen across Indian Island, and the sea is calm, with small waves beckoning on the shore. This is where I end my story. Lou's letters to me and mine to him (which may still survive somewhere) were constructing a future for us, one that, while not destined to happen, was yet full of expectation and belief. That place somehow remains, even as a ruin in the light of a distant time.

Lou's pastel of the Acropolis, Athens, 1951.

ACKNOWLEDGMENTS

A memoir of this scope would not be possible without the institutions that supported my research and the individuals who provided help and encouragement along the way. I am grateful to the Graham Foundation for Advanced Studies in the Fine Arts; the AIA New York Chapter and the Center for Architecture Foundation, which awarded me an Arnold W. Brunner Grant; Alphawood Foundation Chicago; and the Architectural Archives of the University of Pennsylvania, which houses the Louis I. Kahn Collection in the Harvey & Irwin Kroiz Gallery. I am grateful also to Larry and Korin Korman and the Korman family for their generous support.

I am deeply thankful to Sue Ann Kahn for her gracious permission to publish Louis Kahn's letters and to Alexandra Tyng Kantor for her constant encouragement. I thank Charles Linn and Julia Moore Converse for their early support, and Jamie Bischoff of Ballard Spahr for her wise counsel. I also wish to thank the Pennsylvania Volunteer Lawyers for the Arts. Crucial for my research were two books: *Louis I. Kahn: In the Realm of Architecture*, by David Brownlee and David De Long, and *What Will Be Has Always Been: The Words of Louis I. Kahn*, edited by Richard Saul Wurman. Also essential were Susan Rose Behr's insights and key discoveries about Lou's origins, including his birth name and early life in America. I am thankful to Charles Birnbaum, founder and director of the Cultural Landscape Foundation, for his interest in my career and for his superb work in promoting the art of landscape architecture.

Since beginning this project over a decade ago, I have benefited from the help of my family and friends, among them the authors Victoria Villamil and Martha White, who kindly read early drafts and provided much helpful advice. I am grateful to Sue McDonald, who carefully critiqued the manuscript, as well as to Virginia Peterson, Dorothée Metlitzki, Rafael Villamil, Corey Stone, Kenelm Winslow, Judson and Marya Flanagan, Taylor Allen, Gillian Speeth, Ed Marshall, Joanna Bassert, Dan Cristol, Andrew Feinberg, Susan Karp Carson, Douglas Crosby, Warren Hope, Jack Terrill, and Alice and Peter Hausmann. I am thankful also to David Slovic, Anant Raje, Laurie Olin, Cornelia Hahn Oberlander,

James Timberlake, Shilpa Mehta, Jock Reynolds, and Constance Clement for their encouragement, and to Heie Treier, Elisabetta Barizza, and Michael Merrill, who have done their own excellent work on Kahn and who kindly helped me with mine.

I owe deep debts of gratitude to filmmaker Christopher Speeth, who spent weeks scanning Lou's letters and memorabilia of half a century ago with the same care he gave to his own beautiful documentaries. And to Diana Wright, who carefully read the strands of my text and braided them into a document suitable for submission. And to the writer Rosemary Mahoney, whose constructive criticism helped deepen the manuscript.

This book would not have been possible without the ongoing assistance of William Whitaker, curator of the Architectural Archives of the University of Pennsylvania's Weitzman School of Design. Bill's knowledge and insight helped me every step of the way, and he and his colleagues, Nancy Thorne, Heather Isbell Schumacher, and Allison Olsen, supplied a wealth of illustrations and documents relating to Lou and his world.

I am deeply grateful to Laura Lindgren for bringing the book to life with her keen editorial skills and stunning mastery of design. Her caring and patient work transformed the text and illustrations into a work of coherence and beauty.

I am grateful to my book agent Zoë Pagnamenta, and for the dedication and expertise of Yale University Press. My thanks go to director John Donatich, senior editor Katherine Boller, managing editor Kate Zanzucchi, and design and production manager Mary Mayer for the realization of this handsome volume. I also thank freelance copyeditors Miranda Ottewell and Zoë Slutzky, proofreader Jessica Skwire Routhier, and indexer David Luljak.

My profound thanks go to my son, Nathaniel Kahn, whose patience, insights, and sensibilities helped immeasurably in crafting this book. No one could have been a more enlightened editor than he.

Of course, half of this book was written by Louis Kahn, in his letters, postcards, and notes to me. I am forever grateful to him for so much that has been good in my life. I hope that in publishing and illustrating some of his words and mine, I have brought the reader a measure of knowing him.

—HP

INDEX

Note: Page numbers in italic type indicate photographs or illustrations.

Holman, Libby, 52
Holocaust, 61, 222
Honickman, Harold, 359
Honickman, Lynne, 358–59
Honickman House plan, Fort
    Washington, Pennsylvania, 358–60, *361*
Howe, George, 60, 362
Huff, Bill, 68
Hurva Synagogue, Jerusalem, 249–50,
    250, 251, 273, 278–79, 281, 292–93, *292,*
    348, 358, 411
Huxtable, Ada Louise, 181
Hyde, Niall, 165

Ina (invented word), 20–23, *20–21,* 276
Indian Institute of Management (IIM),
    Ahmedabad, India, 68, 94, 109, 116,
    142, *143,* 158, *159,* 160, *200,* 281,
    284–85, 285, *286, 287,* 414–15
Indian Island, Rockport, Maine, 80–81,
    81, 297–99, 306, 311–12, *323,* 329, *330,*
    337, 374, 405, 421
International style, 216
Isfahan, Iran, 316–18, *316, 319,* 385, 394
Islam, Muzharul, 169
Islamabad, West Pakistan, capital complex
    project, 153–57, *154, 156,* 167–74, *171,*
    172, 176–77, 181–83, *183,* 185–86,
    191–93, 214. *See also* Assembly Building,
    Islamabad, West Pakistan; President's
    House, Islamabad, West Pakistan

Jacobs, Jane, *The Death and Life of Great
    American Cities,* 163
Jacobson, Ada, 60–61, 79
Jacobson, Mrs. (Ada's mother), 79
Jaeger, Werner, *Paideia,* 354
Jakmauh, Ed, 412
Jefferson, Thomas, 216
Jekyll, Gertrude, 239, 388
Jellicoe, Geoffrey, *Italian Gardens of the
    Renaissance,* 164
Jericho, Israel, 253, *253*
Jerusalem, Israel, 249–52, *252,* 258,
    278–79, 281, 292–93
Jerusalem Hills project, Israel, 278–79, 358
Johansen, John, 126

John F. Kennedy Library competition,
    144, *145,* 160, *161,* 163
Johnson, Lyndon, 187, 214
Johnson, Philip, 14, 63, 194, 381; Amon
    Carter Museum of American Art, 263
Jones, Amos, *141*
Jones, Charles, 89, *89,* 93, 96
Jones, Susannah, 87–89, *89,* 93, 96, 141, *141*
Jones, Tim, *141*
Jordan, Joe, Philadelphia Center for Older
    People, 412
Judd, Donald, 231
Jung, Carl, 327

Kahn, Bertha (née Mendelewitsch), 58–59,
    59
Kahn, Esther (née Israeli), 61–62, 63, 86,
    94, 194, 235, 295, 301, 321, 328, 352,
    375, 405–8, 411
Kahn, Leopold, 58–59, *59,* 63–64, *63,* 66,
    74, 77, 241, 359
Kahn, Louis: architectural principles and
    ideals of, 163, 193, 215–16, 224, 276,
    312, 332, 360, 378, 381, 398, 415; on
    architecture as a business, 42–43, 67,
    71, 111, 114–16, 122, 133, 142, 155, 167–
    71, 173, 185–86, 191, 201, 209, 279, 281,
    302–3, 308–9, 311, 313–14, 371; awards/
    honors received by, 328–29, 335; career
    of, 11, 60, 62, 94, 378; childhood of,
    58–60; and competitions, 126, 144, *145,*
    160, *161;* death of, 403–9; finances of,
    94, 133, 143, 201, 207, 233, 314–15, 337,
    352, 375; Le Corbusier's significance
    for, 15–16, 187–89; notebook for trip
    to Iran, *319;* office of, *11,* 53, 57, 144,
    168, 267, 352–54, 374, 407, 411; piano
    playing of, 60, 364; and religion, 79,
    106, 221, 250, 292; "The Room, the
    Street, and Human Agreement," 334,
    335, 337; Roosevelt's significance for,
    381; "Silence and Light," 276–77;
    statements on architecture and work,
    38, 112, 129, 168, 211, 296, 299, 317,
    335, 413, 420; as teacher, 15, 57, *152,*
    353, 406; unbuilt projects of, 207, 218,
    219, 222, 226, *228,* 229, *230,* 231, *231.*

PHOTOGRAPHY CREDITS

Numerals refer to page numbers.

American Wind Symphony Orchestra: 334

The Architectural Archives, University of Pennsylvania (hereafter AAUP): 150

AAUP, First Unitarian Church Collection: 43

AAUP, Louis I. Kahn Collection (on permanent loan from the Pennsylvania Historical and Museum Commission): 14, 48, 71, 72–73, 106, 111, 114, 115, 143 top, 154, 159 bottom, 161, 183, 190, 196 top, 197, 200, 217, 218, 230 bottom, 231, 247, 251 top, 264–65, 268, 269, 270–71, 277, 310, 315, 333, 335, 338 bottom, 344 top, 347, 350, 361, 366, 386–87, 393 top

AAUP, Louis I. Kahn Collection, photo by John Ebstel © Keith de Lellis Gallery: 11, 13, 62, 68, 195 top

AAUP, Louis I. Kahn Collection, photo by Lionel Freedman: 2, 12

AAUP, Louis I. Kahn Collection, photo by George Pohl: 84, 171, 399, 400–401

AAUP, Louis I. Kahn Collection, photo by Ezra Stoller: 82

AAUP, Nathaniel Kahn Collection: 214, 242 left, 280, 338 top

AAUP, Harry Palmbalm Collection: 258

AAUP, Harriet Pattison Collection: 164, 166, 238, 240, 300, 339, 358, 359, 384 bottom, 390, 393 bottom, 395, 396 top

AAUP, Harriet Pattison Collection, photo by Heinz Volte: 276

AAUP, George Erwin Patton Collection: 6, 236, 239

AAUP, photo by George Alikakos: 168, 250, 251 bottom

AAUP, photo by Urs Buttiker: 344 bottom

AAUP, photo by David L. Leavitt: 104

AAUP, photo by Marshall D. Meyers: 196 bottom, 212

AAUP, photo by John Nicolais: 198–99, 303

AAUP, photo by Sasha Pabst: 324

AAUP, photo by George Pohl: 53, 151

AAUP, photo by Anant Raje: 159 top

AAUP, photo by Martin Rich: 152–53

AAUP, photo by Joan Ruggles: 352

AAUP, photo by Yukio Saito: 364

AAUP, Venturi, Scott Brown Collection, photo by George Pohl: 234

AAUP, Henry Wilcots Collection: 193, 203, 368–69, 370

AAUP, Richard Saul Wurman Collection: 63, 167, 266

© Iwan Baan: 410

Courtesy of Elisabetta Barizza: 242 right, 271 bottom, 356, 357

Collection Cheryl Barton, FASLA: 107

© Cemal Emden: 284–85, 346

Fisher Fine Arts Library, University of Pennsylvania: 318

Werner Forman Archive © HIP / Art Resource, NY: 290 top

Anton Henze, *La Tourette: Le Corbusier's erster Klosterbau* (1963): 16

Collection Nathaniel Kahn: 39, 59, 61, 69, 77, 126, 177, 241, 256, 278, 317, 321, 365, 383, 384 top, 401 bottom, 421

Collection Nathaniel Kahn, photo by Harriet Pattison: 326, 389, 405

Sue Ann Kahn Collection: 222, 397

Courtesy of the Kiley Family: 108

Kimbell Art Museum: 288

Kimbell Art Museum, Photo by Robert LaPrelle: 376–77, 378, 379

Collection Larry Korman: 360, 362